Ol' Buddy Marty

Ol' Buddy Marty

With Average Ability and Supreme Effort, All Things Are Possible

A Memoir
Sprinkled with Wit, Wisdom, and Inspiration

Marty Devlin

Goofer Press
www.martydevlin.com

Cover design by Tara Devlin
Book design by Rachael Hixon

© 2023 by Marty Devlin

ISBN 979-8-218-12474-8

For my family, my late tag-team buddy Stan Dlugosz, my teachers, coaches, teammates, and students, and for anyone who ever thinks success is unattainable.

For more stories, go to www.martydevlin.com

Contents

FOREWORD

I first met Marty Devlin when I was a sophomore in high school. I was competing in a Middle States Tennis Association men's singles tournament at Frosty Hollow Tennis Club in Langhorne, Pennsylvania. I was the #1 player at my high school and a highly ranked junior. I had easily won my first two matches. Marty was next. I knew some things about Marty and his impressive athletic career: that he'd been a professional baseball player, coach, and manager; All-American swimmer and diver; Intramural Director—and that he was a top-ranked tennis player. He was someone to be reckoned with. I also knew that there were 25 years between us. Marty was 40 years old, and I was 15, one year away from being able to drive. My Dad, also my coach, put some pretty high demands on me. That was okay because I put higher demands on myself, for reasons I'm still trying to figure out. While driving me to the third-round match, he tried to prepare me. He told me that this quarterfinal match would be especially challenging because of Marty's unorthodox style.

Unorthodox was an understatement. I walked onto the court, and he immediately started calling me "Ol' Buddy." I was proud of my sprouting mustache, but at 15 there wasn't much of me that was Ol'. Marty was friendly and polite as we warmed up. That threw me off. I was used to competing in the 18-and-under category against players who tried to psych me out with intimidation. As we prepared for the match, I realized more of what my father meant by "unorthodox." I was playing a guy who had no backhand—but two forehands.

We started the match. I served and volleyed, coming to the net whenever I could. I won the first set and was feeling good about my game. Then, in the second set, Marty changed his approach, and I was bombarded with more lobs in one game than I'd seen in an entire match. Balls kept coming back at me. I was playing a human backboard! He was relentless. Marty got the advantage, won the second set, then the third and the match. How did that happen? I knew I had better strokes, hit the ball harder, and had better style. But none of that mattered. I'd been defeated. When we met at the net to shake hands, Marty told me I was the better player and encouraged me to continue to develop my game. At that time, I had no idea the impact Marty would have on my life.

A few years later, Marty reached out to me and connected me with the Parkview Tennis Club, an outdoor summer club that used the courts at Rider College. We had some tennis buddies in common and I gained more through Marty. During the summer, I was also working for my father, who was now Director of Tennis at the Trenton Country Club. Marty, Scotty Stoner, and Jon Kraut would come to TCC and work out with me during my lunch hour. I was playing with the best in the area.

It was Marty who introduced me to Prince tennis rackets and to Jim Baugh, Director of Sales at the company. I began to test rackets that Prince was developing and played with them at satellite tournaments in the Netherlands after I graduated from George Washington University. After a short stint playing professionally, I was hired as manager of the Hamilton Tennis Club. By then, Marty had joined Prince as manager of their tennis ball machines.

Marty was and is a connector of people. He introduced me to Jack Murray, President of Prince. One morning while I was teaching tennis to Jack and his children, Jack said, "If you ever get tired of teaching tennis, give me a call." It didn't take long for me to act on that intriguing invitation. I waited until after noon that day and then called Jim Baugh to ask what Jack meant. Jim laughed and invited me to interview with Jack later that week. After the appropriate preliminaries, I accepted a job as Product Manager of Accessories and in September 1980 began working alongside my Ol' Buddy Marty Devlin.

The opportunities I had in my career to assume leadership positions in tennis and the business of sports I owe in many respects to Marty's guidance, example, and friendship. Since the time I first met him as a 15-year-old on the tennis court, he has supported me as only Marty can.

Ol' Buddy Marty tells the life story of an ordinary man with extraordinary style, creativity, and passion. Marty describes the formative years of his youth in his introduction, "Imagine being told as a little tyke that you are a jackass." Perhaps it was that feeling of being an underachiever that lit the fire and motivated Marty to accomplish so many great things and achieve more in his life than his parents or even Marty ever thought possible.

Through his experiences—his physical endeavors as a youth; playing professional baseball and managing a professional baseball team and soon a collegiate athletic program; traveling the world while putting on clinics and demonstrating the ball machine in over 30 countries—Marty has motivated thousands of consumers, tennis players, and athletes. He applied what he learned on the athletic field to business and academic settings. When you meet Marty, you see the drive of an athlete, a high emotional IQ, and the inimitable interpersonal style of a leader and motivator.

You can see why I enjoyed reading Marty's life story, and I know you will too. From the stories Marty shares of his athletic, business, and motivational experiences, you can take away ideas from Ol' Buddy Marty and incorporate them into your own life. Some of my favorite sections in the book are on positive mental attitude, positive thoughts/self-efficacy, and positive self-projection. When Marty and I were working together at Prince, he helped ingrain these habits and qualities in me, which still help me in my business and personal life.

Marty wrote this book to motivate and encourage people who perceive themselves as having little or no talent to push and cycle upward, to adopt a positive attitude, and to develop the belief and confidence to take on new challenges. In short, to live an inspired, and inspiring, life.

His hair color has changed, but at 89 years young, Marty's life still reflects that unorthodox style—creative, effervescent, supportive, and indomitable—my father told me about many years ago. Fifty years after that quarterfinal loss, I'm still learning from Marty Devlin. He shares his life lessons so we can all incorporate them into our daily lives. I was so fortunate to meet Marty when I was young. He has left an indelible mark on me and the thousands of friends he has made over the course of his life.

A few years ago, when I was visiting the U.S., I arrived unannounced at his New Jersey home, at what is affectionately called "the Swamp," the tennis court where I often played over the years. I knocked on Marty's door. We had not seen each other in almost a year. We sat and spent a happy few hours shooting the breeze and catching up on life and our friendship. Now, through his memoir, you can sit down with Marty too, and I encourage you to do so. Enjoy the journey that Marty takes you on!

Dave Haggerty

Member, International Olympic Committee (IOC)
President, International Tennis Federation (ITF)
Member, United States Olympic and Paralympic Committee (USOPC)

London
2022

PREFACE

Imagine being told as a little tyke that you were as dumb as a jackass. Imagine going through your youth believing it. That's how my life story began. Despite this, I managed to overachieve. Much of my success was in sports, at a high level, even though my physical stature didn't come close to that of a world-class athlete. I shared a tennis court with Pancho Gonzalez, Stan Smith, Chris Evert, Arthur Ashe, and Don Budge. My baseball teammates and competitors included Tommy Lasorda, Sparky Anderson, Don Zimmer, Willie Mays, Satchel Page, Brooks Robinson, Dick Groat, and Luis Aparicio. I was even named one of the greatest sports stars of all time in Trenton, New Jersey.

For many years, my friends and acquaintances tried to persuade me to write a book. I guess they felt I had something to say. Eventually, I began documenting my experiences and thoughts. This process helped me understand myself better and how I was able to achieve so much.

Yet the more I reflected on the past, the more I also thought I was an idiot to even think about what I wanted to accomplish, let alone do it! My closest friends and family had no idea of the challenges I faced—physically, socially, mentally, and emotionally. I was small in stature. I struggled to fit in socially. I struggled in school and by my senior year in high school I had read only one book (three times!). Yet despite all this I found myself in leadership roles throughout my life. I was asked to be a speaker at a college graduation. I was inducted into five Halls of Fame.

Ultimately, this memoir is about overcoming challenges and making something out of nothing. The first part is my life story, my emotional brain at work. Unlike today, when kids learn in organized sports leagues, my incredibly risky and crazy childhood experiences helped develop my skills, work ethic, and love of physical exercise.

The second part of the book contains the lessons I've learned, which I incorporated in my motivational speaking. This was after years of competing in four sports, serving as a college tennis coach, intramural director, and athletic director, conducting tennis clinics worldwide, serving as a ski patrol member, and coaching golf, wrestling, and swimming.

Preparing my talks was like a lightning bolt striking my brain that brought my emotional brain, my life experiences, and thinking brain together. I read the books listed in Acknowledgments. I reviewed newspaper clippings, magazines, and photographs. I talked to others, listened, and I researched. In Part II, I take you through the essence of the presentation I made at top universities. I include the humor and hyperbole my friends and students hear often. There is order and logic to what, how, and when I say it in Part II.

I've had many nicknames throughout my life. As a kid, my family called me Marty-Hit-the-Ball. In professional baseball I was called Whitey, Twinkle Toes, The Torpedo, The Recording Machine, Motivator, Loud Mouth, and Drunken Babbling Idiot. But the title of the book and the name that stuck was "Ol' Buddy," what I call everyone I meet because I can't remember names.

Many times, people discouraged me from whatever I was about to embark upon, or they told me I shouldn't say what I wanted to say, but that hasn't stopped me.

Gratification comes from the multitudes of people who have told me how much I have inspired them and from knowing that, through this book, my grandkids will get to know their Pop-Pop better and learn his values.

I first realized that I was a motivator and teacher when I was heading up the intramural athletic program at Rider College. Dr. Ken Runquist, Chairman of the Health & Physical Education Department at Trenton State College (TSC), asked me to be a guest lecturer at a three-hour graduate class at Columbia University in New York City.

The faculty at TSC knew me as a student who had difficulty just answering multiple-choice questions on tests. (I always saw something good in all the options.) Nevertheless, I conducted the three-hour class without a note. On the train ride home, Dr. Runquist said, "Marty, we as educators know all the material in the psychology books, but we can't apply it. You know nothing about what's in the books, but you showed us how to apply them."

I wrote this memoir to motivate, encourage, and inspire anyone who perceives themselves as having little or no talent or who lacks confidence. If you are one of those people, I want to encourage you to cycle upward by pushing through areas of discomfort. I hope my story inspires you to have a positive attitude and continue to have the desire, belief, and confidence to take on new challenges. I'm having a great ride. Come along!

CHRONOLOGY

1933	Born in Trenton, New Jersey
1937–1946	Blessed Sacrament Elementary School, Trenton
1946–1947	Junior High School No. 3, Trenton
1947	Entered Trenton Central High School
1948	Trenton Post 93 Schroths American Legion Baseball Team – won the National Junior Championship
1948	Recognized within the Baseball Hall of Fame in Cooperstown as a member of the Trenton Post 93 Schroths American Legion championship team
1948–1952	Four-year player for the Schroths
1949	Named All-City High School Quarterback
1949 and 1950	Named to All-State High School Diver
1950	Named to All-State Baseball Team
1950	Graduated from Trenton Central High School (named Best Boy Athlete and Best Boy Personality)
1950–1952	Attended Duke University and played on baseball and swimming teams
1952 (summer)	Semi-pro baseball, Clarksville, Virginia

1952	Signed with Brooklyn Dodgers; played for Greenwood (Mississippi) Dodgers, C ball; voted most popular player
1952–1967	NJSIAA football and swimming official
1953	Inducted into U.S. Army
1953–1955	U.S. Army, 39th Regiment – played on baseball team at Fort Dix, NJ, and went to Dodgers spring training during 30-day leave
1953	Contracted spinal meningitis while in U.S. Army
1954	Manager of U.S. Army 39th Regiment baseball team, Ft. Dix
1954	Captain of John A. Roebling Steelworkers baseball team (county league)
1954	Contracted hepatitis while in U.S. Army
1955	Mobile Bears (AA Southern League) and Elmira Dodgers (A Eastern League)
1955	Insurance salesman for Bankers Life Company of Des Moines
1956	Fort Worth Dodgers (AA Texas League); voted most popular player
1956–1957	Played winter baseball in Maricaibo, Venezuela, for Cabimas
1957	Fort Worth Cubs (AA Texas League)
1958	St. Paul (AAA American Association) and Montreal Dodgers (AAA International League)
1958	Won the International League pennant with Montreal; played and lost in Little World Series
1959	Player–manager for Orlando Dodgers (D Florida State League) – told I was the youngest player manager in the history of professional baseball

1960	Enrolled in Trenton State College
1960–1972	Managed swimming program at Greenacres County Club during summers
1963	Graduated from Trenton State College with a BS in Health & Physical Education
1964	Health & Physical Education Teacher, Hopewell Valley Central High School
1965	Earned Master's Degree from Trenton State College
1965–1982	Developed and administered Intramural Program, Rider College
1969	Began playing tennis at 36 years old
1975	Served as a chairperson on Mercer County Park Commission for development of new tennis facility in Mercer County Park
1976	Assistant Athletic Director at Rider College, scheduled women's sports
1976–1981	Coached Rider College men's tennis team
1978–2000	Member of National Ski Patrol, Ambassador at Mount Snow
1980	USTA National Hardcourt Tennis Champion, 45 & Over, La Jolla, California
1980–1989	Product Manager of Prince Ball Machines
1981–	Married Mary Ellen Hirst and had two children, Kyle and Tara
1981	USTA National Indoor Tennis Champion, 45 & Over, Salt Lake City
1981	Ranked No. 1 in nation and No. 10 in the world in the 45s in tennis
1981	Represented the U.S. at the Potter Cup in Spain and member of the winning Stevens Cup team

1982	Recipient of New Jersey Sports Writer Achievement Award
1983–1991	International Manager of Tennis Clinics for Prince Manufacturing
1984	Recipient of James E. Cryan Achievement Award
1984	Began making motivational speeches
1986	Constructed tennis court at house
1986	USTA National Clay Tennis Champion, 50 & Over, Sarasota, Florida
1988	Member of the State of New Jersey Governor's Council on Physical Fitness
1989–1990	Athletic Director for Rider College
1990–1999	Taught tennis and swimming at Hopewell Tennis and Swim Center
1990	Named Boy Scouts Man of the Year, George Washington Council
1990	Member of the Advisory Staff for two major tennis corporations
1992	Inducted into the inaugural Mercer County Tennis Hall of Fame
1998	Inducted into Trenton Baseball Hall of Fame as a member of 1948 Schroths National Championship Team (50th anniversary, 1998)
1999	Taught tennis at home and Hopewell Valley Tennis and Swim Center
1999	Voted as one of the top tennis players of the century in Mercer County and one of the top 15 athletes of all time in Trenton by the *Trentonian*
1999–Present	Teach tennis at home and at Bucks County Racquet Club and Hopewell Valley Tennis and Swim Center

2002	Inducted into the USTA Middle States Hall of Fame
2002	Member of inaugural class of Mercer County Sports Hall of Fame as a member of the 1948 Schroths Post 93 American Legion National Championship Team
2003	Inducted into Rider University Athletics Hall of Fame
2003	Retired from Hopewell Valley Tennis Club
2003–2004	Built swimming pool at home
2013	Inducted into USPTA Middle States Hall of Fame

PART I – MY STORY

Your brain gets information from two different sources. Your senses tell you what's going on in the outside world, while your emotions exist inside your body to tell you what these events and circumstances mean to you. Just as hunger motivates you to find food, emotions motivate you to take care of other needs—like safety and companionship—that ultimately promote survival and reproduction.

—*American Museum of Natural History brain exhibit*

My Family

I came from a family of brainy achievers. My bantamweight grandfather, Martin P. Devlin, migrated from southern Scotland to Center Street in Trenton. He worked in a pottery plant during the day and attended law school at night. He was what they now call an activist. He rallied the workers to strike for a raise in pay and later became a prosecutor and a confidant and adviser to New Jersey Governor Woodrow Wilson. James Kerney, editor and publisher of the *Trenton Times*, wrote that Martin Devlin was the Trenton lawyer who helped make Wilson a progressive. Kerney also wrote that while he was in the White House, Wilson said that he "had probably permitted Martin Devlin more than any other person to influence him"[1] My tough little grandpa died a few months after I was born so I never got to know him.

---

1   James Kerney, *The Political Education of Woodrow Wilson* (New York: Century, 1926), pp. 93, 112–13.

His wife Mary, my German grandmother, must have had brains because she married my grandfather. She raised four kids. One of those kids was my father, Martin P. Devlin, Jr., who went to Lafayette College and then law school. Those who knew him thought he had brains. He became a great lawyer, prosecutor, and judge. He drank, smoked five packs of cigarettes a day, was active in Trenton society life, and sought to move up in the world. My social climbing consisted of sneaking onto the Trenton Country Club golf course at the 15th hole until I'd get chased off.

My mother, who I call Saint Viola, was self-taught and well read. Before she married my father, she worked as secretary to the publisher of the *Trenton Times*. Mom raised five kids, one of whom was my father. The rest of us boys came one after another, less than a year apart, as abstinence was the only form of birth control my parents knew. It was me, John, and Donald. Then, six years later, my sister Trish.

Mom had brains and common sense—and she held the trump card. She was the boss and disciplinarian who ruled over my father and us kids. Whenever my father came home drunk on a Friday night, he slept in a side bedroom and did the dishes. He did a lot of dishes.

Mom had reddish brown hair and was beautiful, neat, and precise. She cooked dinner all dressed up. She wanted to look nice for my father when he came home from work. Not a single bite was taken until mom took off her apron, sat down, and grace was said. The damn meal was cold by then. Mom became a Catholic to marry my father and turned out to be the best Catholic of all of us. Her respite from the chaos of raising us was Mass, the Stations of the Cross, and the Rosary. She also read anything she could get her hands on. When she wasn't cooking or cleaning, I'd see her sitting in her bed reading or on the porch with a book.

Like my father, my brother John went to Lafayette College. And like my father he became a successful lawyer. He is sensitive, loves animals, and is generous to a fault. If it wasn't for his sensible wife, he would buy drinks for the entire college on homecoming weekends.

Donald, who we call Pancho, is third in line. He became an educator and taught business courses in high school. He was beloved by all his students. Donnie has always tried to take on the world and do good. John and Pancho were my rivals and buddies growing up.

Trish was raised by her three older brothers. She was tiny and impish, growing only to 5 feet tall, but she was a tomboy and tough. (At the age of 50 she played on a women's hockey team called the Mother Puckers.) Trish, who taught school, was loved, feared, and respected and married her grammar school boyfriend, who became a superior court judge for the State of New Jersey and the fairest judge this side of heaven. Trish's social skills are so good she can tell the pope to go to hell and get away with it. She took my mother and father into their home when they got old and sick, and she is the glue that holds the family together.

Born into a family like this, where does this leave me, Martin P. Devlin III, oldest son and heir apparent to his father and grandfather, two prominent attorneys? Brother to a future attorney and educators? Someone who loathed reading, writing, arithmetic, science, Latin, and studying and school in general? Who was told he had an IQ of 80, a low or below-normal intelligence? Who avoided social life? Who, at the age of 10, believed what his grandmother told him, that he had no brains and was nothing but a dumb jackass?

The Devil's Gifts and God's Gift

Growing up I was a loner—shy, self-centered, scared, uncomfortable, insecure, and afraid of girls. I loathed mixed parties. If you asked me my name, I'd be hard pressed for an answer. Speaking was worse than death. From an early age, I was confrontational and negative. I didn't feel I needed people. I had what I considered a ten-cent brain and hated school. I had no knowledge of how to change myself, much less influence other people. Without brains, how would I succeed at anything?

My mother nagged at me to be more social. When my mother wanted me to go to a party, I would tell her I didn't want to go. Her response was always, "How are you going to get along in life?!" In her mind, you made your way in the world by being part of society. Without social skills, you can't function in the world or be successful. You might just as well go hide in the woods.

And what about my physical gifts? I inherited my grandfather's build: Popeye-cartoon forearms and big shoulders, small feet, excessively short from the knees down, a big butt, long waist, big belly, short arms, little fingers, small hands. And I have astigmatism, which created a lifelong depth perception problem.

The way I saw it, I had no brains, no social skills, and stood no chance physically.

Yet God gave me a powerful gift—a force that would guide me throughout my life, a secret weapon that we all have in varying degrees. It's called the emotional brain. It's one of the two brains that helps us survive. If you've heard about following your heart. If you've had a feeling in the pit of your stomach, had a sense of something, that is from the emotional brain. My emotional brain guided me and communicated to me through my feelings, instincts, and intuition.

My emotional brain told me from early on that physical activity was of utmost importance to me. Funerals, weddings, school, jobs, my wife, holidays, my kids—none of these ever stopped me from getting exercise of some kind. I will need my daily workouts until the day I die.

It was in physical endeavors that I experienced my first success. These successes would eventually lead me to developing socially and mentally and becoming successful in life in ways I could not have imagined.

My First Playgrounds

My birth year, 1933, was during the Depression. I was delivered by our family doctor, my uncle, Dr. Jim Murphy, in an English Tudor house my father bought from builder Charlie Teunan for $5,000. Our house, at 132 Abernethy Drive, was in the Glen Afton section of Trenton, New Jersey. It was the biggest little house I've ever been in and was made of real 2x4s. At the time, there was only one house nearby. Our house stood between two canals, near the Trenton Country Club and the Delaware River. For 17 years, this house and its surroundings were my first playgrounds.

After my sister Trish was born, my father added a dormitory on the third floor to house us three boys. My brothers and I would line up our three beds in a row to serve as a wrestling mat or diving pool. We'd get a running start and catapult ourselves onto the beds and a brother. When we missed both, we'd crash into the wall, leaving holes that, if discovered, were sure to bring on the wrath of our father, "the General." We became so good at covering up the holes we could have been in the furniture-moving business.

The stairway going down from the third floor served as a racing run. We inserted our legs and butts into pillowcases, leaned back, and zipped down the stairs like race cars on a speedway. The pillow provided us a little protection from the wooden steps. The cellar was better suited to our ambushes. Its four concrete walls were safe from our assaults and somewhat soundproof. That room gave us a chance to let off steam on the rainy days.

But most of our time was spent outdoors, in every season and in all weather. Twenty-five yards from the back of the house was a berm. On one side of the berm was a railroad track and on the other the Delaware and Raritan Canal. Just beyond it was the 4th hole of the Trenton Country Club, the TCC, where my family were members.

During the winter, when the canal froze over, I imagined I was Hans Brinker, the fictional ice skater from the Netherlands. I'd strap on my skates and my feet would glide for hours, arms cutting into the air. One day the neighbor's dog, Freckles, followed me. After covering 20 miles, the dog's tongue was nearly resting on the ice. I damn near killed the dog!

The canal was also where we played ice hockey. Trish was the goalie, but with no pads or mask. I don't know how many teeth she lost. Another game we played on the canal we called Ticky. We'd take turns skating over a weak part of the ice until it got weaker and finally gave way and one of us fell in.

When it snowed, we strapped on wooden skis with bear-trap bindings and raced down the hilly 4th hole of the golf course. Gaining speed, we hit the berm and were launched into the air and onto the canal ice, imagining we were Norwegian ski jumpers. Mid-flight, I remember hoping the ice would hold on landing. When it did, we kept going, reaching the berm, and flying across the railroad track hoping a train wasn't coming.

One snow-covered February day, Mom ordered my dad to look for the four of us. He found us soaking wet playing in the creek near the green of the 13th hole of the golf course. By the time he got us home we were shivering from the cold. I drew a warm bath, and John jumped in.

"Get out or I'll poop on you!" I shouted at him.

Hearing the commotion, the General came storming up the steps to check on us. John was a good trooper and didn't squeal on me. He covered up each piece of feces with his hand as it threatened to pop up in the water. We didn't get caught, but my dad caught pneumonia.

My brothers and I had a good old sibling rivalry, and following the code of the time, if someone got you, you got them back. I was top dog and liked being in charge. My brothers were always eager to pick a fight with me and try to take me down a notch. They only really got me once.

Pancho and John challenged me to a boxing match. Like trainers getting a prize fighter ready for the ring, each of them slipped a glove on my hands and tied it on tightly. When I started boxing, I could feel my hands slipping and noticed a distinct, familiar odor coming forth from the gloves. They had loaded my boxing gloves up with their own feces! I couldn't get the gloves off. When my brothers finally untied them and took them off me, I had to get the stuff off my hands. It took much longer to get rid of that smell.

My mother called me a bully because I always wanted to be in charge and saw my brothers as the underdogs in our family. I swear my mother was in on it!

She understood boys and had a sense of humor about us. She also may have been getting her own revenge. When I was a toddler, Mom couldn't wait to show off her white-haired Afro cherub son to her bridge club, which she was hosting in the backyard. Much to her chagrin, when she went to introduce me, I was wrestling with the contents of my diaper. It was in every orifice of my body and all over the crib. Mom and her friends spent the whole afternoon cleaning me up. I don't believe they played bridge that afternoon.

Even though my mother would get on me, we were close. When I was old enough,

I helped her scrub the floors and watched her as she cooked. I learned how to cook just hanging out with her in the kitchen.

During the school year, I rode my Flexible Flyer sled to school. Equipped with wheels like a scooter, it got me to grade school and back—five miles each way. Kneeling with one leg on the sled, I propelled it down the highway, pushing with my other leg.

Between school and home was a new gas station on Sullivan Way, right across from the Water Power Canal. Earl Stevenson ran the place and would give us free Cokes when we stopped by after school and pay us the deposit money when we'd bring empty bottles to him. At the time, Coke came in glass bottles and cost a dime. You paid a deposit when you bought a bottle and got the money back when you returned it empty. As kids, we'd collect bottles that were left lying by the side of the road or in a field, and Earl gave us a few cents for each one we brought to him.

One day he found out my buddies and I were collecting the deposit for the empty Coke bottles he stored in a wooden case behind the station. Earl went after us, and when he caught us, he grabbed us by the necks, stuck our heads in the gas station toilet, and threw us off a nearby bridge over the canal into the water. I was building my diving skills.

After the toilet episode, we forever called him "Stinky Earl." The only time I took the bus to school was to get back at Stinky Earl. For days I rode the bus and each time we rode past the station, full of customers, I got the kids on the bus to holler out the window, "Hey, Stinky Earl!" The bus was rocking, a turbulent sea of raucous kids, heads poking out the window. It's a wonder the bus didn't tip over. This taunting wasn't serious, and neither was Stinky Earl's "corporal punishment." That was his way of evening the score. Getting the kids to taunt him was mine. He just laughed it off.

The same canal Stinky Early threw us in ran in front of our house. Three football fields away, it was called the Raritan Water Power Canal. Beyond it was the glorious Delaware River. In the summers, my brothers, my best friend Hanky and I built kayaks out of barrel staves, covered them with muslin, smeared the muslin with paint, and sojourned up and down the canal for miles. What started as a splashing game turned into a sinking game and sometimes escalated into a destroying-boats game, as we attacked each other's kayaks with our paddles and smashed them up. After the onslaught stopped, we salvaged what we could and rebuilt the kayaks or built new ones if they were a lost cause. Then we'd carry them back to the canal and start the process all over.

The Water Power Canal was our barometer each spring for when we'd start swimming. There was a monkey swing we used to propel us over and drop us into the canal. Each year we challenged ourselves to beat the previous year's record. At first, we went into the canal in May, then April, then March.

The Delaware River was just beyond the canal. Hanky had been admonished not to go in the river. I assured Hanky that we'd never get caught, that it was extremely safe.

"I know every rock in the river," I told him.

We lowered ourselves into one of our homemade kayaks and took off. We hadn't even reached the first rapids and were swimming for our lives. That wasn't the only kayak the Delaware River claimed. The second one we donated after a snake found its way to the bottom of our prized possession. As soon as we saw it slithering near our feet, we jumped ship.

We spent days playing "King of the Rapids." We'd swim out into the river to fight the rapids and one another to see who would suffer a "take down" and be pulled through the churning waters and sent down the river. Whoever lost responded by clawing their way back for another bout. We played from can't see to can't see, from morning till night, dawn till dusk.

One day, we decided to swim out into the river to Rotary Island, a long strip of land in the middle of the Delaware not far from home. We removed our clothes. If we made it to the island, we would run to the other end and plunge back in the river, hoping we could successfully battle the current and end up close to where our clothes were. The bigger danger was missing the island completely. If that happened the current would take us all the way to downtown Trenton without a stitch of clothing. We took off swimming and made it across the rapid-laden river to the island and back to the riverbank, but we still had to duck cars, jump guardrails, and run like scalded dogs to retrieve our clothes. My running and jumping skills improved dramatically.

Beyond the canal behind our house was a fairway and the swimming pool at the TCC, where the Devlins were members. It was so close to our house you could hear sounds from the pool at night. But getting to the pool wasn't easy. There were three ways to get there from our house: get a ride, walk a mile along the railroad tracks, or swim across the canal. While the Water Power Canal at least had a few fish in it, the one behind our house was a cesspool. I had a lot of energy—and an equal amount of laziness. I chose the quickest route. I was covered in mud and crap that dried on me by the time I crossed the 4th fairway. Then I would hide in the bushes until an opportune moment, when, encrusted with smelly gunk, I would run to the pool and dive in—and be immediately ordered out by the lifeguards. After I was back in their good graces, I'd spring off the diving board and cannonball the well-dressed ladies coming from lunch at the clubhouse. I was sharpening my diving skills.

———————————— • ————————————

Paradise was Lavallette at the Jersey Shore. Hanky's dad, Frank Casey, my father's law associate, rented a house there every summer. I was invited for a day, I stayed for a month. On one side of the house was the ocean, on the other side was Barnegat Bay. The bay offered seining for fish bait and softshell crabs, crabbing by boat using mutilated fish parts, fishing for baby blues off the docks, swimming with shoes on, and crewing in a sneakbox, a small, light, shallow-bottomed boat. Hanky and I raced against sixty yacht racers and catboats. Sneakbox racers needed additional weight on windy days and the boat we had leaked like a sieve. With my Popeye arms, my job was to bail it out with a hand pump. We always led from start to finish.

Hanky and I also raced the Lavallette lifeguards in their Durham-like rowboats from out in the ocean to the beach. If the two little kids in Hanky's aluminum canoe won, all of Lavallette would know, and the guards' reputation would be destroyed.

Hanky and I never won those races. We never once made it all the way to the beach. The canoe was so light, the bow dipped down with each movement of the waves. Hanky always sat in front and had to scramble to the back of the canoe at just the right time to shift the weight so the canoe wouldn't nosedive to the bottom of the ocean. If he didn't make it in time, the canoe would flip over. I would be catapulted clear of the boat, but it would come down on Hanky. Whenever we crashed and burned, we swam the waterlogged canoe to the beach, emptied its contents, and paddled through the surf again to meet our challengers, who had some belly laughs at our expense.

The canoe also served as our fishing rig. Once we made it through the surf, we'd paddle miles out in the ocean to the fisheries and drop our fishing lines into the nets where the fish had already been caught. We still caught nothing!

We used to pray for Nor'easters to make the ocean as rough as it could be so we could play a game we invented called "Driftwood." We'd lay on our backs in the sand at the edge of the water, hands joined. We were not allowed to move as the big boomers at high tide would batter and somersault us like a piece of driftwood. When that game was over, sand was in every crevice of our bodies.

Once I needed a workout and decided to go for a swim during a fierce storm. The first wave took me down and around, beneath the roiling surface of the ocean. I did not know which way was up or down. I gained a newfound respect for the ocean. That was my first and last time swimming in a hurricane.

The ocean was a great haven for me. In fact, it was heaven. Days were filled with swimming from lifeguard stand to lifeguard stand, body surfing, fishing, and racing. Hanky and I would body surf all day, from can stand to can't stand, exhausted from battling the waves. I would dive under the incoming waves and then go to a peaceful, quiet place where I could tread water and look for the perfect wave. When I saw the swell of the ocean, I put my head down and my arms started flailing. Feeling the goose of the wave reminded me to keep kicking. When caught by the wave, I put my arms to my sides and held my breath until my lungs felt like bursting. Then I'd raise my head and enjoy the beautiful view of the beach. Hanky and I body surfed like this till our bellies needed sustenance and we'd head for dinner and fresh corn and tomatoes.

When my father came to pick me up after that month was over, he wanted to go out into the ocean with me in the canoe.

"How do you manage the waves in the ocean?" he asked me.

"It's easy," I bragged. "Have you ever handled these big waves before?"

"No, but I ran the river. I shot the rapids. I'll show you."

Whoa! We're in trouble now, I thought to myself. *The river rapids weren't a piece of cake, but the ocean has monster waves! He has no idea what we're in for.*

As we were heading out from the shore, a big old wave crashed over us. The boat flipped over, separating me and my old man from the canoe. He went flying one way, I went the other, and the paddles somewhere else. The lifeguards saw what happened and climbed down from their perches and swam out to rescue us. What a commotion! I nearly drowned myself laughing.

My father, to his credit, took it in stride. But his life wasn't the outdoors and vigorous physical activity. It centered on the country club and cocktail parties and doing what he could to maintain his place or climb in society.

The month I was at the shore, Hanky's dad would join us on the weekends. I'd see him treading water, floating, swimming out into the ocean after dinner as the sun was setting. He would float and bob on his back in the water and to enjoy the view. That was how he dealt with the stresses of his job. The idea of how an adult could relax and enjoy life put a picture in my mind that never left me. It grabbed me right and intrigued me. He was way the hell out there looking for enjoyment. That was a beautiful way to do things.

Blessed Sacrament and Junior High School #3

Blessed Sacrament Elementary School and I were not compatible. I had a hard time with schoolwork. I was restless. I daydreamed. I couldn't pay attention or sit still. I had way too much energy and couldn't help but get in trouble.

I did like Sister Antineta, my first-grade teacher. She was warm-hearted and seemed to like me. I liked her so much I'd have married her. She wrote in my report card, "Martin only wants to play." She got me.

Our house at 132 Abernethy Drive, Trenton, New Jersey

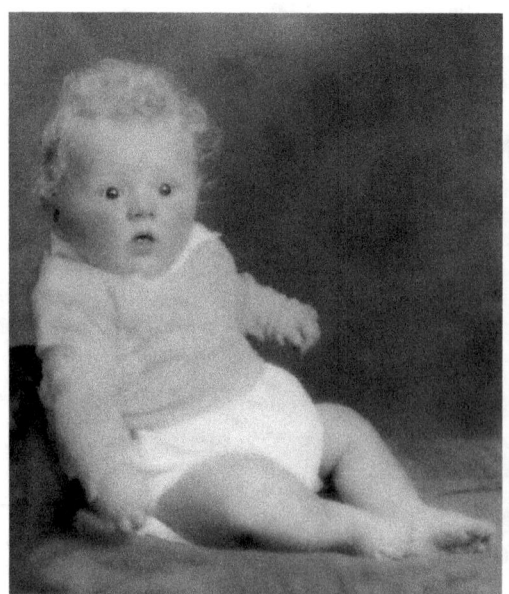

Here I am as a baby

My grandfather, Martin P. Devlin

The Devlin kids at the Trenton Country Club pool

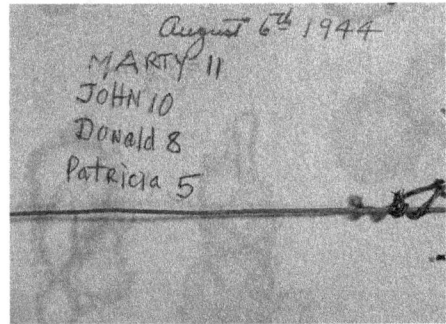

Our diving board ages, from right to left

The Devlin kids, years later: (L to R) Donald, John, me, and Trish Devlin Delehey (C)

My mother, Viola Mae Attwood Devlin

My father, Martin P. Devlin, Jr.

My salvation was recess in the pit and Father Degnan and his 16-ounce boxing gloves. The church must have run out of money to build a playground. The pit was a big hole in the ground. During recess we played baseball there using our arms as bats and striking the innards of a tennis ball with our hands. Recess gave me a break from hate camp.

In class I had trouble following what was going on. I'd sit in the back of the classroom until the teacher would move me up for talking or pulling a prank like dipping a girl's pigtail in the inkwell. At Blessed Sacrament the nuns hit you with a ruler for goofing off or not paying attention. When they really didn't know how to deal with you, they sicced Father Degnan on you.

Father Degnan was less than 5 feet tall and loved to box. In the eyes of the nuns, his job was to keep us in line and teach us a lesson, but for me, I had no reason to be good. I'd get sent to the old gym/auditorium and get my butt kicked by Father Degnan. I loved to box, and I loved Father Degnan.

I even became an altar boy so I could serve Mass with him, but I never did. Father Hayes, the pastor, was in charge of the altar boy schedule and always had me serving for him. On the days I served Mass, I went to a second Mass just to hear Father Degnan. Once in a sermon he compared the effect of God-give grace to spinach and Popeye. Even though I never understood the grace and God part, I sure knew about spinach and Popeye. Father Degnan was down to earth, someone I could relate to.

One day I went to school, and Father Degnan didn't show up. A few days I found out that he'd died. The story was he had gone to New York City and was injured in a fight that proved to be fatal. I cried when I found out. I felt lost. I was 11 years old, and I now had no reason to go to school.

Once I was so scared of failing a test, I feigned sickness, and the school gave me permission to go home after lunch. I took my Flexible Flyer to Arctic Ice Cream and spent the afternoon—and all my money—ordering sugar cones. By the time I got home at the end of the school day, my parents had gotten a call from the school checking in on me. I soon met up with my father's belt! Corporal punishment was considered a way to motivate you.

It did no good for me. I never could understand what was expected of me in school. Latin made no sense to me. Math was too abstract. I never learned to diagram a sentence. It was like a foreign language. The only subject that made any sense to me was catechism. It was black and white.

I had to find a way to get through the 12 years of school required of me. Soon I discovered the halo effect. I learned that if I smiled a lot and looked like I was listening, I wouldn't get in trouble. My grades were still not great, but I was passed through and the teachers liked me.

I was relieved when my eight years of Blessed Sacrament were over. My next school was Junior High School #3. Fortunately, the skills I'd developed—from my cannonballing at Trenton Country Club to monkey swinging into the canal to flying-through-air-off-bridges—were finally in demand. I became a diver on the swim team and played basketball and baseball.

That fall, basketball was my first organized team activity. At my height I was an unlikely player, but I loved being physical and had unbound energy. I dove after balls and hustled. At first, I was quiet and shy. I had no idea how to be on a team. Then I started to learn to laugh, to holler and support my teammates and lead by example. I was named captain of the basketball team and the swim team and even ended up making the basketball All-Star team. In the spring, the school offered baseball. This provided me with another refuge from the classroom. I became captain as a freshman.

While I still had to go to class, all I did—all I needed to do—was show up, keep my nose clean, smile, stay quiet, listen, and follow directions. I made it through that year in junior high because I was socially promoted. I still dreaded going to class and taking tests. I had no study habits, no idea of how to study. I went into tests not knowing the answers or even what the teachers wanted from me. I was scared and thought I was dumb.

Playing sports was where I was most comfortable. It was how I was learning to fit in, where I was starting to become successful, and where I started seeing that I could be pretty good at something.

With my Junior High School #3 basketball team. I was the captain (holding the ball), my first leadership role

Schroths Baseball and My First Job

The summer before I entered high school, I tried out for the local American Legion baseball club and made the team. The best teams go to the county, state, regional, and sectional tournaments at the end of the season, and a handful compete for the national championship.

The Schroths, Trenton Post 93's American Legion baseball team, had always been a winning team. They were the runner up in 1945 and 1946 and had won every American Legion title except for the national championship. At 14 years old, I was the youngest player on the team.

In my first summer with the Schroths, baseball wasn't enough physical activity to keep me happy. I was used to playing long and hard every day, and my father wanted me to learn the lessons of work. As president of TCC, he asked the golf course superintendent about job openings. As you might expect, the superintendent created a job for me. The guy must not have been happy about it because he asked me to rake hay out of a gully the size of a football field. I was done in an hour.

When I came back to his office, he asked me, "Why are you back so soon?"

He must have thought I was quitting. When I told him I'd finished, he couldn't believe it. Then he gave me another job—this one in the middle of the night. I was to water the fairways by setting up the watering units into receptacles and drawing water out of the Raritan Water Power Canal. Here I was, 14 years old, with no driver's license, and driving the jeep across the whole green golf course. I was on top of the world and felt like a king.

There was no way my folks would drive me to the country club so I could get to work at 2 a.m. I wouldn't swim that cesspool at night, so to get there I walked two miles on railroad tracks in the dark. Muskrats scared the devil out of me as they scurried to the canal, dragging their scaly tails across the ground. When I heard a freight train approaching, I hopped off the tracks. As the summer went along, I got bolder and would grab onto the bar on the side of one of those boxcars and ride shotgun. If I had miscalculated or slipped, I would have been chopped liver.

Once I made it to the country club, I had the cushiest job there. They left me keys to a jeep. I drove to each of the holes, setting sprinkler heads and drawing water from the canal to water the greens, fairways, and tees. I worked through dawn. It was the best, most fun job on the golf course. This was my first real job, and I had money and time to myself and was unbothered by social demands.

After I finished up my work at the golf course at 10 a.m. I'd go home, get a few hours' sleep, and go to baseball practice. Other than sleeping, I was in motion all the time.

The following summer I was 15 and didn't work. I was too busy with baseball.

Kelly (Carl) Palumbo, my coach on the Schroths, had been a prisoner of war in World War II and received the Purple Heart. Unlike a lot of coaches at the time, he never yelled at us and wasn't an authoritarian. He was soft-spoken and a gentleman who acted more like a teacher. He paid attention to the small things, like noticing how strong a throwing arm the catcher had before deciding whether to put on a steal. He taught us to look for cues so we knew what to expect in the game and we'd be prepared to take advantage. Besides batting, fielding, and throwing the ball around the horn, he made sure we practiced what to do in game situations whether we were in the field or at bat. That is common now, but it wasn't then. He helped us outthink the opposing teams. We knew what to do. Knowing what to do, we never doubted ourselves.

That year we kept on winning even though we couldn't break a pane of glass with our bats or hit our way out of a paper bag. We were called the hitless wonders. Our trademark was hustle and picking each other up. We'd scrap for runs—steal, dive, and disrupt the other team. We applied what we learned from Coach Palumbo about the strategy of the game. Kelly Palumbo outcoached the other coaches, and we outhustled the other teams.

We won the county, state, regional, and sectional tournaments and made it to the national championship in Indianapolis. I enjoyed the whole experience with my teammates. Dizzy Dean, one of the greatest pitchers of all time, was there for the tournament. We beat Omaha and then Belleview, Illinois, made it to the national championship game and beat the team from Jacksonville, 4–1. "Quick thinking and fast base running enabled Trenton to cash in on every break," wrote Jim Burris of *The Sporting News* (Junior Baseball Edition, Sept. 1943, p. 6). I played third and stole three bases in the championship game. It was 1948, and we were the first New Jersey team to win it all: number 1 out of more than 14,000 American Legion teams across the country.

When we arrived back in Trenton at the South Clinton Avenue train station, five thousand people turned out to welcome us home. We were driven in open cars through a parade route. Along with local dignitaries, major league ballplayers attended a dinner given in our honor. The fine knuckleballer Dutch Leonard was there. Rogers Hornsby, Robin Roberts, and George Sisler, all now in the Baseball Hall of Fame, were there. Bert Shotton, manager of the Brooklyn Dodgers, attended too. Our local baseball hero George Case from the Washington Senators spoke. We truly had a heroes' welcome in our hometown.

It was an incredible summer. My teammates and I had become local celebrities. We got loads of attention from the media and appeared the following year in *Look* magazine ("American Legion Junior Baseball," August 16, 1949). Winning the championship was one of the highlights of my life. In many ways, the experience brought out what I already had inside of me. I understood the importance of a great work ethic, I had high standards, and I expected to succeed at whatever I threw myself into.

I wasn't always all that focused on the attention we were getting until it got in the way of what I wanted to do. That September we were going to be honored at the first game of the World Series between the Boston Braves and the Cleveland Indians. But I didn't want to go. I didn't care about that kind of stuff. I had just entered high school and I'd just started playing football. I loved football. I loved the physicality of the game. When I found about the trip to Boston, I cried, sobbed, and was inconsolable. It took lots of talks from Coach Palumbo, my father, and Trenton High's football coach, Pat Clemens, and Coach Clemens assuring me that I wouldn't lose my standing on the football team when I returned from the trip. Once I finally believed him, I went and had a good time. The Schroths were also recognized as a team by the Baseball Hall of Fame in Cooperstown.

I continued to play for the Schroths during the next two summers and served as co-captain after the 1948 championship season. I was the first player to be on the team for 4 years. I had a direction in life. The physical guided me, and I achieved success. As my name started appearing in the sports sections of the newspapers, my parents began worrying less about my grades. My parents, especially my father, began to look at me differently.

Trenton High School and College

At 135 pounds I was a Lilliputian among giants on the football field. To compensate, I worked at football like a one-armed paper hanger, like a one-legged man in a butt-kicking contest. Running, passing, catching, throwing myself through the air to block, and tackling with my head. I loved the physical contact. In the NFL today, I'd be penalized and fined.

Like many people in Trenton, Coach Clemens knew the reputation of my father and grandfather in the law and in society. He made me the quarterback on the assumption that I had their brains and could manage the position. When we shifted from the T-formation to the single-wing, I became the blocking back for big, burly fullbacks. I still wonder how my tiny feet could punt a football, how I could grip the football with little fingers and small hands, how I could throw

With my Schroth teammates posing with a parade car before the championship. I didn't know what a big deal this was—I was just having fun!

We won! The Shroths after the American Legion championship game in Indianapolis, September 11, 1948. This was my second organized team; I played 3rd base and was co-captain the next year. (The names of the Schroths are in Photo Credits.)

Part of the crowd of 5,000 that met us when we returned from the championship game in Indianapolis. I'm in the middle at the Clinton Street (Train) Station in Trenton.

The Schroths with Mr. Raymond Schroth (top row, 2nd from L), the soft-spoken, thoughtful man, who sponsored our team. This was taken during a photo shoot for the Look *magazine article "American Legion Junior Baseball," August 16, 1949.*

the ball for distance with short stubby arms, how I could throw passes over huge linesmen or even see who I was passing to, especially given what I learned later was a depth perception problem. To get the football by the giants coming at me, I had to throw it early or fling it sidearm. I played safety on the defense. I don't know how my short legs could chase down broken-field runners and block and tackle players twice my weight. I was the last resort before they made it to the goal line. I believe I succeeded because *can't* wasn't in my vocabulary—at least as it related to athletics.

The sport that followed football season was swimming. Our coach, Al Neuschaefer, had been an All-American offensive lineman for Rutgers University football team, where he played with the great Paul Robeson. After college he even spent a year coaching pro football for the Staten Island Stapletons, a team in the National Football League, before coaching football at Trenton Central High School. He was a tough guy who taught his football players dirty tactics like tossing dirt into the eyes of opposing linemen. As punishment he was made the swimming coach, even though he couldn't swim a lick.

I was a diver on the swim team. Al Neuschaefer carried a clipboard and a kickboard as he walked the side of the pool watching us. Any time he thought I wasn't executing a dive with enough effort, he'd fling a kickboard at me. It flew at me like a missile and would pick me off midair. The swimmers had heavy-duty desk chairs thrown at them. The pool water was so cold we sneaked into the showers to get warm. Once he learned what we were doing, he locked us in the pool during practices. We accepted this treatment. It felt right for the times. He demanded the most out of us, and I respected that.

Year after year this big, burly coach won interscholastic meets held from Maine to Florida. He coached the swimming team from 1932 to 1960. During that time the team won 19 state championships and 10 Eastern States titles. He went on to become the first high school coach in the International Swimming Hall of Fame. He was tough mentally and physically and had high expectations for us. I became an All-American diver twice under his tutelage and co-captained the swimming teams. My big rival was Bobby Clotworthy from Westfield High. I came in second to him in the big meets. He eventually became an Olympic champion. He won the bronze in 1952 and the gold in 1956 on the 3-meter board.

Unlike me, Bobby devoted the whole year to diving. I played sports year-round and needed to do something physical and keep fit between the football and baseball seasons. I liked competing, but I never loved diving. I hated the cold water, and if you missed a dive and had a bad landing, hitting the water felt like crashing into cement. You'd get battered and bruised by a hard shot into the water.

As for school, I had to endure three more years of hate camp in one of the most populated high schools in the state. While I was a dynamo in physical endeavors, I struggled in the classroom and was shy, awkward, and introverted. I never went to parties. I was schooled properly by my parents in manners but was never in an environment with girls and didn't want to be. I was only comfortable with boys who spoke my language—sports and play. Finally, in high school I managed to get my first girlfriend.

Nancy Ide was on the girls' swim team. She got me out and about and I started to gain a few social skills. I learned the basics of how to talk in social situations just to be polite. I gained more confidence and began to feel accepted and came out of my shell a little more. I was a one-girl guy, and for three years Nancy and I were inseparable. She helped me tremendously in my social development. We went to parties together and were very popular, though we rarely went out on the weekends. It was then I rested up from all my physical activities.

The spring sport was baseball. I starred on the diamond but was having my usual trouble in the classroom and with my grades. My coach, Tom Murphy, taught math. He once prepped me for a test by writing the problems and solutions on the blackboard and encouraging me to memorize them. I didn't even succeed at doing that! I'll never know if I could have done the work. I believed I was stupid and couldn't learn so I never really tried. The only book I read in high school was *Home Run Hennessey*. I wrote three book reports on it, one each year in high school.

Of the three sports I played at Trenton Central, the sport I loved most was football. I was selected to the All-City Football Team and began to have aspirations of playing and then coaching college and professional football. But when Coach Clemens resigned as football coach after my junior year, I gave up the sport. I'd been loyal to Pat, but with him gone, and, given my success on the diamond and my lack of size, I devoted myself to baseball, where I thought I had a future. My senior year I became an All-State player, batting .390. A newspaper article said that my "speed, rifle arm, and ability to hit in the pinches brought much misery to opponents." Baseball was my sweet spot.

All-American diver, All-City quarterback, All-State baseball player, and the Schroths' national championship: people were starting to take notice of my accomplishments. One coach said, "Marty Devlin could be a big league ball player, an Olympic swimmer, a successful performer on the tennis and golf tours, or a champion bowler. He could do anything in sports." My name and photo appeared in the local newspapers, and I was recognized for my "star-studded school-boy career" and called a "brilliant all-around athlete." The *Trentonian* named me one of the top ten athletes to come out of Trenton ("Trenton's 15 Greatest Sports Stars of All Time," December 31, 1999, p. 40.)

My parents were proud of my achievements. In my father's eyes, my success enhanced him in society. I'd found a way to fit in. I sure looked the part of the all-American boy. I had the big smile, and with my blue eyes and blonde hair I looked like an innocent cherub. I'd get 200 points just for putting my name on a piece of paper. I managed to graduate from Trenton Central High School with C grades for just behaving. A star athlete, my future was being laid out for me. I had a partial scholarship to play baseball at Lafayette College, but I wanted to go elsewhere. Despite my mediocre academic record, I applied and was accepted at Duke University. Duke had the reputation as the "Princeton of the South," but I wasn't going to Duke for the academics. I was going to play baseball.

Duke had the best college team in the country and was one of the Big Four of college baseball, along with Wake Forest, North Carolina State, and North Carolina. We'd play the top schools, and with the warmer weather in the South we'd get to play more games than the teams in the North.

First-year players practiced with the varsity, but NCAA rules at the time prohibited them from playing varsity baseball. I played third base for the freshman team and dove for the swim team. I also played handball with my buddies, honing my eye–hand coordination and my ability to use both hands equally well.

In every job I held from college on, I was paid for having fun. It started after my freshman year at Duke. During the summer, along with many college baseball players, I was tagged to play in a small-town semi-pro league. Jack Coombs, the baseball coach at Duke, had been a star pitcher for the Philadelphia Athletics. He fit in at Duke in many ways. He wore a suit around campus and was educated and well spoken. He also had connections and sent me play for the team in Clarksville, Virginia.

Technically, we couldn't get paid for playing baseball. To comply with NCAA regulations, we had to work. Summers in Virginia were scorching. My job was on a construction site, to oil a crane that never ran. This was fake work, an excuse for paying us under the table while we honed our baseball skills.

How many times can you oil a crane that's never used? I hid under the idle crane for shade and slept all day. How long can you do nothing for 8 hours day after day? I had way too much energy for that. I wasn't happy and told the foreman in charge to give me something to do. He gave me a job driving a scoop mobile. I learned to operate this machine that looks like a backward tricycle with a big bucket on the front end. I'd pick up a load and drive it to an area on the job site. After working 8 hours a day, I played baseball in the evenings.

After that summer I returned to Duke, but a semester into my sophomore year my academic shortcomings and goofing off caught up with me. I went to movies, played pool, got drunk, and drove around in my new Model A Ford. I even asked Dick Palatine, one of my roommates, to write a paper for my Greek Mythology course. I failed the class anyway.

I was lost academically and fearful. I figured I'd get through school the same way I did before. By being a yes man. By smiling. I had been socially promoted until I got to Duke. Here the halo effect didn't work. The faculty at Duke didn't give athletes a pass like they did at Trenton High, and I found myself academically ineligible to play baseball in the spring. But I wasn't sorry. I was happy. I majored in pre-law to please my father but had no interest in becoming a lawyer. A year and a half of failed classes meant that at 19 years old I finally had a chance to do what I really wanted: play professional baseball with what friends of my parents called the "dregs of society."

I was a two-time All-American diver at Trenton Central High School.

Number 33, I was an All-City quarterback for Trenton High School—here leading the blocking.

TIMES, MONDAY, APRIL 12, 1948

Trenton Sports Figures by Joe Masick and Bill Dwyer

HE HAS TOURED THE TRENTON C.C. LAYOUT IN THE "EIGHTIES."

MARTY PLACED 2nd IN THE EASTERN INTER-SCHOLASTIC and THE STATE INTERSCHOLASTIC DIVING CHAMPIONSHIPS.

MARTIN P. DEVLIN, III

15-YEAR-OLD TRENTON HIGH SCHOOL SOPHOMORE IS ONE OF THE MOST VERSATILE SCHOOL-BOY ATHLETES IN THE CITY

YOU COMIN' IN WRONG!

YOUNG DEVLIN PLAYED A LEADING ROLE AT THE QUARTERBACK POST LAST SEASON FOR THE RED and BLACK GRID SQUAD.

HE IS A MEMBER OF THE T.H.S. BASEBALL SQUAD and HOPES TO BE THE SCHROTHS REGULAR THIRD-BASEMAN TILL 1950!

I received lots of media attention early on, creating new meaning to the word exaggeration!

I played baseball at Trenton High School along with a lot of my teammates with the Schroths.

Starting Out in Professional Baseball

Big league scouts had been following me since high school and I'd batted .383 for the freshman team at Duke, so when I left school, I knew I'd have options and felt confident I could sign on with a team. Lefty Lloyd, a scout for the Philadelphia Athletics, the team nearest my home, liked me, but Connie Mack, who owned and managed the team, had a reputation for being cheap so I didn't seriously consider the Athletics. I was also being scouted by Rex Bowen with the Pittsburgh Pirates and Marty Jones from the Brooklyn Dodgers. The St. Louis Cardinals had invited me to camp, but the Dodgers and the Pirates agreed that I could spend half of spring training with each team, with the understanding that I would take the best offer from one of those clubs. I saw that as my best opportunity.

I showed up at spring training in Florida excited about my future. Then, halfway through the preseason, someone on the Dodger staff told me my father had had a heart attack. It was a massive one. The Dodgers sent my butt home immediately. My father survived the heart attack but was in bad shape. I took the train back to Florida and my first spring training, still without a contract to play professional baseball, but confident it would come.

Toward the end of spring training my mom worked with me on negotiating the contract. Al Campanis, the Dodgers' scouting director, first offered $2,000, but I wouldn't take it. I didn't respect him and felt he didn't respect me. When Fresco Thompson, the head of the Dodgers' farm system, got involved the offer was doubled. The Pirates offered me the same $4,000 signing bonus, but the Dodgers had made the offer first. I could have bargained, using one team against the other—I knew stuff like that happened—but I kept my promise to Fresco when I first came to spring training that I wouldn't do that. It was taboo for me anyway, even this kind of negotiating was common at the time. I would respect the Dodgers, and I wanted them to respect me.

Four thousand was big bucks, the biggest signing bonus the Dodgers could offer without putting me on the major league roster. My parents didn't have insurance and with my father unable to work and my mother with three kids to feed, all the money I signed for went straight to Mom and Pop. I didn't care. I was grateful to my parents for letting me play baseball.

What I didn't appreciate was my father's acquaintances blaming me for my father's heart attack. The scuttlebutt in his social circles was that my leaving Duke had caused it. That wasn't the reason. My dad wasn't in good shape. He drank hard, smoked five packs of cigarettes a day, and never exercised. During the Depression everyone drank like camels and smoked like choo-choo trains. He had a great mind, but he was physically lazier than homemade sin.

The way the minor leagues are set up, there's a hierarchy of teams that serve to test and prepare players with the hope that some will climb up the ladder all the way to the major leagues. Branch Rickey, the father of this farm system, created for the

Here I am at Duke. The baseball in my left hand says everything!

I finally realized my dream of playing baseball. Here I am with teammates walking around a minor league town.

Dodgers the most advanced minor league system of any major league club. With 17 minor league teams throughout the U.S. and into Canada, they created loads of competition for a spot on the big league club.

At the lowest level were the D league teams. If you started there, you'd tried to move on up the ladder to C, B, A, AA, AAA, and then, hopefully, the major league team.

I was vying with at least 32 players for a position and over 400 players competing to play for the big league club. After a reorganization of professional baseball in 1963, minor league classifications changed and there were far fewer leagues and fewer players, but when I entered the pros, the size of the minor league systems meant fierce competition to move up in the system.

My first contract was with Elmira (New York), A baseball in the Eastern League, but my first pro baseball team was the Greenwood Dodgers, C baseball in the Cotton States League.

My Career with the Dodgers

Greenwood Dodgers	Cotton States League	C	1952
U.S. Army, 39th Regiment			*1953–54**
Elmira Pioneers	Eastern League	A	1955
Mobile Bears	Southern Association	AA	1955
Fort Worth Cats	Texas League	AA	1956, 1957
St. Paul Saints	American Association	AAA	1958
Montreal Royals	International League	AAA	1958
Orlando Dodgers†	Florida State League	D	1959

* Participated in spring training during 30-day leave.
† Player–manager.

INTEGRATING BASEBALL

From the 1880s until 1947, the major leagues had been a whites-only league. I was entering professional baseball around the time major league baseball clubs began signing players from the Negro Leagues, which was stacked with talented players who were blocked from playing in the major league. In 1945 the Boston Red Sox were pressured into giving these three players a tryout: Sam Jethroe, the quickest man in baseball, Marvin Williams, and Jackie Robinson. It lasted just 90 minutes. The players were dismissed without being given so much as a reason why.

That same year Branch Rickey was considering whether to sign Jackie Robinson as the first player to break the color barrier. He sent Buzzie Bavasi, future vice president of the Dodgers, to observe Rachael, Jackie Robinson's fiancée and future wife. Buzzie is said to have told Rickey: "If Jackie married Rachael, Jackie is smart enough to be in the major leagues." In 1947, Jackie signed for $4,000—the same amount as Marty Devlin a few years later. Big money then! Never mind Jackie Robinson's impact on baseball and civil rights vs. Marty Devlin's contributions. How important was Jackie Robinson? Martin Luther King Jr. once said of him, "I didn't start the Civil Rights Movement, Jackie Robinson did."

The Greenwood Dodgers

The Dodgers had their own plane to fly the big league team to games around the country during the season. At the start of the season, they used the plane to shuttle minor leaguers from spring training in Florida to their minor league teams. I found myself on one of those flights with my new teammates, headed from Florida to Greenwood, Mississippi. "Bump" Holman, the young pilot, invited me to sit in the jump seat right behind him and the co-pilot. I was so shy I felt more comfortable there than sitting with my teammates. When the co-pilot had to relieve himself, Bump invited me to sit in the co-pilot's seat and fly the plane.

I was 19 years old and flying the Dodgers plane, a DC-3 that had been repurposed from the war.

I didn't know at the time that you made passengers more comfortable by flying the airplane straight. My teammates were sicker than hell and began shouting words I never heard before, demanding that I relinquish my chauffeuring duties immediately.

"Get that SOB out of there!" "What the ---- are you doing? Trying to kill us all?!"

I responded by defending my airplane-flying ability and shouting some choice words back to them. I don't remember exactly what they were, but I do know that my vocabulary expanded dramatically on that flight.

That crazy experience started to bond me with my teammates. I was learning more about how to lower barriers between me and the rest of the world.

Not long after I'd settled in at Greenwood, Chuck Lamberti, a pitcher from Albuquerque as small and skinny as a toothpick who'd been in the minors for a while, talked me into playing pool at a bar. He was a Bobby Riggs–type—a big talker, a bit of a con man. I hadn't swung at a single pitch as a Greenwood Dodger, and I was minus my first paycheck—$250 a month. That was my welcome to professional baseball and the real world.

Stan Wasiak was my manager at Greenwood. Like Kelly Palumbo, my American Legion Schroths' coach, and Tom Murphy, my high school baseball coach, Wasiak endorsed hustle and aggressiveness. The Greenwood Dodgers were an exciting team whose roster included Danny McDevitt and Karl Spooner, players who later made the big leagues. I stole 48 bases that year.

Greenwood was a small town, like many of the towns in the league. If you had a good night at bat, you'd stand on a street corner, light up a cigar, and look for a date while watching the girls go by. That season at Greenwood I had my second girlfriend. I met Ann Turner while she was life guarding at the local pool. She was beautiful, had brains, and a sense of humor. She came to the home games to see me play and wrote to me while I was on the road. Now I had no reason to light up cigars in Greenwood or in any town on the road—in Natchez or Meridian

(Mississippi), in Monroe (Louisiana), in Hot Springs, Pine Bluff, or El Dorado (Arkansas).

That season Danny Lynk, a bonus baby who had spent the year before riding the bench for the Dodgers, and I both rented rooms for $20 per month from eighty-year-old Mrs. Seng and hung out together. There were certain beliefs at the time that discouraged cross training. You could get fined if you were found swimming on a game day—it was seen as weakening your muscles. There was a also belief that playing golf would mess up your swing. Stan, our manager, happened by the driving range one day and spotted Danny and me hitting golf balls.

He got out of his car. He was angry and yelled, "Do you think that'll help you bat any better?!"

"I couldn't be doing any worse!" I responded.

Stan didn't think it was funny and fined us each $10—a lot of money at the time!

On the road, we spent a lot of time on the bus and found some unique ways to entertain ourselves. Danny had a ukulele and showed me how to play a few chords. On one trip, I bragged that I could play the instrument. I sat in the back while Danny put down signs like a catcher from the front of the bus, letting me know what chords to play to make a song. My teammates couldn't believe it!

I was new to pro baseball and realized I needed to learn to project better to the fans. I had to overcome my shyness and become more extroverted. I used what got me through school—smiling and being friendly. I began to wave to the fans. I'd say hello and talk to them before the game. Doing that lowered barriers. I tried to project well in the way I played. I stole bases, dove after balls, and always encouraged my teammates. That energy is powerful. People pick up on it. I was rewarded when the fans voted me the most popular Greenwood Dodgers player and presented me with a wristwatch that my daughter Tara wears to this day.

◆———————— • ————————◆

Throughout my baseball career my mother was one of my biggest supporters. She'd get subscriptions to the local newspaper, track my progress, and keep the clippings of my exploits. She also pushed me to educate myself. She prodded and taunted me about not knowing what was going on in the world or who important world figures like Stalin were.

"How can you be so ignorant?!" she would say.

I was happy to be out of school and playing pro baseball, but that season with Greenwood I began to hate feeling like a dumb jock. My mother's nagging started to get through to me. I started to read, to educate myself. I became curious about what was going on in the world. Reading was difficult for me, but I pushed through it. My buddies went to the movies to watch Bugs Bunny and the Road Runner. I started reading the *New York Times*, *Time* magazine, *Reader's Digest*, and the local papers. Reading made me more aware of what was going on in the world and gave me more of a thirst for knowledge and learning.

On the field, it was bawdier and brawlier. At the time players wore sliding pads on the sides of their hips under their uniforms but no underwear. Once I slid into third with a triple and my uniform tore. I had a gaping hole down the center of my pants and bared my rear-end to some 3,000 patrons. I set a speed record from third base to the clubhouse that day.

On another occasion I slid into second base with my spikes up and found myself looking up from the bottom of a pile of opposing players who were out to get me. Then the pile cleared faster than it formed. Apparently, Bobby Dolan, our speedy shortstop, ran out of the dugout and clocked my opponent on the side of the head because the entire pile of players left me to get him. The last thing I remember seeing was Bobby climbing over the outfield fence, leaving the ballpark faster than he got there. Confrontations like this happened all the time. The "rules" were different, and players settled scores themselves. This was my first year in pro baseball. I was in the lineup every day and batted .240.

We made it to the playoffs that year, which meant more money. Winning the championship would have secured us another small bonus, but we lost to the Natchez Indians, and our season was over. But by the end of my first year in pro ball, I was considered a prospect, a ballplayer who might move up in the organization.

Stan Wasiak told me, "I can get you down to Panama. Want to go?"

I went back home to Trenton to wait for my ticket south.

Army Baseball and Another Spring Training

Instead of a ticket to Panama, I received a letter from Uncle Sam saying he wanted me—for two years. I went out to the railroad tracks behind my house and cried like a baby and swore like a trooper. I was so frustrated, angry, and bitter I'd have punched the pope out. I'd give Uncle Sam 10 years when I was 50 but not 2 years of my baseball life now. But this wasn't a negotiation. I had no choice. I was going from a democratic society to go-clean-the-toilet, from following my heart to following orders. It was the biggest blow since Father Degnan died. I thought my dream of playing baseball was destroyed. I was inconsolable.

I had just gotten off the bus at the induction center at Camp Kilmer, New Jersey, when a driver showed up in a car to pick me up. I hadn't even gotten my induction pills and found myself being driven to Fort Dix. I had been assigned to the 39th Regiment Company C. The car? It was a Captain Moorman's.

Normally, recruits don't see a captain until after basic training, let alone ride with him in his personal car before it starts. Turns out that generals like sports and winning teams. God bless Captain Moorman, who wanted to please the general. And God bless Arky Arkalian. Arky was a lowly private who filled quotas and cut orders, which gave him more power than God. Arky had gotten wind of my time with the Dodgers and delivered me to the 39th.

Basic training for me meant marching out to one of the firing ranges and then getting picked up and taken back to camp to practice baseball or dive for the regimental swim team. If I'd ever been shipped to Korea, I would have been a dead man. The only training I had was firing an M1 rifle and throwing three hand grenades. Since the Army wanted grenades thrown as far away as possible and no live ammunition returned to the base, I complied. I threw each grenade like a baseball over three shooting ranges. One long, one short, one in the middle. I don't know that I killed anybody.

— 35 —

Uncle Sam got me!

Devlin, Meningitis Patient, Improved But Still Serious

Martin P. Devlin 3d, son of Mr. and Mrs. Martin P. Devlin Jr. of 132 Abernethy Drive, and well known Trenton athlete, is recovering in Fort Dix Hospital from an attack of spinal meningitis. His condition was reported to be "greatly improved, but still serious" today.

Devlin's career as a professional baseball player was interrupted when he was called into service some weeks ago. He is the property of the Brooklyn Dodgers and had played one full season with Meridan, Miss., in the Cotton States League. He entered the Army on February 25 and was in basic training at Fort Dix when stricken.

Prior to signing a professional baseball contract, Devlin had played with the Trenton Schroths, Trenton High and the Duke University freshmen. While at Trenton High School, he was a varsity

Martin P. Devlin 3d

swimmer as well as baseball player.

I was in the hospital while my team played in the All-Army finals in Colorado.

NAME	NO.	UNIT	HOMETOWN	POSITION	TEAM PLAYED WITH BEFORE
Cahir, Thomas	7	Co C	Providence, RI	Outfield	St Louis Cardinals (property)
Carcaterra, Ciro	1	Co E	New York, N.Y.	Shortstop	Pittsburg Pirates (property)
Ciarrocca, Lou	14	Hq Co	Newark, N. J.	1st Base	Geo Washington Univ.
Creazzo, Augustine	9	Co G	Massena, N.Y.	Pitcher	Levis, Quebec (Free Agent)
Devlin, Marty	16	Co H	Trenton, N.J.	3rd Base	Brooklyn Dodgers (property)
Forizs, John	2	Co K	Stamford, Conn	Pitcher	Brooklyn Dodgers (property)
Govin, Joseph	11	Co G	Spencer, N.J.	Utility	Spencer Mass. (Free Agent)
Gurell, Gerson	4	Co L	New York, N.Y.	Outfield	New York Univ. (Free Agent)
Kerr, Billy	4	Co H	New York, N.Y.	Shortshop	Tarbord, N.C. (Free Agent)
Linsalata, Ben (Mgr)	8	Btry C	Brooklyn, N.Y.	2nd Base	Washington Senators (Free Agent)
McDede, Peter	20	Hq Co	Fanwood, N.J.	1st Base	Adephi College
Metecki, Ted	13	Co I	Trenton, N.J.	Pitcher	Brooklyn Dodgers (property)
Molinari, Steve	3	Co L	Medford, Mass	Outfield	St Louis Browns (property)
Napoli, Michael	10	Hq Co	Brooklyn, N.Y.	Catcher	Brooklyn Dodgers (property)
Onorato, Frank		Hq Co	Bronx, N.Y.	Trainer	
Sanders, Robert	24	Co G	Plainfield, N.J.	Pitcher	Phila Athletics (property)
Sowers, Gerald	6	Hq Co	Elmira, N.Y.	Utility	Brooklyn Dodgers (property)
Sullivan, Dick	19	Co K	Fall River, Mass	Outfield	Brooklyn Dodgers (property)
Swanson, Bob	15	Co H	Cranston, R I	Pitcher	Pittsburg Pirates (property)
Palica, Erv	12	Hq Co	Brooklyn, N.Y.	Pitcher Outfield	Brooklyn Dodgers
Portacarrero, Arnold	17	Co M	Bethpage, N.Y.	Pitcher	Phila Athletics
Tindall, Dick	8	Co H	Trenton, N.J.	Catcher	Chicago Cubs (property)

I managed the 39th Infantry Regiment team. Almost all of us had signed with major league organizations.

BASEBALL AND THE MILITARY

There's a relationship between baseball and the military (Harrington E. Crissey, Jr. has written about this history.) During the Civil War, baseball started to be played by all social classes in the military, and it is written that a crowd of 40,000 soldiers once watched a game in South Carolina. Troops played baseball during the Spanish American War in 1898 and during World War I, when 76 American major leaguers were in the service.

The U.S. military draft was instituted in 1940, and many outstanding ballplayers were drafted and served during World War II. From then until the Japanese surrendered in 1945, a number of players lost 3 to 5 years of their prime playing years to the service and two major league players lost their lives. Blacks and whites played together on service teams overseas during World War II, including in the Services World Series in Hawaii, but back in the states, service teams remained segregated until after the war.

Fewer players served in the Armed Forces during the Korean War (1950–1953), and there was an entirely different public sentiment than toward World War II. Much of America wasn't even sure where Korea was and didn't know what America was trying to accomplish. I was drafted, but I didn't have to go to war because I played regimental baseball for the Army, as did future Hall of Famers Whitey Ford and Willie Mays.

I was on the 39th regimental baseball team. We traveled to other military bases to play other generals' teams. Dick Tindall was on the team and had been signed by the Cubs. Almost a third of the players on the team had signed with Brooklyn. I knew some of the players we played against too. At South Boston, Virginia, we competed against Dick Groat, my old teammate at Duke. Dick had been a year ahead of me at Duke where he was an All-American baseball and basketball player. He was a tremendous athlete, and I looked up to him. When we played touch football games at college, he could change direction so fast my head would spin right off.

When I was at Duke, I came in the dorm drunk as a skunk one night and he chewed me out. That night I saw Dick at Fort Belvoir, and the tables were turned. He was drunk and smoking cigarettes. I used some of the words I learned on the Dodger plane and gave him one of my best lectures.

"You, SOB! What the ---- do you think you're doing!"

I can't take credit for it, but Dick later played for the Pittsburgh Pirates where he also won the batting title and the league MVP.

We were bussed to Virginia to play at Fort Eustis, where Willie Mays was stationed. Willie Mays was from a small town. He was quiet and shy, but, boy, could he play! He'd just completed his rookie season in the biggies and won the World Series with the Giants when he was drafted into the Army. Willie's first time up, Ted Matecki struck him out. We gloated over Ted's accomplishment. Two doubles and a home run later, we were humbled. Like me, Ted had signed with the Dodgers. Ted and I had played baseball against each other in American Legion ball and in high school football where he played for our biggest rival, Trenton Catholic. Those games were packed with fans. One time, I was on the ground in a pile of players. As the play ended, I sucker punched one of his teammates, knowing the refs wouldn't see it.

"What a chicken shit thing to do!" Ted yelled at me.

I knew I was wrong. That was the action of a bully. I got in my share of fights playing ball, but I never pulled that kind of stuff again.

◆———————— • ————————◆

My overseas duty was playing baseball in the Bahamas, where I learned to sleep on the metal luggage racks of buses and on the seats of cargo airplanes. I spent a whole night there eating in the Air Force commissary to put back the weight that I had lost marching during basic training.

After eight weeks, basic training was over, and Arky cut my orders to stay at Fort Dix as a platoon sergeant. My voice has always been an asset to me. I loved marching the troops bellowing out, "Here comes Company C!" It was a great outlet for my energy, but as soon as Arky found out that the job interfered with baseball practice, he moved me to special duty with H Company.

Every morning from 6 to 7 a.m., I was a gas station attendant at the motor pool. After an hour's work, I was free until practice.

Shortly after this reassignment, I passed out on the shooting range. The next thing I knew I was in a hospital. I had contracted spinal meningitis. It was so bad my family was contacted and came to see me. The Army brought in a priest to give me the last rites. The mortality rate was 98 percent at that time, and the 2 percent that survived often had paralysis and brain damage. When I was first hospitalized, I couldn't move my limbs and a corpsman had to wipe my rear end. But I always believed I would recover. Eventually, I was released from the hospital and sent home. I made the Army All-Star team but missed out on going to the All-Army playoffs in Colorado. When I recovered, I returned to my hour-a-day job pumping gas.

My mother kept in touch with Fresco Thompson. She reassured him in a letter that my muscles were not permanently damaged and that I'd be able to play baseball. He wrote back to her, "It would have delighted you to have seen the concern of Marty's teammates and friends in the Brooklyn organization when we learned of his misfortune. He has made a lot of friends because of his baseball ability as well as his personal charm." My social skills must have been improving!

When the Army gave me 30 days' leave, I asked the Dodgers if I could go to spring training. It was unheard of for a soldier to relinquish his furlough that way. But I wanted to play pro ball. Once I got there, Dodgers' owner Walter O'Malley and his staff went nuts and let me loose. I played hard and got all I could out of that month in Florida. Once the Dodgers let me play three games in a single day—a game in the morning with the A team, a game with the AAA team in the afternoon, and even one with the Dodgers, the big league club, at night against the Pittsburgh Pirates. On the way to the game, I rode the bus with the great Pee Wee Reese. Don Zimmer played shortstop that game and I played second. Zimmer and I managed to double up Sam Jethroe, the fastest man in baseball, and I went two for four.

As a pro ballplayer you were always being evaluated—for a possible trade with another team and for your place in the pecking order. That spring I suppose they were evaluating their players' speed. The Dodgers put me in a foot race against four of the fastest players in the organization—Willie Davis, Tommy Davis, Maury Wills, and Bobby Dolan. Each of them could run a pork chop past a wolf. We lined up in the outfield grass. The command was "ready, get set, go." I heard "take your mark," "get set." Anticipating the start, I took off and was leading for the first 30 yards. I finished fifth.

One day Fresco Thompson approached me with an unusual request: "Would you be Therese O'Malley's date for dinner and dancing this evening?"

It might have been my relationship with Fresco. Or that I came from a good Catholic family (O'Malley was Catholic). Or that they had admired the nicely tailored suit my father bought for me before I visited their Brooklyn offices on Montague Street. Or they liked that I kept my nose clean. They may have thought I had an intellect because I went to Duke. For whatever reason, the Dodger brass seemed to cotton to me. What was I going to do? I was not going to say no to Walter O'Malley's daughter! I went out with Therese and a group of the executives and their wives for dinner and dancing that night. I must have been the worst dance partner she ever had.

The next day, I was playing in the second game of the day. Vin Scully was on the PA system. As I walked up to bat, I heard him announce, "Next up, Marty 'Twinkle Toes' Devlin." Fresco had started calling me Twinkle Toes, and word got out where I'd been the night before. The players in Dodgertown gave me all kinds of grief!

"That's the only way you can get to the major leagues, Devlin!" was one of the nicer comments.

By the time my action-packed 30 days of spring training were over, I was almost glad to get back to Uncle Sam. "Twinkle Toes" was wearing on me, and I was ready to start my last year of service baseball, my last year in the Army.

I considered myself lucky. Most of the other guys in the service weren't playing at all. They were fighting in Korea.

That second year in the Army I was named manager of the 39th Regiment team and played third base. I held the tryouts, ran practices, and chose who was on the team. I was 19 years old and was managing major league players and minor leaguers who were big league prospects in a very competitive environment. The pressure in playing service baseball was knowing you had to win and perform at a high level or be cut from the team and sent to war. It was real! Our team won the regimental title and went to the All-Army tournament. While I was playing for the Army, I played semi-pro baseball for Roebling, a top team in a Mercer County (NJ) league. We played on weekends against teams from Lambertville, Trenton, Atlantic City, and Hightstown. I captained that team too and managed to live at home, 20 miles from the base, during the weekend, taking the liberty of sleeping in my own bed with my M1 rifle with me for safe keeping.

That second year I teamed up with Angelo Santoro, a little Italian man, an excellent professor who hardly spoke English. I spent my days sitting with him on two-and-a-half–ton military trucks getting the greatest of educations. We'd tear those trucks apart and put them back together. Whenever my buddy Angelo needed help in the motor pool, I volunteered. We'd fix a few trucks, take a break, sneak into the chow hall, and cook ourselves a magnificent breakfast. One morning I was so hungry I forgot to wash my hands. They were covered in grease. Within a few weeks, I started to feel weak. Soon after that I was so sick, I ended up in the hospital again. This time I was diagnosed with hepatitis. It was serious.

They got my records mixed up with someone else's and sent me home early by mistake. I got worse: I was weak, nauseous, and felt like a vegetable. Soon I was back in the hospital. Normally, hepatitis is a six-week illness. Six weeks turned into six months of lying on my back. The Army moved me to Murphy Army Hospital in Massachusetts. I spent that time sucking on hard rock candy to help my liver bounce back and regenerate itself. Either the Army felt bad or didn't want a lawsuit, but they let me out of the service three months early, in time for spring training but as weak as a baby kitten.

The Dodgers trained in Vero Beach, Florida, at a new spring training facility called Dodgertown. Walter O'Malley had bought the Dodgers during the Depression.

When everyone was pulling their money out of everything, he bought in. He not only acquired the Dodgers, he also purchased a Navy base with lots of land and barracks to house the ballplayers. It became the most modern training facility in baseball, and all 400 ballplayers, major leaguers and minor leaguers, trained there. It was state of the art, with sliding pits, pitching machines, batting cages, locker rooms, and amenities.

I was so feeble from lying on my back for six months that each day after morning drills, I would gobble down lunch and take a nap so I could get through the afternoon session. I had no physical strength and couldn't pull the trigger quick enough on a blazing fastball to hit it. This turned into an opportunity for me. I had to find ways to adapt. I did it through anticipation. I'd look for cues from my opponent to get a jump on the ball and start the bat swing sooner to time the pitch. That year I would have the best baseball year of my life.

From the Mobile Bears to Elmira

In the 1955 season, the Dodgers sent me to Alabama to play third base for the Mobile Bears. Mobile was a member of the AA Southern Association along with other substantial towns like Birmingham, New Orleans, Chattanooga, Nashville, Little Rock, and Memphis. Players from this league were two steps away from the majors and could easily be sent directly to the biggies. I had played only one year of pro baseball, but I already had three spring trainings under my belt—the first before I was drafted into the Army, the second during my 30-day furlough, and the third the one I'd just completed. At Mobile, I was teammates with future Dodger manager Tommy Lasorda and the big slugger Jim Gentile.

The Southern Association was a pitchers' league. The pitchers had good command of three pitches—the fastball, curveball, and changeup—and could keep you off balance by mixing them up. If you did manage to get your bat on the ball and hit it on the ground, you had a good chance to get a hit. Ground balls ricocheted off the rock-baked diamonds and skipped fast through the infield. At night, playing defense, it was hard to see the ball. The lights were not great, and the balls looked like beebees coming at you. I was at third and had to stick up my glove in self-protection when right-handed sluggers pulled line drives at me in the twilight. We wore steamy old ill-fitting flannel Dodger uniforms, hand-me-downs from the big league club. Mine was so big I almost needed two belts! With no air conditioning at the hotels for the away games or in the room I rented, it was so hot I could lie in bed naked with the fan on and sweat. I didn't care. I was playing baseball.

Since I had just gotten out of the service, I was counted on the NDL, the National Defense List. The NDL didn't count against the regular roster, so teams could go over the limit on the number of players they had. I must have butchered playing third because they tried me at shortstop, then right field. It wasn't easy being moved around, making those changes, but I just wanted to play and was happy to play anywhere I was asked.

At one point in the season, we were on a losing streak that wouldn't quit. Clay Bryant, our manager, tried everything to change our luck. His livelihood was on the line. After another loss, he was so frustrated, he dropped cases of beer in the clubhouse and locked us in until we drank it all. We could only crawl out to the bus. When that didn't work, my teammates took another approach. In baseball no one was sacred, and my upper middle-class upbringing made me "proper" and a target. They decided I should try chewing tobacco to change our luck. I'd never chewed tobacco before in my life. I got a hit that night and stole second. As I slid into the base, I swallowed the tobacco and threw up. We won, and my teammates wouldn't let me stop the tobacco. Fifteen games later, we were still winning. I was still chewing tobacco and getting better at it.

Clay was quoted in one newspaper as saying, "Devlin doesn't hit the ball out of the park and he doesn't have a shotgun arm. But he's the loudest, nerviest, most dedicated holler guy the Bears have had in years."

Then, in the middle of the season, my old friend Bobby Dolan got beaned in Elmira in the Eastern League, and they needed someone to fill in. The Dodgers asked me if I'd go down to A ball and learn to play second. The Bears were leading the league at the time, and I was hitting almost .300, but I agreed to make the move.

It was unusual that the Dodgers asked me about taking the assignment to Elmira. Normally a player was just told where they were headed. That's why most ballplayers hated the organization. They were treated like pawns. There was so much competition to survive in the minor league system, let alone make it to the majors, they often became bitter and resentful when demoted or when they were not moved up the ladder. Unlike today, players were tied to the organization for life. Relationship between the ballplayers and front office was adversarial.

I had a good relationship with Fresco Thompson from the time I started with the Dodgers. Even though I took a pay cut to go to Elmira. I agreed to make the move because I was a team player and because I knew I'd always be in the lineup and would learn to play one position, second base, instead of being moved around. I thought that might help me get to the bigs.

Other teams in the Eastern League were Albany and Binghamton in New York and Williamsport, Reading, Allentown, and Johnstown in Pennsylvania. Pitchers in the Eastern League were a bunch of flamethrowers. There was heat all over the place. Unlike in the Southern League, these pitchers didn't know much about pitching. They had only barely begun to learn to throw the curve, and when they threw any pitch, they didn't know where it was going. One baseball could be in the dirt and land at the backstop while the next one could be coming at your ear. This was dangerous at twilight when you couldn't see the ball at all. If you went to the plate during the early innings and didn't get hit by the ball, it might as well count as a lost time at bat. You had no chance to hit it.

I got off to a bad start at Elmira. I was 0 for 17, no hits after seventeen at bats. One game I made three errors and went off. I swore, cursed, and threw my bat after I made an out. After the game, I got drunk. This was a low point for me, and I knew I had to change. I was aware of how the negative would bring me down and I fought like hell against it. I finished the season hitting .319, made the All-Star team, and was voted the most popular player by the fans. In one newspaper article, Fresco Thompson was quoted as saying, "Marty was one of our most pleasant surprises of 1955."

My manager, Ray Hathaway, said, "Give me eight guys like Devlin, let them all hit .210 and we'd win the pennant." I believe that was a tribute to my hustle and positive attitude.

I still had the naysayers. Buzzie Bavasi didn't see my value to the team. A sports-writer reported overhearing his comment during spring training: "'You guys can have that Devlin,' said Buzz. 'If you had a team full of players like that you'd be happy until you woke up one day in seventh place and you wonder why'" (Alan Gould, Jr., *Elmira Star-Gazette*, July 23, 1955). I was batting in the .300s by then and proving him wrong.

My social skills were also improving dramatically. I became less shy. I was acquiring my own sense of humor and could bust balls with the best of them. You needed that to survive in baseball. I had a teammate who wore thick glasses. He couldn't see worth a nickel without them. He was so vain, he never wore his glasses when he went on a date. Once I gave him hell by telling him afterwards that his date was not the most attractive. He got so mad he wanted to fight. This was the kind of sense of humor you needed to fit into baseball and be accepted by your teammates—the kind of humor I gave up later.

Having a laugh with pitcher Tom Bigham (L), my teammate with
the Single-A Elmira Pioneers in the Eastern League

132 Abernethy Dr.,
Trenton, N. J.

October 23, 1956.

Mr. Spencer F. Harris, President,
The Fort Worth Baseball Club Inc.,
La Grave Field,
Fort Worth 2, Texas.

Dear Mr. Harris:

    I am sending your letter of October 18 to my son,
Martin P. Devlin, who is now playing ball in South
America.

    To expedite matters I am enclosing a check for
$9.18 to reimburse you for Marty's exceeding his food
allowance in San Antonio. It seems all his life he has
been doing that, along with his two brothers and sister.

    Marty enjoyed playing ball in Fort Worth and liked
the town and its people very much. I hope he will
enjoy his stay in South America as much.

                    Sincerely,

Letter from my father to the president of the AA Forth Worth Baseball Club (the Cats) after the 1956 season. My father had a sense of humor, but the pay and the food allowance on the road in the minor leagues were skimpy!

Baseball in Venezuela and Other Winter Jobs

After that season Fresco Thompson asked if I'd like to play in the Occidental League in Venezuela. I'd missed out on going to Panama, so I jumped at the chance, even if it meant being away from home year-round. I was to play short-stop for the Cabimas for $625 a month plus $350 living expenses (housing free). That was big money. (When I played for Fort Worth (AA) that summer, in 1956, I received $500 a month and had to pay for my own housing).

In Venezuela I played with future major league players, including my teammates Jim Gentile, Danny McDevitt, and Don Demeter. Luis Aparicio, a future Hall of Famer, also played in the league. Aparicio was such a skilled fielder he could cover more ground playing inside the line between second and third than I could playing on the outfield grass.

To compensate for my physical shortcomings and survive at this level of com-petition, I did what I could to find an edge. I studied hitters and pitchers, so I knew their tendencies. I studied baseball-playing situations like I'd been coached by Coach Palumbo with the Schroths. For two winters I played shortstop in Venezuela. I batted third and hit well over .320. In high school I'd learned some Spanish and made an effort to talk to everyone. I became one of the most popular baseball players in Venezuela. I had a lot of nicknames in Venezuela: El Torpedo (The Torpedo Boat), Rockola (The Juke Box), High Fidelity, the Motivator, Loud Mouth, and Drunken Babbling Idiot.

The fans in Venezuela reflected the society. The wealthy, rich off the country's oil, had seats at the games. The poor people had to stand, jammed into the stadiums like cattle. You'd hear set off firecrackers in the middle of the game. I saw one fan put a firecracker in another guy's pocket. I even saw someone throw a rooster on the field. There was singing throughout the game. This was the atmosphere. It was one big, loud party.

We played from November through January. My first season in Venezuela a group of my teammates and I stayed in a resort hotel on Lake Maracaibo. We played just three games a week—one Friday night and two on Saturday. The rest of the time we swam in the Hotel del Lago pool, played a little volleyball, and sunbathed. Here I was, 22 years old, being paid to play baseball. I saw gray-haired tourists who just got off the boat after saving money all their lives with barely any time left to enjoy themselves. I knew I was fortunate.

The second winter in Venezuela we were housed in a big home with a Chinese cook and a sun-tanning roof. My ballplaying American buddies couldn't speak or understand Spanish and didn't trust the local barbers, so I cut their hair. I'd cut a little hair up one side of the head and try to even the other side. They were nearly bald by the time I got through! Much later, I attempted to use my barbering skills on my son. That's how my first son Butch got his nickname.

One day my teammates and I were in Caracas sitting on the hotel roof. Planes were buzzing above us, doing what we thought were fly-bys. We waved to them. Unbeknownst to us, they were on their way to strafe the government building. We were right in the middle of a coup! We still played the game that night.

For two years I was fortunate to be paid to play baseball year-round. More often, professional ball was a seven-month job with winters off to work legitimate jobs. The Army and pumping gas took care of two of those winters. The other times I held various jobs.

One offseason I was a dairy farmer at a farm near Yardley, Pennsylvania. It was good, hard physical exercise. I helped milk 80 cows twice a day and cleaned up their pigsty of a barn. Old straw was piled up to the ceiling, and the elimination troughs filled to the brim. I had to back a manure spreader between two troughs without driving the tractor or spreader into either one of them. I shoveled old leftover hay, full of urine and manure, into the spreader and had to drive it to the pasture before it leaked out. Spreading it evenly in the pasture was a real challenge. The spreader would send the homemade fertilizer high into the air. If I didn't calculate the wind correctly, there would be more fertilizer on me than in the pasture. It was a seven-day-a-week job, and I loved it. At that time in my life, I was a good Catholic boy who never missed church. It was Christmas and I left the farm wearing my manure-scented work clothes to attend 5:00 p.m. Mass. The church was packed—standing room only. I found myself alone in the back of the church as people moved away from me.

Another winter I worked for George Case at the sporting goods store he opened in Trenton after he retired from baseball. George had been a famous outfielder for the Washington Senators who was so fast he once raced against horses before a game and barely lost out to Jesse Owens in a 100-yard dash put on by the owner of the Cleveland Indians, Bill Veeck. The newspapers followed my pro baseball career, making me something of a local sports celebrity. George hired me because I might attract business.

I don't know that I brought in much business, but my social skills and confidence took a leap forward with this job. I talked to customers and learned the selling points of the various sporting goods—baseball gloves and bats, golf clubs, tennis rackets, skis, hockey sticks. I paged through the catalogs and talked to the wholesalers whenever they stopped by the store. I learned how to explain the products and brands and sell over the counter. I was becoming more motivated to learn and began to believe I could.

I still found ways to stay physical. George had me build a duck blind in the marshes of Barnegat Bay out of an old sneakbox. I spent hours shoveling in the mud to camouflage the blind.

These photos show the high and the low, the huge gap between the rich and the poor in Venezuela, where I played winter ball for two seasons, 1956 and 1957. This is a market in the poor section of Maracaibo.

Our home stadium in Cabimas

A view of Lake Maracaibo from the Hotel del Lago pool

A little boy on a burro, a form of transportation

My teammates and I getting on a plane for an away game

My mouth is closed in this photo, but the newspaper reported that I was so loud supporting my Cabimas teammates during games it was hard to hear the announcer!

Oil rig being built on Lake Maracaibo

The Fort Worth Cats

Tommy Holmes was the best hitting instructor I ever had. He averaged over .300 during his time in the biggies and managed the Boston Braves before he joined the Dodgers. During my fourth spring training with the Dodgers, he taught me the advanced hitting technique. Advanced hitting meant positioning your body so that you could smack the baseball where the manager wanted you to, especially in hit-and-run situations. It allowed you to hit the ball to a place vacated by a fielder.

It was my third season playing pro baseball, and I was back with Clay Bryant, this time in AA Fort Worth. Seven or eight of the players on the team would make it to the biggies, including Jim Gentile, Don Demeter, Norm Sherry, Larry Sherry, Dick Gray, Stan Williams, and Dick Tracewski. The whole league was talented, with Brooks Robinson playing for San Antonio, Albie Pearson for Oklahoma City, and Ruben Amaro for Houston. While I had been in the lineup consistently in Mobile, my second year at Fort Worth, I was in and out of the lineup and Clay had me playing different positions: third base, shortstop, second base, left field, and pinch hitting. He liked me best in the infield where I could exert more leadership. I became a student of the game. I would tell the outfielders where to play, letting them know who was a pull hitter and who hit behind the runner.

Of all my managers, Clay got the most out of me as a hitter because he picked up on my ability to use the advanced hitting technique. When he put on the hit-and-run, he pointed the place on the infield occupied by the shortstop or the second baseman. When the runner on first took off for second, the fielder would run over to cover the base, leaving a hole I would shoot for. Thanks to Tommy Holmes, I could place the ball where Clay wanted, which got me many easy hits.

I was hitting over .300 for the Cats when I tore an abductor muscle in my inner thigh. Soon after I'd recovered and got back to playing. I did chores around the house for my landlady, cleaning the house, cutting the grass, and washing floors. Once when I was washing the kitchen floor I slipped and ripped the muscle again. That injury nagged at me much of the season, often keeping me out of the lineup. I was never 100 percent and ended the season batting .286 in 88 games.

We were a talented club but lost in the playoffs. I was voted by the fans as the most popular player. I was awarded a TV and gave it to my landlady.

During that season the Dodgers sent me to Texas Christian University to rehab my leg injury. The last time I'd been on a university campus was at Duke. At the time, all I wanted to do was leave Duke for pro ball. While I still wanted to play baseball, now I was older and thinking more about the future. I liked the feel of being in a learning environment. *This would be a nice place to be,* I thought to myself.

Before my fourth season in pro ball, I was sold to Rochester, in the St. Louis Cardinal's chain, and went to spring training with the Cardinals in Daytona Beach. The Louisville Slugger company provided prospects like me with bats with my signature on it and with golf clubs. After dinner, I'd go back to the ballpark, throw my clubs over the fence, and practice my short irons on the baseball diamond. I don't know if there was any correlation, but that same year I was sold back to the Dodgers.

Before the Dodgers moved from Brooklyn to Los Angeles for the 1958 season, they shook up their farm system. Fort Worth was now affiliated with the Cubs, but the Dodgers kept some of their players there. I was one of them. The teams in the league were the same: Dallas, San Antonio, Houston, Austin, Shreveport, Tulsa, and Oklahoma City. The Dodgers gave me the option of moving up the ladder to Montreal in AAA. I chose AA Fort Worth. That was a no-brainer for me because I'd have the chance to play regularly there. This second time in Fort Worth I played second base.

At the beginning of the season, I wasn't well regarded by sportswriters, but by the time it ended, they wrote I was the best second baseman in the history of the Texas League. I made the All-Star team and set a league record by striking out only 8 times in over 500 times at bat—and 3 of those times I took the third strike. That meant I swung and missed the ball for an out only 3 times in 647 times at bat even though I had a major depth perception problem, severe astigmatism the Army found when I took a motor vehicle exam. I also had a .988 fielding percentage and didn't make an error the last 37 games of the season.

I usually got along with my managers, but that year I ran into problems. I tried to explain to my skipper, Gene Handley, that I had a skill no other player on the team had, the advanced hitting technique, and that he should use it with me. I told him I could hit the ball wherever he wanted me to direct it. All he had to do is give me the signal and point his finger where he wanted the ball to go. Either I didn't get that point across or I just rubbed him the wrong way. Handley criticized me in the local newspaper for trying to manage the team. It was a hard lesson in the importance of good communication.

All the Way to AAA: St. Paul Saints, Montreal Royals, and a Treasured Ring

I don't know if the Dodgers just sent me to St. Paul or if Max Macon, the manager, asked for me, but I was still moving up the ladder. St. Paul was AAA baseball in the American Association. It was the summer of 1958, and Jack Spears and I vied to play second base. We were both versatile players, but he moved gracefully and seemingly without effort. You were more likely to get a chance to play in the big leagues if you looked good doing it. I never looked good. I was like more like an Eddie Stanky–type of ballplayer. I couldn't run, hit, or throw, but I hustled, got a lot of walks, and harassed the opposing team by being aggressive on the base paths. Max eventually chose Spears as the starter. I would have picked him too.

During my time at St. Paul, I played sparingly against the teams from Charleston, Denver, Omaha, Louisville, and Minneapolis. I never made it to Indianapolis, Wichita, or Charleston. Mid-season I was shipped from St. Paul to Montreal. A team of sportswriters picked us to finish fourth in the Triple A International League.

It was called "international" because we crossed borders six times on a three-week road trip going from Canada to Cuba. We played in an airplane league. We'd travel to Buffalo, Toronto, Rochester, Columbus, Havana, Miami, Richmond, and finally home to Montreal.

Clay Bryant was my manager again. This was his third time managing me. Clay had been a pitcher for the Chicago Cubs when they won the National League pennant. He had the biggest back on a man I've ever seen and frightened my teammates. Like the Catholic Church, he ruled by fear. If the team lost, right after a night game he'd keep us at the ballpark and make us practice in our sweaty uniforms. We couldn't take a shower until he was done and gone, and he might not talk to us for two days. He was rough and uncouth. If he was swearing in the dugout, we knew we did something wrong. "Jesus F...ing Christ Almighty!" he'd yell. Never any explanation of what you did wrong. No direction on how to improve. He was primal. Just working from the emotional brain.

When I was taking infield practice and he was wielding the fungo bat I'd yell at him, "Hey, you gray-haired SOB, hit the ball!" The other players cringed, thinking I was going to get it from him. My teammates couldn't believe I would go toe-to-toe with him verbally. But he loved it. They saw him as an authority figure. I wasn't burdened by those kinds of societal expectations and related to him as a human being.

I often pitched batting practice. One day before the game Clay gave me a big bag of brand-new baseballs.

"You're pitching batting practice.... I want them all back!"

That was the wrong thing to tell me. I liked to stage home run hitting contests. The balls started soaring over the outfield fence. We weren't five minutes into batting practice when I dropped the empty bag at his feet. You could have heard him all the way from Montreal to Los Angeles!

The Montreal team was like my 1948 American Legion championship Schroths team. No big shots, just a bunch of guys pulling together in the same direction. We managed to win the International League pennant. The day after we clinched the pennant, we were scheduled to play Rochester. We went to the bar and partied all night right up to game time. Drinking was a major activity on baseball teams anyway, but now everyone was in on it and drunk as a skunk. I was the only one sober enough to catch. Bob Lennon, a minor league slugging champion, staggered to the plate and on the first pitch parked one over the fence. He looked like a drunken sailor on a motorcycle circling the bases. It was a sight to behold! Even Clay Bryant was in stitches.

We went on to play Gene Mauch and his Minneapolis Millers of the American Association in the Triple-A World Series and lost four straight. Mauch went on to become a successful big league manager with the Philadelphia Phillies, and many of my teammates in Montreal—Tommy Lasorda, Sparky Anderson, Tommy Davis, and Sandy Amoros—went on to have legendary careers in the bigs. To this day, I treasure and wear that diamond pennant ring.

Since my last season in Fort Worth, I couldn't catch a rhythm. I didn't have an everyday position in Montreal. I believe to this day that I was more important to Clay not starting at one position because he knew I'd pitch in wherever he needed me. I threw batting practice, played first, shortstop, left field, even catcher. I figured my best way to the majors was my willingness to play anywhere. The Dodgers were loaded at second: Dick Young, Junior Gilliam, Charlie Neal, Sparky Anderson, Don Zimmer, and Jackie Robinson were ahead of me. By now I had developed a sense of humor, I hustled, and I used my booming voice. I had learned how to fit in with my teammates and managers, and my managers loved me and the way I played. I had gone from C ball all the way to AAA, one step below the major leagues.

Player–Manager of the Orlando Dodgers

After the season was over, I returned home to New Jersey to my wife and my brand-new son, Martin P. Devlin IV, and to some serious soul searching. My limited playing time at St. Paul and Montreal was the catalyst. I'd spent five glorious years being paid to do what I loved. I had traveled to many places and gotten a great education in life. I endured joys and tribulation. I had been living on the road in hotel after hotel, catching buses, going to different countries, cities, and ballparks, meeting new people from big shots to riff raff, dealing with injuries. I determined that the best I could do was become a Rocky Bridges, who spent 15 years playing for the Dodgers as a utility baseball player in the bigs. Not a bad life. Looking back, if I'd learned to switch hit, like Maury Wills had, my chances to make it to the major leagues would have been better. I'd devoted my life to playing baseball, but I was tired of traveling and I began to see that my dream of playing in the big leagues wasn't likely to happen.

Martin Patrick Devlin IV ("Butch"), with me in Vero Beach, Florida, April 1959

A few years earlier, posing at the orange juice stand in Dodgertown during Spring Training. You could have all of the orange juice you wanted. When I got off the train from Trenton I had a cold; the next day it was gone!

'Not Many People Here Tonight'

'That Pitcher's Throwing Close'

'If We Can Just Get One Run'

'It's Been A Long, Hot Summer'

YOUNG ORLANDO PILOT GIVES SIGN
. . . he leads team batting with .307 average

Giving signs as player–manager for the Orlando Dodgers

The Dodgers had taken care of me from the time I signed my first contract throughout my baseball career, and I had a good relationship with the front office. I shared my feelings with Fresco about it being the end of my playing days. At Christmas time he wrote me asking if I'd like to be player–manager of the Orlando Dodgers in the Florida State League. He stated that he thought I would do an excellent job and would have a "hustling ball club." At that point, I had developed the physical side of my game, I had become more adept socially, was getting better at dealing with people, and I knew a lot about the mental side of the game. I'd played on at least 23 sports teams and had leadership roles in 17 of them. I jumped at the opportunity.

I would be one of the youngest playing managers in the history of professional baseball, managing players only a few years younger than me.

After a year in AAA, one step below the major leagues, I was moving down to D ball, managing players five steps away from the bigs and playing second base on the team.

My rule as a manager was "Don't embarrass yourselves, the Dodgers organization, or me." When I went to play winter baseball in Venezuela the letter I got from the president of the National Association of Professional Baseball League, George Trautman, reinforced that to me. Don't do something stupid and derogatory that wouldn't reflect well on you or the U.S. I'd seen the kind of stuff ballplayers would do, and I didn't want a part of that. It was good, sound guidance and I've tried to follow it throughout my life.

The differences between D baseball and higher leagues were the players' skill levels and their knowledge of what it took to improve. Al Ferrara and Choo Choo Coleman were a cut above the rest. Al grew up in New York, where he took piano lessons to please his grandma. He became a concert pianist, even playing at Carnegie Hall. If he went into a batting slump, he knew how to work it out himself. Choo Choo, our catcher, had the quickest hands I've ever seen. Playing

One of my biggest failures in life has to do with going along with society's values. It happened during my time with the Orlando Dodgers. When I was playing with the Schroths, we had one African American kid on the team. I roomed with him, probably because my manager knew I just saw him like anyone else, as a teammate. When I managed the Orlando Dodgers, the South was segregated. Two of my players, Choo Choo Coleman and Donald Ellis, were African American. They weren't allowed in the hotels where the team was staying, and they weren't allowed to eat in the restaurants where we ate. I was instructed to have our white players bring their meals back to them as they waited in the bus and to drop them off at their nonwhite hotel while their white teammates and I stayed at the main hotel. I did what I was told. If I'd had any intestinal fortitude, I'd have quit managing. I was living the other side of the Jackie Robinson story and was just like all the other bigots in society.

second, I could see my bonus-baby pitchers cross him up time after time, throwing a fastball when he'd called for a curve. Most catchers would be injured if they were crossed up so often. The umpire would be just as vulnerable to those pitches bouncing off the dirt or flying wildly above the catcher. Choo Choo protected both himself and the ump. The Dodger execs told me to leave Al and Choo Choo Coleman alone. They thought managers would mess up their prized players by coaching them. I felt I could have helped them but left them alone. Choo Choo and Al made it to the majors anyway, along with Bill Kelso.

The rest of the guys were head cases and needed help. One game, my centerfielder dropped a fly ball. When I asked him what happened, he said, "I lost it in the moon." I looked up in the sky. Sure enough, it was up there. I could only laugh.

I taught my players when to take extra bases, when to steal, and where to throw the ball. I taught them how to win. They busted their chops for me, and at mid-season we were in first place. The Orlando Dodgers had earned the right to play against the rest of the league's all-stars and host the all-star game. We kicked the all-stars' butts. That was the high point of our season.

In baseball, there's the trickle-down effect. When the Dodgers cut players from their roster, the cut players were sent down the ladder to the AAA club. To make room on that team, some AAA players would be sent down to AA. This slide continued all the way to D ball. After the all-star game, the Dodgers asked me to take players from B and C ball. That would have meant cutting some of my players from the roster. As I saw it, my players supported me, and I supported them. I cut no one. I refused to take the trickle-downers.

During the second half of the season, the other teams had taken on trickle-downers from the more advanced leagues and the competition got tougher. On top of that, late in the season too many early season rainouts led to too many doubleheaders. My pitchers' arms were shot.

This gave me the chance to bring myself in to pitch in one game.

I told Choo Choo, "No signals, just give me a target. I'm gonna change speeds and hit spots with only a fastball."

Two strikes on a batter and we would stick the pitch in their ear—a brush back pitch to get them to back off the plate. Damn, if I didn't finish the game. I had just completed playing every position in baseball!

The beauty of managing in the Florida State League was that we played in major league spring training facilities. They were classy compared to the run-down minor league fields and locker rooms I'd played in before, but there was still the travel. On one road trip I asked Fresco Thompson if I could drive my car instead of riding the team bus. I had my wife and young son with me. He okayed my request but told me I had to follow behind. Five miles from home, and I sped ahead. Then, Murphy's law. The bus broke down and "Bussy," the driver, had to walk five miles to get help. When word got back to Fresco, I got hell from him by letter. It hurt. I respected Fresco.

After the season I still had no thoughts of quitting baseball. I hated living out of a suitcase but still loved the game. Then Uncle Sam threw another curve at me seven years after my draft letter. This time he wrote me that my GI benefits would run out if I didn't take them. If Uncle Sam was going to pay for college I would have to enroll now.

I was married and had a wife and son to support, and knew I needed to think about my future. Walter O'Malley told me there would always be a job waiting for me with the organization. If the Dodgers had told me more clearly what they had in mind for me, I might have thought differently, but that kind of communication didn't happen back then. I believed I'd have made a good manager, but it took me just a week to decide that my 8-year stint with the Dodgers, from before I was drafted into the Army until now, was over. It was time to move on.

What a ride it was! I had eight glorious spring trainings (1952–1959) with O'Malley and company. I had opportunities to rub noses with legends like Jackie Robinson, Pee Wee Reese, Roy Campanella, and 400 other players on my spring training trips. I won a ring with Montreal and managed three players who would make it to the bigs. When just one player from a minor league team makes the big show, the franchise pays for itself. Choo Choo, Al Ferrera, and Bill Kelso all made it.

When the Army discharged me, they sent me to Stevens Institute of Technology for occupational testing, and I learned I could have been a lawyer, social worker, teacher, or priest. Managing that one year for the Dodgers reinforced for me that I could be a good teacher.

If I hadn't gotten that letter from Uncle Sam, I believe I'd spent my life managing in baseball. But I never had regrets giving up the game. I knew that there were other good things ahead of me.

Back to School

It was 1960. I applied to Trenton State College. I was planning to major in health and physical education with the idea that I would become a teacher. But first I had to get in.

I had to be an idiot to think I would get accepted into college, much less succeed. I hadn't made it at Duke and hadn't developed one positive study habit during my 13 years of schooling. I'd been passed through grades 1 through 12 without learning much of anything. I knew the importance of training the body for playing sports but had no idea of the value of training the mind. I had lacked the passion, motivation, and the belief that I could do it. Maybe if they'd explained the why, I would have applied myself.

I sweated it out waiting to hear about my application. When I got my letter of acceptance, I was excited and relieved. Thank goodness I had the guts to apply!

Ed Brink, a professor in the phys ed department, had gone to bat for me, and other professors in the department did too, but there were still naysayers. Every student entering the college had to be interviewed by the director of admissions. From the time I sat down in his office and heard his questions, I could feel he wasn't supporting me.

"Devlin? I don't think he'll make it," is what I heard he said about me behind my back.

If I needed more fuel for the fire, I just got it. The GI Bill would pay for my education, rent, books, tuition, and a small stipend. I knew I had to make the most of this opportunity. I came this time with a load of life experience. I learned how to learn in other arenas—baseball, fixing trucks, reading. With a wife and kid to support never once did I consider failure. I wanted to teach and would do whatever it took to succeed at school.

I made it through anatomy and physiology, but biology was kicking my butt. I needed to pass the class to get my degree so I went to the professor, Dr. Treuting, during his office hours to see what I could do.

"Come in here tomorrow morning at six," he told me.

For an entire semester, five days a week, I showed up at his office at 6:00 am for tutoring and extra work. I didn't miss a day and got a B in the class.

I had to bull my neck and work hard to acquire good study habits. I was never good with concepts or abstract thinking, so I worked my tail off memorizing what I needed to learn, outlining, and memorizing again. (This is where my Catholic school education helped!)

But I didn't want to just make it through school, I wanted to make sure I would never be labeled a dumb jock. When I started out in baseball one of my teammates at Greenwood, Bill Crawford, was so articulate. He had an unbelievable vocabulary and used language beautifully, in a way I admired. I wanted to learn and broaden myself. I took art, history, and literature. My favorite book in college was *The Man from La Mancha*. I loved reading about Don Quixote and his misadventures. He was someone I could relate to—the dumb things he did. Like me he did the things that other people told him he couldn't or shouldn't do. I loved that stupid book! I loved the stories in Greek mythology too. I never forgot *Lysistrata*, a story of the women all agreeing to refuse pleasure to their husbands to stop the war. Women should rule the world!

I was developing the confidence to know that I could take anything on, and I was so thirsty to learn I even enrolled in a philosophy class. The professor told me I couldn't cut it, and I dropped the class. I regret believing him.

The phys ed department was stacked with professors who'd gone to Springfield College, the top school in the country for PE. I'd gotten to know them through the admissions process. Along with Ed Brink, there was Roy Van Ness, Dr. George Krablin, who was in charge of the department, and Mel Schmid. They had studied under Peter Karpovich, a giant in the scientific study of exercise and sport who was unconventional and ahead of his time. He taught about balancing the development of the muscles and endorsed weight training for athletes, proving that it did not have to hamper flexibility.

My body had gotten me this far in life. Now I acquired a knowledge of what was going on inside it. I studied the major muscle groups, their origin and insertion, and their actions. I also learned the importance of the cardiovascular system, balance, agility, flexibility, strength, quickness, fitness, and the value of cross-training. How, as we get older, our arteries, veins, and capillaries become constricted and our strength, agility, balance, and quickness deteriorate faster if we don't exercise properly. It wasn't just the body I learned about. The department taught us to look at the health of the whole person—mental, emotional, and social. I am grateful for that view and for learning the basic principles of teaching. I got a great education.

With my background I had more street smarts than the whole college put together. My studies just put the icing on the cake. My experience playing baseball and my work ethic, attitude, and motivation sent me through school with flying colors. Anatomy, physiology, psychology, kinesiology, world literature, art, teaching methodology, they all grabbed me. I no longer tolerated feeling ignorant.

I wasn't eligible to play sports at the college because I'd played professional baseball, so I was recruited to be the third-base coach for the baseball team, the spot usually occupied by the manager of a college team. Bob Salois turned the reins over to me. It took a lot of guts for him to do that. I also helped out the divers on the swim team and pitched in where I could, but I was most proud of getting my degree.

After graduation, I stopped by the admissions director's office, dropped my diploma on his desk, and walked out without saying a word. Two years after that, I earned my master's degree in physical education. More icing on the cake. I thank Uncle Sam, my attitude, and God for sending me back to school.

I could not have received a better formal education, and I came to love learning so much that I became a principles man. Studying gave me a framework for understanding what I already knew intuitively. Principles and good values were becoming the foundation of everything I did in life.

My next job was student teaching at Hopewell Valley Central High School in nearby Pennington, New Jersey. While I was finishing up my masters, I taught health and physical education. Ed Brink observed me teaching only once. After that they let me loose.

I coached golf and wrestling, a sport I knew nothing about, and helped out a little with the baseball team. I'm convinced you give a good man any job and he'll get it done, whatever the endeavor. That first semester health class required the most preparation. I turned some of it over to the students and had all of them give presentations on a topic of their choice. They did the research, prepared overheads, and presented to the class. They did a great job. I gave all of my kids A's. They'd earned them. But the administration wanted me to change the grades.

They wanted me to grade on a curve. I refused. I loved teaching and I did things the way I thought was right.

The next semester I had a student in my health class who had spina bifida and wasn't going to live much longer. He wanted to give his presentation on the disease. The administration found out and didn't want me to allow it. They thought talking about this fatal condition would be too hard on the young man and too hard on the class. I supported the young man. He went on with his presentation and did a bang-up job. He was proud of himself, his classmates learned more about the illness he was dealing with, and other teachers and the chair of our department sat in on his talk and had tears in their eyes by the end of it. I did too. I was so proud of that kid. He did what others said he couldn't or shouldn't do.

Rider College Intramurals

After my year student teaching at the high school ended, the Board of Education of Hopewell Township decided to create a position for me on the faculty. I was happy as a clam teaching and was looking forward to the school year. Then I got a call from Bob Kilgus, the athletic director at Rider College. He explained it was only a matter of time before Tom Petroff, the baseball coach at Rider, would move on to bigger and better opportunities. He knew I had managed in pro ball and wanted to cover his butt by lining me up to coach the Rider baseball team when Tom left.

Rider would create a position for me directing the intramural athletic program, so I'd be there when the baseball job opened up.

I was caught between a rock and a hard place. I loved teaching high school, but I now viewed a college or university as a nice environment that would be stimulating for me. I accepted the job at Rider.

At the time, all I knew about intramurals was from an illustration in my PE textbook, a triangle that conveyed the hierarchy in college sports. The top tier of the triangle represented the elite, the athletes who represent the college in competitions against other colleges and universities. The widest tier, the bottom of the triangle, represented students enrolled in physical education courses, normally required for all college freshmen. In the middle tier were the participants in intramural athletics. These were students who competed against other students within the walls of the college.

There was no phys ed program at Rider, so intramurals were the only opportunity for students who weren't in collegiate athletics to participate in sports. I saw expanding the program and improving its status as an opportunity and challenge. At the time three sports were offered in the intramural program. The intercollegiate coaches pitched in to help run the intramural program during their offseasons. If I needed further fuel, a faculty member in the phys ed department told me that it would be impossible to improve on the existing program. That was the wrong thing to tell me.

My job didn't officially start until fall. Over the summer, I read a book on intramural athletics outlining the principles of a sound program and began to think about where I could take it. I scouted the facilities I had to work with and began to daydream and plan my course of action. Rider had one auditorium/gym shared with the intercollegiate coaches and a 40-acre field. The county had off-campus facilities we could use to supplement what the college had. Mercer County had a lake, a steep ski hill called Bell (Bump) Mountain, and a golf course. The 40-acre plot on campus was big enough for six football fields, four soccer fields, and a cross-country course running through and around the other games. There were the woods for archery. Golf could be off campus at the Mountain View Golf Club, just seven miles away. There was room at the auditorium/gym facility for table tennis on the stage and wrestling in the cloakroom. By erecting partitions in the gym, it would accommodate single-wall handball. Three-man and five-man basketball could take place later at night, along with volleyball and badminton. The pool could house modified versions of competitive swimming, water polo, and diving. These ideas began forming when I learned I'd be starting the job and evolved as I saw opportunities to grow the program.

When I took the position in the fall, I was ready to go. I started with the 40-acre field. I used weedkiller to line the football and soccer fields. These fields would also be used to play push ball, a competition where six-man teams sought to wrestle a 6-foot ball across a line at the opponent's end of the field. The lake would be used for tug-of-war, with a rope spanning the lake. A new track was being built so I knew I could offer track and field in the spring, along with softball on the football and soccer fields. For volleyball and tennis, I would make net posts using car tires, cement, and poles and use clothes lines and tape as boundaries for the courts I set up in the gym.

Another principle of intramural athletics is to have units with the same number of students competing against one another. Rider College had five male dormitories with 60 students in each unit. The five fraternities also had 60 students each. Perfect! We created similar units for off-campus students.

All competition was round robin. Each sport offered points depending on the number of participants. There was an all-dormitory champion, an all-fraternity champion, and an all-college champion. Each unit had a representative who served as a member of a student governing body. The group decided all issues. I was their advisor and scheduled the activities. The students handled officiating, coaching, and equipment sign outs. Entry fees for each sport went toward a year-end banquet where awards were presented.

INTRAMURAL ATHLETICS

In 1965 Rider College enlisted Marty Devlin to develop and administer the program. Marty did his homework, read up on it, and went in prepared. It was wildly successful, with more than 90 percent of the school's male students and 50 percent of female students enrolled in 20+ sports. Athletes were even quitting their varsity teams to join the popular and fun program. It received national acclaim and was unmatched in popularity among the student life programs.

Intramurals are a way to participate in organized athletics without a huge financial and time commitment. The competitive aspect is within the institution. Now, college club sports, a step up from intramurals, have risen in popularity. Club sports are more formally organized, often require tryouts, and are more competitive and lead to national collegiate championships.

On a serious note (the first and last of the book), the *Shadow* would like to honor Martin Devlin, the director of Rider's incomparable men's intramurals program. Known especially for his devotion and honesty, Mr. Devlin has developed the intramural sports system into what has to be the most supported activity at Rider. It is doubtful that even classes draw as many participants as do the twenty-some-odd sports that are supervised by his office.

Although universally (and affectionately) referred to as "Marty", he is spoken to as "Mr. Devlin" and is always accorded nothing but the respect which he has always earned. His influence has benefitted many and his rewards have been in his immense success.

The *Shadow* is sure that the entire Rider community joins us in thanking Mr. Devlin for his creative efforts and may we be the first to suggest the presentation of an annual **Martin Devlin Trophy** to the athlete who most faithfully displays the qualities with which Mr. Devlin has won this campus.

Mr. Martin Devlin.

I am beyond honored! This appeared in Rider College's 1969 yearbook.

I applied all the principles I'd read about—establish units, set up a student intramural council, use a point system, plan round-robin competition, and create a circus atmosphere for each division. The administration gave me everything I wanted. I surrounded myself with good people and later hired Vi Udy to set up a women's intramural program. Students ran the whole thing. It was a working laboratory. We went from 3 intramural sports to 27.

It soon became clear that I needed to cut the program back. I had to eliminate the tug-of-war because students might drown in the lake. Diving competitors had to execute five kinds of dives: front dive, somersault, inward dive, twisting dive, back dive, and gainer. There was imminent danger in trying to perform these dives with no experience—and the strong possibility of crashing into the board or the side of the concrete pool or experiencing the violent jolt of hitting the water the wrong way. Diving went by the wayside.

It was still entertaining seeing all this crazy activity. Another sport that amused me was wrestling. Macho students would volunteer to represent their unit. Win or lose, these out-of-shape competitors scurried to the locker room after the match and got rid of breakfast, lunch, and dinner—sometimes through both ends at the same time. The custodian was not a happy camper.

Students killed themselves to compete and they loved it. If they weren't drowning in tug-of-war contests across the lake or playing water polo (where you were in trouble if you couldn't swim), they were getting beaten up playing with the six-foot diameter push ball (where there were no rules against mounting the ball), touch football (where injuries do happen), and ski racing (with no training). The only one complaining was the nurse. There were more students in the infirmary than in class.

"Marty, what are you doing to these kids!?"

She sent me a strong letter complaining about the implications of the program for her workload.

This voluntary program was so popular students cut class to play. Athletes left their intercollegiate teams. The student newspaper covered soccer and football games. The college radio station broadcast special intramural contests. English professors had students write compositions using intramural events as the vehicle.

Ninety-two percent of 2,000 resident Rider students participated every year of the program—for 18 years. Students were so busy playing they couldn't get into trouble. The program provided physical activity and challenge. It offered a social outlet and taught leadership, team building, and communication more effectively than could be done in the classroom. Sports teaches life, and over the years, the program impacted the lives of the 40,000 people who participated in it.

The baseball job? I knew I would not like recruiting and figured I'd rather have an impact on thousands of students than on the some 25 intercollegiate baseball players I would coach each year. When Tom Petroff moved on, I turned the baseball job down.

I had a model program that impacted so many people. I could see how it could easily be adapted for the community at large as a recreational athletics program. I was involved with the country park commission and proposed to the county that they establish the program for the community. I couldn't sell them on my idea. That was a huge disappointment to me. Only years later did they see the value and implement a recreational sports program for all county residents.

Home on the Delaware

While I was in school at Trenton State, I rented an apartment for my family in Pennsylvania. My wife wasn't Catholic, so on Sundays I went by myself to mass across the river in New Jersey at St. George's in Titusville. One Sunday I discovered a house not far from the church and about a soccer-field's length north of where George Washington crossed the Delaware River in December of 1776. The house was empty at the time, so on Sundays I would sit on the back porch and gaze at the river below. It was so close to the river I almost felt suspended over it. I dreamed of living there one day. Wouldn't you know it happened!

I paid $18,000 for the house. The mortgage was $118 a month and the utilities $118 a year.

The flood of 1955 hadn't gotten the house, and it was so high on the bank I knew no flood could get us. It had a large picture window facing southwest and overlooking that glorious river. I added another room that looked out over the water, and I put in a wood-burning stove. Every day I sat in that room enjoy watching the water's ebb and flow and the hundreds of geese that flocked there in the morning and honked their way to sleep at night in the cornfield across the river in Pennsylvania. I never felt alone. The geese were my buddies.

One winter night, I heard the cracking and roar of large ice floes, dangerous and strong, making their way down the river. It was 2 or 3 a.m. There was a full moon. I got my son Butchie out of bed—he was two or three at the time—and I carried him to the riverbank. I held him up to show him the power and beauty of nature so I could enjoy watching this show with him.

The river was high and flowing fast beneath a thick layer of ice. Huge chunks of ice, like fast-moving glaciers, rode on top of a what looked like one giant wave that pushed the ice down the river and up onto the riverbank. As the ice cracked, the floes dropped into the river and raised the level of the water. The force of the water and the jagged edges of the ice toppled the trees alongside the river like they were ten pins. I loved that house.

The house also provided a great opportunity and challenge to me. I wanted to beautify the bank from the house to the edge of the river. Once this idea came into my head, I knew I'd find a way to do it. One day I noticed almost-new railroad ties lying along the sides of the railroad track. This was the same track that ran behind the house where I was born and grew up, six miles to the south.

I thought to myself, *Maybe I could use these to terrace the bank.*

I inquired about the ties. The railroad authorities said I could take them because they were installing new ones. They also told me there were many more ties on the Main Line to New York and Philly, on the tracks north of Trenton. I rented a 2 ½-ton truck and coerced my brother Pancho into helping me. We threw them on and off that truck over several trips. With each trip, my driveway looked more and more like a logging camp. These babies were about 8 feet long and weighed some 200 pounds. When we were done, we had transported 500 of those bad boys.

The authorities told me there were many more ties north of Trenton and north of my house. These ties weren't accessible with a truck. I thought about how I could solve this problem. What if I flipped each tie end over end into the river and let the current transport them down to my house? As they floated by, Pancho could paddle out like a Labrador retriever going after ducks and swim them to my riverbank. Pancho, who's as crazy as I am, might see this as a fun challenge and help me, especially if I fed him. My mistake was feeding him before we started. He ate so many meatballs and so much spaghetti all he could do was throw up. He was useless as teats on a boar hog. I swam to get them myself. Terracing the ties into the bank was fun. I gained so much strength moving those ties.

After completing that project, I had another idea for beautifying the property. I wanted to build a supporting wall along the river beneath the wall I'd already built. I had a pram and Pancho had one of his own he wasn't using and a 3½-horsepower engine to go with it. He offered it to me. He wasn't expecting me to destroy it. With these two aluminum boats at my disposal, I would tie one pram to the other, ride in the front pram, and tow rocks in the second.

I put on old sneaks, a bathing suit, and a mask, and when I saw a keeper, I dove down to get it. From July to November, when the river was low, I fetched rocks from the bottom of the river. Every now and then an eel would slither from under the rock I was lifting and scare the hell out of me. My rock-hunting territory was from Washington Crossing to the rapids north of my home so the river current could help me float downriver to my home.

Lifting the rocks in the water was easy compared to flipping them over the gunnels. With the buoyancy of the water, these huge rocks felt almost light. Lifting them out and letting the big boomers fall into the pram, though, required a lot of effort. It was hard work—and was hard on Pancho's pram. By the end it had so many dents in it, you could barely recognize it as a boat.

Every day I filled the boat to three inches from the gunnels, hoping it didn't sink in the wakes of the speedboats and water skiers that streamed by. I only sank one time. My river buddies helped me right the pram, recover the sunken treasure, load the pram up again with boomers, and sent me on my merry way.

It took me three years to complete the project. I had a gorgeous wall two hundred feet long and ten feet high. A bonus was that when the river was high, river debris floated above the wall and backfilled the space between the wall and my property. What I didn't know at the time was that taking even one rock from the riverbed is illegal!

The house gave me challenge and enjoyment for many years. It was heaven for my son Butch too, who grew up a river rat. He and his friends spent days buzzing back and forth on the river, on our 75-horsepower Starcraft motorboat.

Some of the 500 ties I retrieved and terraced at my first house on the Delaware River

Country Club Swimming Director

Greenacres County Club needed someone during the summer months to ready the pool for the season, administer the swimming program, and put the pool to bed in the fall. I started working summers at Greenacres after my years with the Dodgers were over. The pool at Greenacres was tailormade for my workouts. It was tough duty watching women in bathing suits, guarding their kids, and teaching swimming.

One of those I instructed was Stacy Isaacson. Stacy had suffered brain damage at birth. I taught her swimming and diving. She would keep trying until she got it right. Greenacres held an end-of-season program where kids could either compete or demonstrate what they learned to parents and family. For years, Stacy's family felt embarrassed when she was put in front of an audience. Stacy and I had been working together all summer, and when the time came to show what she could do, she mounted the diving board, hesitated, smiled, walked to the end, jumped in, and swam across the deep end. The house went down.

Stacy eventually learned to swim a quarter mile with the most beautiful strokes. As an adult she swam every day in her resident facility. I'm proud to have given her a gift for a lifetime.

The approach I used with Stacy was the same one I used to teach every other swimming student. The swimmer has two kickboards. One remains intact, the other was one I'd cut in half. Over time I'd cut the half-board in half again until the board was the size of a pencil. The swimmer started working on skills like arm strokes or breathing with the regular-sized kickboard, then progressed to thinner and thinner boards and eventually no board at all. This technique allows the swimmer to practice the same skill in a gradual and progressive process. It's fun, challenging, and motivational because it gradually instills skills and confidence in the swimmer.

Tennis, A Passion for Life

On days of inclement weather, I began to rally with some of the ladies who played tennis at the club. There were two of us guarding the pool, so I could leave the pool in the hands of the other lifeguard and spend time on the tennis court. I could run every ball down, hit every ball back, and make it fun and a great workout for the ladies, and they kept asking me to come and play with them. Stan Dlugosz was the tennis pro at Greenacres. He started asking me to rally with them too. I was told by the higher ups that this wasn't my job, but both the ladies and Stan kept asking me to play and I kept playing. I didn't have any technique, but I did have hustle, decent hand–eye coordination, and could keep a rally going.

Once I get hooked on anything, passion does me in and leads me where it wants to go. All I could think about, all I wanted to do, was play tennis. Then I started thinking, *how could I play this silly game and get paid for it?* One summer while guarding the pool at Greenacres, I could see the tennis courts across the way at Rider College. The wheels in my head started to turn. Rider, where I was working during the school year as intramural director, had 12 tennis courts. Why not talk the school's administration into renting them to the community during the summer and hiring me to oversee the program?

It worked! Goodbye, 12 glorious years at Greenacres. Now I was at Rider year-round and had a salary, benefits, and insurance.

It was 1969, I was 36, and was also about to immerse myself in a brand-new sport.

When I first played Stan, I could barely win a point. He had skills that I couldn't match—a rocket serve, a beautiful backhand, and the ability to lob a ball over me and place the ball where he wanted it. He had me running around like a crazy person. I was so dumb when I started. While I could run down every shot and return it, I was one dimensional and had no idea what I was doing. I realized I couldn't beat Stan with hustle alone, especially because I couldn't hit the backhand. I was getting better, but after six months my backhand still sucked. Until I mastered that I wasn't going to be able to compete. Then it hit me: *I played handball to train for professional baseball and used my left and right hands to strike the ball. Why not use two forehands?*

I tried it out, switching hands, hitting right- and left-handed. After just the first week, my left hand was 100 times better than my backhand had ever been. I never looked back.

I kept looking for an edge. At the time, the ball was slower and the rackets, still wood, were less powerful. I tracked down a high school woodworking teacher who added 4 inches on my racket so I could better reach the ball.

I'd played team sports for much of my life and loved it. But with tennis, victory or defeat came down to me alone—my skill level, my desire, my competitive fire. And there was the challenge of figuring out the game and learning how to win. I began to play for hours a day on weekdays and all day on the weekends. When the weather was bad or the courts occupied, I'd play on the court I rigged up in the Rider gym or just hit the ball against a wall. For 18 years the brilliant Ken Wilson, my doubles partner, would come to Rider to play me during his lunch break from his work at Educational Testing Service (ETS).

I wasn't getting enough competition and decided to compete in the open division of U.S. Tennis Association (USTA) Middle States tournaments. I began to play competitively and became known as the guy with two forehands. By the end of that summer, I had been exposed to every conceivable type of game and was ranked number 36 in Middle States in the open division. I was on my way.

Five years later I was ranked among the top ten players nationally in my age group.

After I left Rider for a new opportunity with Prince, the tech reps for Prince were instructed to schedule tennis matches for me in their state or country so I would host a prized Prince clinic. My secretary was a wizard at scheduling my tennis clinics alongside national and international tournaments. I'd put on a clinic, then play in the tournament. It worked out well for Prince and for me. I had the opportunity to meet and compete against top players in the world.

The USTA awards a gold ball when you win a national championship. When I started to play the senior grand slam tournaments, my goal was to win one gold ball before I died. Most of my life I didn't plan goals, I just felt them. This time I laid it out clearly and pursued that goal.

I went to the hard courts in California unseeded. It was going to be a tough draw for me at the La Jolla Beach and Racquet Club. I met Ron Livingston, the scourge of the Far West, in the early rounds. I beat him 6–0, 6–0. Boy, did this open the eyes of the Californians! I went on to beat Clif Mayne in the semis and Lorne Main in the finals on the same day. Both were top players, and both were seeded.

They were backboard guys who could hit a million balls in a match, so I was running miles that day. The tournament directors gave me a lunch break between matches but playing them back-to-back with so little rest between matches was like playing Nadal and Federer. The semifinal round was over three hours of continuous play, with a one-hour break for lunch and back on the court for another three-hour match—a total of six hours of tennis. You might think I was in training to be a Navy SEAL. Both matches were three-set cliffhangers.

While I was playing, my father was dying of a brain tumor. I used him to motivate me through the tournament. *If he had the courage to die, I'd better have the courage to play,* I told myself. I couldn't tell you the scores. The only score I could tell you: it was one for the old man. When the finals were over and I was the victor, lactic acid invaded my muscles. I was so mentally, physically, and emotionally drained from focusing on every single point, it was difficult to summon the energy to climb the stairs of the airplane that would take me back to New Jersey. I slept all the way home. I'd achieved my goal, though, winning my first gold ball.

I had mixed emotions about my accomplishment. I was hurting so much physically and mentally I could hardly walk on and off the plane. I didn't want to see a tennis racket for weeks. I don't remember feeling any elation over winning my first national championship, and I never discussed the experience with my father. He knew I'd won and talking about it didn't seem important given he was dying.

TENNIS IN THE 1980S

The 1970s and 1980s were one of the most exciting eras in tennis history. The quality of professional tennis was top notch, the rivalries were intense, and there were recognizable stars with distinctive personalities, players to cheer for and to cheer against. Many of the world's best players were Americans.

During this time there was a major evolution in rackets from wood to graphite. More recreational players took up the game. This period was accurately described as a "boom." After 1968, professional players were allowed to compete in the Grand Slam tournaments and the Davis Cup. This ushered in an unprecedented level of interest in tennis. In 1968, the U.S. Open was broadcast on television for the first time. In 1988, tennis became a full sport at the Olympics for the first time in 64 years. By the 1990s, the sport had dropped back to an interest level that has remained steady since.

After I won my first gold ball, I set a new goal for myself. I wanted to win a gold ball on every surface. My second national championship, in Salt Lake City, was a very different experience. Jim Nelson was a serve-and-volley player. He attacked on every ball—his serve, his return of my serve, and off the ground. I lost to him before and noticed he floated his approach shots. My game plan was to jump on his approach shots by taking them early out of the air. I'd attack an attacker. I beat him to the punch and won gold ball number 2.

For my third championship I felt like I was in a boxing ring. I was playing Lester Sack, a former Canadian Open winner, on clay in Sarasota. On clay you hit a lot of balls during the match. My opponent was a baseliner who could effectively manage a weighted tennis racket, which gave him more power. All I had were my legs, which could run all day. It was a long, drawn-out war. Besides running all over chasing down balls, I read cues my opponent was giving me. That was the difference in the match. From Lester's behavior later in the match, I could see he was cramping. I became a great actor, never letting on that I was cramping too. Gold ball number 3. The icing on the cake for me was when my 2-year-old daughter Tara waddled out on the court to hug her daddy after match point.

The only surface that eluded me was grass. Winning the grass championship would allow me to brag that I won a career grand slam. I had never wanted to play on grass to begin with. (I told my buddies that grass was for cows.) They talked me into playing a practice match. I stepped into this new arena and relished the opportunity and challenge of learning how to play on a foreign surface. I played doubles with Stan Dlugosz on grass, competing in local, regional, and eventually national tournaments. In one tournament we won several rounds, including one over the legend Pancho Gonzalez and his partner.

The following year my friends convinced me to play the national 45-and-over grass court championship at Germantown Cricket Club in Philadelphia. In the quarterfinals, I beat John Powless, who was ranked number 10 in the United States. I didn't win that tournament and spent the next 40 years competing only on grass. I never won on that surface. Still, three out of four gold balls gave me a lot of satisfaction. I played against the best senior players in the world, was in the finals eight times in singles and once in doubles, and won titles on three of the four surfaces.

By traditional standards, I was lacking as a player. I had no backhand, no over-head, no volley, no serve, no powerful ground strokes. I did have the ability to run every ball down, pass players at the net, and I never missed. I used both a left- and right-handed forehand. This became my trademark on the tennis court. I had discovered tennis at age 36 and became a national senior champion at 45. During the ten years I traveled throughout the nation giving clinics on behalf of Prince and playing in tournaments, I was always ranked in the top 10. In 1981, I was ranked by *Tennis* magazine as number 1 in the country and tenth in the world in the 45-and-over age group. In 2000, a *Tennis* magazine article referred to me as the "most prominent dual-forehanded player on the planet."

Besides the gold balls, I would become the G. Nelson Green Tournament champion 17 times, and I dominated Middle States and Mercer County tournaments in singles and, with Ken Wilson, in doubles.

Over time I started to lose the edge I had with my hustle. I had good eye–hand coordination, but I didn't have powerful ground strokes. The game changed when the newer rackets allowed for more power. I tried bigger and longer rackets to reach more balls. I tried every wrinkle I could to get better, but I could not win at the power game.

I still played competitively into my 80s.

A Painful Failure and a New Beginning

While I was the intramural athletic director at Rider, the college offered students a month-long interim study program that began after Christmas. Students could choose any program of interest to them. Dr. Derrill McGuigan and I tag-teamed to lead a study abroad to the Alps. I would teach skiing during the day, and he would teach psychology in the evening. I liked to ski, and while I wasn't an expert, I knew the basics of teaching so I could make it work.

Dr. McGuigan was born and raised on a farm in Nova Scotia. His family had few of the amenities of civilization most of us in the United States took for granted. His bathroom was an outhouse during the day and a bucket under his bed at night. It was so cold that whatever he deposited in the bucket at night was frozen solid by morning. He hated this existence so much it drove him to leave the farm and look for a more refined way of life. He found it through education and acquired two undergraduate degrees, two masters, and two doctorates.

He was a brilliant, classy man and very proper. Dr. McGuigan strove for the niceties of life and acquired a beautiful home near the New Jersey Governor's Mansion in Princeton. Never married, he taught psychology at the college. He was an excellent professor—firm, fair, consistent—and the students loved him. He loved to ski and so did I. I loved his brilliant mind. I guess he enjoyed my questions.

Student fees from our combination skiing/psychology course would pay for Dr. McGuigan's and my expenses. My wife wanted to go along on the trip, but we didn't have the money. I went to Europe without her. She never forgave me, and we were no longer happy. I can't say I was blameless, but I decided I had to get out and leave the home I loved so much.

I had to do some real soul searching and eliminate conceptional barriers that had been with me as long as I could remember. I was born and raised a staunch Catholic. Marriage was supposed to be forever, and getting a divorce was scandalous in the eyes of Catholic society at that time. I'd gotten far in life by getting along. I didn't like the prospect of not being liked. Then I had to wrestle with how to let people know. Do I bring everyone in the family together and tell them all at once that I'm getting a divorce, or do I inform family members one at a time?

When I told my wife, it didn't go over well. She never got out of a state of denial. Next, I took Butch, who was 15 at the time, out to dinner to tell him. To my surprise, he said "Dad, I totally understand." He was the easiest of the lot. We had a few beers together and I poured him into bed that night. That didn't go over well either.

I dreaded having to tell my mother- and father-in-law. I loved them, and they loved me. They never interfered with our marriage and always gave us such support. When I talked to them about the divorce, I was a basket case, but they listened to what I had to say. (Later my then ex-wife told me that her mother gave *her* guff for letting it happen.) Now to spread the news to my mother and father. I don't even remember how they reacted, but they informed my brothers and sister for me. I was numb by then.

The process of getting a divorce is the best diet you could ever go on. It was so devastating to me I dropped from 170 to 150 pounds. I couldn't hit a tennis ball with any consistency. I hadn't even been to see the judge in the court of law and was already traumatized.

My brother John represented me. In court he asked me questions like, "When were you born?" "When were you married." I always had trouble remembering birthdays, anniversaries, deaths, but this was worse. I was drawing blanks. John ended up providing the dates and asking me to respond with a yes or no. That's called "walking you through it." We laugh about that now. Not then.

According to the Catholic Church, marriage was a lifetime commitment. I didn't make it. The Church excommunicated me. In addition to having to tell my family and being banned by the Church, I had to put up with what society thought. This biggest hurt I ever experienced was my failed first marriage. After my divorce I vowed to never get married again.

●————————— ● —————————●

I was playing a sanctioned Middle States tennis tournament in Atlantic City in the 45 and over division. It wasn't far, so I commuted there.

Women's divisions were offered at the same time, and I was asked if I would give a young woman a ride to the tournament. I agreed. This beautiful woman had Hedy Lamarr–like legs, a washboard belly, and a model's waist. She was cute as a button and a jock to boot.

In the car I was distracted by her presence. I kept asking her questions so I could keep focused on the road. For the 1½-hour trip to Atlantic City, it was like talking to a wall. All I could get out of her were yes and no answers. I finally gave up and turned the radio on.

Mary Ellen was 20 years younger. Was she petrified of me and afraid to talk? One day after the tournament was over, I was surprised when she asked me to hit tennis balls with her. American culture was not as liberal as it is today, so a divorced 40-plus-year-old man had to watch his p's and q's and be careful not to rock the cradle for fear of being the victim of unkind remarks. For 8 years, I rocked that cradle and our friendship developed into something more.

There was one catch. Mary Ellen told me that she wanted to have a child before she was 30. Every woman deserves to be a mother if she wants to be. She was 29 years old, and I was 49 or 50. If I got married, I could be raising a family again. Then one day it was like a lightning bolt hit me. I had spent eight glorious years with this woman. If I married her, I could be with her the rest of my life.

ADVENTURES WITH MARY ELLEN— AND ANOTHER AIRPLANE INCIDENT

Mary Ellen and I flew across the country with tennis player Jim Orange and his wife in his plane to Southern California. We were playing in a tennis tournament in LaJolla.

I was at the controls trying to fly the plane via short-range radio signal straight to the next VOR (VHF Omnidirectional Radio Range) when it looked like a missile had been shot from the ground and was coming right at us toward the cockpit. Jim saw the plane the same time its pilot saw us. It was a commercial airplane. We were on different radio frequencies so there was no communication. Jim wrested the controls from me. Both pilots made right turns. We missed one another by feet. I cannot imagine what the passengers on that commercial airplane experienced. Damn, if we didn't make it to the tournament on time. When we landed in Oceanside, Jim filed his report to the FAA (I am not privy to it, but Jim was in the clear).

Now we had to get home. Mary Ellen flew commercial because she had to get back to work—or at least that's what she said. Jim, Carol, and I went to the Navy commissary, and Carol bought three of the most powerful binoculars in the store.

With Kyle (on my back) and Tara

*Mary Ellen and me on our
wedding day, August 22, 1981*

*With Mary Ellen and Tara on our way to a
tournament in Sarasota*

The week after we got married, Prince held a surprise celebration for Mary Ellen and me.

With Mary Ellen, celebrating our 35th wedding anniversary.

We eloped. We were married in the Rider College Chapel by the chaplain, Ron White. Then we went out to dinner with Mary Ellen's sister Martha, her husband Jimmy, and their daughter Sarah.

We thought perhaps we should tell her mother and mine. Mary Ellen's mother was in bed when we got to her house. Mary Ellen threw our keys up to her second-story bedroom window to try to wake her up. She finally got up and opened the door. I got off to a great start with my new mother-in-law, who was mad because she wanted a party in the form of a wedding. My mother was still living at the house on Abernethy Drive. Mary Ellen and I stopped by to let her know. We didn't need to wake her, she was still up. When she saw the flower in my lapel she asked, "Who got married?" When we told her that we did, she said Mary Ellen would be good for me. Her job was to tell the rest of the family. My mother had Alzheimer's, so when she called everyone to say Marty got married, they didn't believe her. My father had passed away so I couldn't tell him.

Afterwards Mary Ellen drove me to a tournament. Our honeymoon consisted of Mary Ellen driving all night while I slept so I'd be ready for a tennis match when we got to Bucknell University. She's been a keeper since that day.

Mary Ellen has been an awesome wife and mother. I watched this woman with impeccable credentials and experience in the medical profession perform for 30 years. She worked in the Labor & Delivery operating room as a surgical tech for most of these years. I'm so proud of her. She bore me a rich man's family—a talented and beautiful daughter and a handsome, smart son.

We have been together for more than 40 years and I couldn't be happier.

Coaching Rider College Tennis

In 1976 the Rider tennis coach up and died. I was still heading up the intramural program and had only started playing tennis seven years before. I collected another job, coaching the men's team at the college level. When I took the job, I refused to actively recruit. I wanted kids who truly wanted to play. I maintained a no-cut policy and worked with anyone who came out for the team. They chose whether they were on the team and cut themselves if they did not show up for daily practices. The no-cut policy was so unusual for an intercollegiate athletic program it made it into the *New York Times*. Earle Rommel, the PR guy for Rider, was so excited about this little article that he repeated time after time how important it was to the college to get that kind of publicity.

We learned, had fun doing it, and still had winning seasons. The team adopted a fine system. Anyone on the varsity could fine a teammate for mental mistakes that occurred in practice or in matches. The "accused" could appeal their case in the locker room court, which took place once a week. The judge was Greg Church, who presided with a robe on his back and a floor mop on his head. Greg never overturned a case. He was a riot in this role and later became an outstanding lawyer. The fines, not more than a dollar each, were used to supplement a year-end party.

Even though I didn't actively recruit, I was glad to talk to parents and students about the college and its programs. One Saturday, I was playing tennis with a friend. A makeshift court was set up in half of the gym, with a wall partition as a divider. I was interrupted by a father and son who expressed an interest in attend-

TENNIS BALL MACHINE

Tennis star Rene Lacoste is credited with creating the first-ever tennis ball machine. It was 1920 and it was hand cranked. The first electric machines appeared in the 1950s but were not available to the public. In 1968, Robert H. McClure designed the "Little Prince," a ball machine launched under the Prince brand, which was later bought out and improved on by Howard Head. These air-pressure machines were the first available on a large scale to the public and revolutionized tennis training. There was little competition among companies making the machines. They served as the standard for many years until cheaper battery-operated portable machines hit the market and, in 1975 came the birth of the modern ball machine. Marty Devlin learned everything he could about the machine and used it in incredibly new and innovative ways.

ing the college. I invited them to play doubles against us. This was an infraction of NCAA rules, but I needed my workout. I ran the old man into the partition so many times I thought I'd have a lawsuit in the morning. The father and son loved my act so much the old man endorsed the college, and the kid, Norm Rebach, enrolled and became one of the most creative tennis players I ever had.

I coached by playing against the kids and observing their strengths and weaknesses. Every day I would play all or some of them. Every day my number 1 player said he had a lab and would be late for practice. He drove to the court toward the end of practice in his TransAm, music blaring, unmistakable with his big Afro. Little did I know he waited for me to be exhausted so that he could take me on while fresh as a daisy. I felt more pressure to win against him than if I played at the U.S. Open, because if he won, it would be all over campus that he kicked my butt. His name was Steve Diamond.

After Steve graduated, when he was playing a sanctioned USTA player he had never beaten, I told him to change pace, use spin, think tactically, use every element of surprise. I wanted him to be a thinking player. He won in straight sets and later became the USPTA tennis pro of the year out of 15,000 tennis pros throughout the country. He became a great buddy and even coached me in the 80-and-over national grass court championships.

A Prince of a Job

I dealt with 2,000 students a year at Rider and one of them really shone. His name was Jim Baugh. We called him Beamer because of his perpetual smile. Beamer was a business major and a manager for the Rider basketball team. He also helped out with intramurals. I loved his work ethic, character values, and his attitude. After he graduated, I managed to get him a job teaching physical education at Blessed Sacrament, where both the nuns and the students came to love him. The only ones who were unhappy were my colleagues in phys ed. I caught smoke from them. They complained that Beamer had never taken a PE course. I didn't care. I knew he'd be great at teaching kids. I gave him a series of physical education principles and turned him loose. He knocked 'em dead at Blessed Sacrament.

A few years later, Prince, a tennis equipment company in nearby Bordentown,

New Jersey, contacted me about Beamer. They wanted to hire him. I knew he'd succeed at whatever he did. Blessed Sacrament's loss was Prince's gain. Beamer was now in a job where he could use his business degree.[2]

A few years after Beamer started at Prince, he brought me into their offices to meet with the bigwigs. They wanted to hire me to negotiate racket contracts with pro players. I had no interest in that kind of work. It was like being a lawyer. A few years later Beamer brought me in again. This time Prince asked me to be product manager of the tennis ball machine. I was ready for a change. I left Rider with a gem of an intramural program, many fond memories, and some apprehensions.

Bob McClure founded Prince to sell his tennis ball machine, which he developed in his garage by reversing the motor on a vacuum cleaner. It became the first commercially successful machine to automatically propel tennis balls. But the company was known mainly for its tennis rackets. I was brought in to develop, market, and sell the ball machine. Just as Beamer had had no qualifications to teach physical education, I had no qualifications to enter the business world. At 45 years old, after 18 years at Rider, I took the job not knowing how I would do it.

I did know I couldn't manage anything I didn't understand. I spent lots of time with the engineers so I could thoroughly understand the product. I learned to take the ball machine apart, build it, and repair it. I tried it out on the tennis court to understand what it was capable of. I thought about my markets. Tennis teaching pros seemed to be a logical market. Why should the tennis pros hit balls to pupils when a machine could do it for them? At Prince they left me alone for months. I spent most of my time at the office learning about the machine and developing a plan to sell it. Then they let me loose.

I wanted to make it easy for the pros to use so I created a program of 80 drills with three settings and three formations. At the time, tennis was declining in popularity and the aerobics craze took over. How about bringing the two together? I talked to the swimming coach at Rider, Dick Coppola, a former classmate at Trenton

---

2   Jim Baugh skyrocketed to vice-president of sales. Later he became president and CEO of Wilson Sporting Goods and was inducted into the Tennis Industry Hall of Fame. He is back in education as founder of PHIT America, a nonprofit promoting kids' mental and physical fitness.

State, to test out my idea. He thought it would work. I created a jogging/aerobics program, using the machine to shoot a full load of 175 balls, plus 20 more, corner to corner on the tennis court. Anyone who did the program jogged and hit nearly 200 balls during a one-mile run. I had an aerobic tennis fitness conditioning program 30 years before cardio-tennis!

Wouldn't it be nice for the pros to be able to evaluate the skill development of their pupils using the machine? I developed scorecards to track the progress of each player. A byproduct was bringing more fun and variety to the tennis court. Creating games and drills made practicing the sport less tedious while giving the teaching pros more tools in their toolboxes.

While I was becoming an expert at moving people from court to court all day long, I knew I still needed to work on a few things. To be successful, I had to become known at the clubs. I was still uncomfortable with people I didn't know and felt awkward introducing myself. One day driving up to set up a clinic, I realized I had to overcome my shyness and put myself out there. I had to make it so that people would be more comfortable with me and more likely to participate in the clinic. To do that, I had to call up all of my courage and change how I'd done things.

Instead of going straight to the courts and getting set up for the clinic, as I entered this tennis club, I went right up to the desk staff and told them why I was there. I made a point to meet the rest of the staff and repeat the message. I sought out the pros and talked to them. At first it was a painful task. I had to fake that I liked talking to them. Just like everything, it took practice. Soon I had done it so much that introducing myself and talking to people I didn't know became easier for me. I became like a politician working a crowd wherever I went. It got so where I could hardly turn it off. Once I was at dinner with Mary Ellen and I found myself introducing myself to people I didn't know in the restaurant! Connecting with people had become a habit. Cultivating this new habit changed my life. What a complete metamorphosis! I was now becoming outgoing and comfortable with my social skills. It only took me 50 years to get there.

I also had to create a network of dealers, educate them on the use and value of the ball machine, and explain the markets so they could sell it. They did—to the tune of a million-dollar business. My brain was continuing to wake up.

More questions came to me. What is the optimum number of students on the court hitting balls off the machine at the same time? How many courts could an individual pro manage? I tried different formats and found that the ideal was six courts with six students on a court at one time, for one-and-a-half hours. This would put lots of money in the pro's pocket. Instead of working with a few pupils at a time, they could maximize their income by working with many at once.

I found other ways to push the limit. With the help of the pros, one day I ran 2,500 people on mega-courts. On more than one occasion, I managed 16 courts at a time. These events attracted a lot of attention and further promoted both the ball machine and the sport of tennis.

Now my wheels were really turning. Prince reps had territories throughout the United States. They had tennis clubs in their territories. If the reps selected a different club to reward each year, I could conduct a free clinic for them and help them sell the entire line of Prince products, not just the ball machine. I learned about all the product lines—rackets, clothes, strings, bags, shoes, and accessories. I compiled my resume, including all my crazy experiences—American Legion champ, All-American diver, All-City quarterback, Army baseball, player–manager in the Dodgers' organization, tennis champion. I packed it all in and made sure my screwed-up resume got to the media. I wanted to pique their interest. The media bought in. They showed up to interview me, often with film crews, in the many cities and towns I traveled to, and Prince got lots of free press. I made sure I was surrounded by loads of Prince products and banners so both me and Prince products were getting free airtime. It was great marketing. All my life I'd been in the newspapers because of my accomplishments. Now I was figuring out how to work the media for Prince. My reputation started to precede me, and the tennis clubs and the Prince reps began clamoring for me to hold clinics.

Our rep would go to the local club and have the pros there. He'd let them know, "There's this guy coming to town…."

As for the showman, he was still waiting to come out. Then along came "Smiley Bones," aka Ken Merritt. If I was Popeye, he was Olive Oil. He smiled all the time and could stand in a shower and not get wet. Tori Baxter, who led Prince's junior program, wanted me to meet with him. We hit it off immediately. I knew he had skills I needed to learn to take the clinics to another level. There was a job opening at Prince. I was now head of international clinics for Prince, and I asked him to join me on the road. We headed out together in the van Prince provided me to travel with my equipment across the country. Smiley Bones helped transform the clinics into events. He was only 18 but was a musician and had played in bands with trumpeter Doc Severinsen and entertainer Sammy Davis, Jr.

The ball machine was the Prince Deluxe 2. I came out to music toting a huge Prince tennis racket, dressed in a regal outfit as Prince or King of the Court. I was introduced as Johnny Carlson (a take on Johnny Carson). Ken was the DJ who orchestrated the show. He made an ass out of me, and I didn't mind. I showed Ken how to move and motivate people, he showed me the art of performance. We created drama and suspense. He introduced an "indispensable member of the Prince team," and the ball machine would emerge in the court with fake smoke drifting all around it. Music was playing everywhere during the clinic.

It was nonstop action, competition, and fun. We set up hula hoop contests, an elimination competition with the kids, the adults, and the pros. In the Hit-for-Prizes competition, I placed Prince t-shirts, cans of balls, rackets, and other branded tennis paraphernalia all around the court. Participants won a prize by striking a tennis ball and hitting these targets. The clinics were becoming carnivals. I did sit-ups on the court, we ran the drills, and measured the speed of serves with a radar gun. It was a three-ring circus.

We kept working on the show, making it better. God knows how many thousands of people we introduced to the game of tennis this way. We conducted clinics in countless cities: St. Louis, Fort Worth, Oakland, Little Rock, Tucson, Dallas, Miami, and places more off the beaten path like Wenatchee, Washington, to name just a few.

After we had a national sales meeting, the reps asked for the clinics to go international. Now I was traveling, holding clinics in Europe and Canada.

We started with one court, one ball machine. I talked Prince into growing the reach of the clinics. Over time we went from one van to five so we could cover more clubs. I trained tech reps, who were added, along with more ball machines, equipment, and apparel, which were being shown across the country. The new tech reps were sharp cookies who got to be awfully good at putting on clinics.

They did a great job promoting the Prince brand and the game.

Tennis had been a stiff and formal game, a gentleman's game. You could listen to the ball coming off the strings. We turned it into showtime, with talking and hollering and music. What had been a staid activity was now a great release.

I had also been given the responsibility of awarding free products to opinion leaders—highly ranked senior tennis players who were tennis leaders in their communities. This helped me network for Prince, embed Prince products in tennis clubs throughout the country, and gave me the opportunity to observe and play against these outstanding tennis players at national tournaments. The reps were charged with getting me daily tennis matches.

One of my opinion leaders was Bobby Riggs, best known for an amazing, hyped-up spectacle. In "The Battle of the Sexes," he played a nationally televised match against Billie Jean King (and lost). Bobby was known as a con man, a hustler who bet on everything. I wasn't surprised to find out that he sold the free rackets and equipment we gave him. That was Bobby. He was a hell of a player and a Wimbledon champion but is still best known for that crazy day in 1973 at the Houston Astrodome that was also a step forward for the women's liberation movement.

One time I was 55 years old and giving tennis clinics for Prince with the Bollettieri Tennis Academy. After the clinic was over, the pros began playing. The organizers were bringing people out of the stands to return Andre Agassi's forehand and Chip Hooper's serves. Hooper was Paul Bunyan, Goliath, John Henry, and Hercules all put into one man. He could fire screaming meemies, hit frozen ropes. Unbeknownst to me, my friends had taken my racket. They shoved me onto the court, put my racket back in my hand. Here I was, having to return Chip Hooper's serve.

Chip served to my forehand and I returned his serve. He served to what would be my backhand side, and I returned it with my left hand. He went bonkers. *What is this guy doing?!* Some SOB in the stands suggested we play out a point! He served and volleyed. I put the ball at his feet, he hit a drop shot. I lobbed, and he ran into a grocery cart full of tennis balls. I walked off the court.

I didn't want to give him another chance. As we were leaving the court, I said to

Here I am at a clinic showing a little guy how to hit a tennis ball

Rackets up! With Prince clinic participants demonstrating the ball machine and ready for Hit for Prizes.

Prince tech reps—the best in the business! They educated dealers and put on dog-and-pony shows. L ro R: John Keller, Tommy Judson, Peitre Overbeeke, Marty Devlin, Ken Merritt, Jerome Jones, Dale Hawkins.

We thought we were in the Prince hauling business! Stew Bunn, a tech rep, pulling the ball machine and getting ready for a clinic

Tommy Lasorda, my former teammate with the Montreal Royals, holding Tara. It was 1984, and I wanted to show Mary Ellen Vero Beach and Dodgertown where I'd trained. The Dodgers happened to be running a fantasy camp when we stopped by.

With Bill Hughes (C) and Steve Garvey (R) at the Germantown Cricket Club

With good buddies Jim Baugh (L) and Dave Haggerty (C)

With Ken Wilson (L), my doubles partner, equally brilliant as a tennis player and a man

Mary Ellen and me with Bobby Riggs (C) at the Germantown Cricket Club in Philadelphia, 1979

him, "Thanks for being a good sport to the old man." And he responded, "Good sport, bull! I was trying to kick your butt."

During my years with Prince, I traveled to 56 cities each year. I eventually made it to all but 2 states in the Union. I conducted clinics in Norway, Sweden, Finland, Denmark, England, France, Germany, Italy, Austria, Spain, Belgium, Switzerland, and other Western European countries. Prince sales soared, and one Christmas, Dave Haggerty, Prince's top dog, presented me with a bonus check for $25,000.

It was nice to receive the money and that kind of recognition, but for me it was never about the money. More important are the people you impact. You never know who, when, where, or how that will happen. I was conducting a Prince tennis clinic at the United States Professional Tennis Association (USPTA) Convention. Thousands of members and their families came to Phoenix for the event. I often worked with young kids. There was one little guy who was clearly incapable of playing the game and needed help. We set up Hit for Prizes, and every time it was his turn, I'd pick him up and help him swing the racket and hit a prize on the court. Unbeknownst to me, this little guy had been deliberately left to die in the desert as a young child. He was found living with wolves who had been "raising" him. His adoptive parents brought him to the Prince clinic to help socialize him. Until then, he had not uttered a single word. After the clinic, the USPTA revealed to me the story of the young boy. I was totally unaware of this amazing story during the clinic. The other part of the story was that after the clinic he began to speak. His new parents were ecstatic and grateful. Until then, he had not uttered a single word.

Rider College Athletic Director

I'd had ten exciting years working at Prince, running clinics for thousands of people throughout the U.S. and Europe, having opportunities to play and promote the game I loved. Then the athletic director position opened at Rider College. By now I'd had my fill of travel. I was ready to get off the road and back to the kids. I was ready for a change.

Rider loved what I'd achieved with the intramural program. I had been assistant athletic director while intramural director and looked like I was prepared for the job. But all I'd done was manage the athletic teams' schedules. I was hired without an interview to run the school's intercollegiate program.

Taking the job with Rider felt like a homecoming for me. I decided to celebrate by holding an event on the tennis courts at the school to mark my transition from the business world back to Rider and education. It was going to be like a Prince clinic. We'd use the 6 courts at Rider, have banners, music, giveaways of accessories and rackets, games, students, faculty, and fun. When I told my new boss about my plans, Bart Luedeke wasn't enthusiastic.

I had made Prince money and attracted people to the sport of tennis through clinics. I figured holding an event at Rider would promote the athletic program, get people excited about the school, and help me celebrate my new job. If it promoted the Prince brand, that was fine too. Everybody won. I held the event, and many people came out and had a good time. To me it was a big success. We were covered in the newspaper. It was a way to get people excited about the school.

President Frank Elliott had hired me. He knew me and loved what I'd done for the intramural program. Six months after I took the AD job, Dr. Elliott retired, and Bart Luedeke became president.

One of the challenges the Rider athletic program faced was that it didn't have a big budget or a football program that could attract big donors. Coaches from all the sports were competing for a small pot of resources. Money was so tight it was tough for me even to get a pencil. I needed to do something to get the alumni to buy in and help fund the athletic program. My plan was to build out the program by bringing in ideas about marketing and sales I'd learned at Prince.

With President Elliott gone, I had to sell my idea to President Luedeke. I was not a numbers guy and needed some help. I'd known Al Sumutka since he was a student at Rider. He'd played on the baseball team. Now he was an accounting professor and faculty representative to the NCAA. I told him about my plans for promoting the school through athletics. We started talking and came up with the plan to fully fund and finance every sport.

He was brilliant. He developed charts and spreadsheets I could use to present my ideas. We met with the president to explain how spreading out the budget across the men's athletic programs and raising their profiles through favorable press coverage, we'd have free publicity year-round. At that time the local papers— *Trenton Times,* the *Trentonian*, and the *Star Ledger*—all had big circulations. To me it was free advertising for the university. Corporations paid big bucks for the kind of marketing that colleges got with their athletic programs—cascades of free press. As I saw it, this marketing the school was here for the taking. It was just a matter of using the publicity generated by the sports teams to market the college.

TITLE IX

Title IX prohibits sex discrimination in educational institutions that receive federal funding. The same Title IX requirements for varsity college sports also apply to club and intramural programs. Title IX was passed in 1972 as a follow-up to the Civil Rights Act of 1964, and Marty Devlin's role in developing and running intramurals at Rider was happening in the midst of these developments. Before he was even aware of Title IX, however, Marty had started the men's intramural program and brought in a woman, Vi Udy, to oversee a women's division. Later, when he was named athletic director at Rider, he oversaw implementation of Title IX for women's intercollegiate sports.

Maybe the plan was too radical. Early on I was told by Rider's PR guy, Earle Rommel, never to use the word *marketing* with the faculty, that it was a dirty word. That was an omen! I don't know if this was the reason, but the president didn't go for the plan. He was a sports enthusiast and supported the athletic program, but most of the resources went to the basketball team. The other coaches who missed out raised hell with me. I felt I was caught between the coaches and the administration. I had a little bit of control as athletic director, but I was used to running the show. I'd been a popular character on campus as intramural director and knew most of the coaches. I wasn't used to being seen as the bad guy.

The other idea I had was the Arete program. Arete is a Greek word that means "excellence," or "be the best you can be." Arete would prepare the athletes with an array of skills that would help both their own development and the school. I started to bring in speakers to talk to both male and female athletes about how to represent themselves, the college, and the athletic department. I wanted the athletes to go beyond the notion they were jocks and learn how to succeed in life. Arete would also prepare them to represent the school so that we could use publicity more effectively. We started the program with top-flight presenters on an array of topics—leadership, study skills, time management, nutrition, training techniques, communications skills, substance abuse, etiquette, stress management, and job search skills. I was excited about the prospect of seeing athletes develop themselves. The school loved Arete.

While I was AD, a big problem I ran into was the focus on NCAA rules. It used to be that the school presidents ran their athletic programs, but in the 1940s the balance of power shifted to the NCAA. The NCAA was like God. The NCAA had rules about recruitment, about when coaches could begin practices out of season, about how long those practices were, and so on. I didn't realize until well after I became the athletic director that a big part of my job was to keep the coaches in line and make sure they were following NCAA rules. If I'd been a lawyer or a cop, I'd have been better prepared.

I was hearing rumors I was in danger of being fired. People who had supported me started looking like they were uncomfortable when they ran into me on campus. I'd held the AD job for a year and a half when I traveled to the NCAA convention with Bart Luedeke. During this trip our conversations made it clear to me that he and I had very different ideas of what my job was. I think that's what they call irreconcilable differences.

Sometimes you have to admit when something isn't working and make a change. I decided to leave on my own terms. I was coaching the tennis team at Rider and loved teaching. When an opportunity came to teach tennis at Hopewell Valley Tennis Club, I jumped at it. The press presented my taking that job as a step down. I knew I would be doing what I loved.

I saw my time as athletic director as a lesson in the importance of communication. I'm happy to say that writing this memoir has also given me more appreciation of what I did accomplish, and no longer see this as a failure. I recently learned that Arete continued at Rider after I left the school. The name later changed but the program continued. I am proud of this, and I laughed when I heard that the program now includes training required by the NCAA, given that the NCAA and I weren't always best buddies!

Teaching at Hopewell Valley Tennis Club

Until now, I had so many jobs you'd think I couldn't hold one. Bill Kurtain, co-owner of the Hopewell Valley Tennis Club, who hired me to teach tennis, was a great boss.

I knew about conducting clinics on multiple courts from my time at Prince and had played competitively at the highest levels. When I coached tennis at Rider, I focused on conditioning and strategy. I knew about ball placement and outthinking your opponent from my baseball experience and my own tennis matches. But I never had formal skills training and knew nothing about teaching tennis correctly. At Hopewell Valley, Bill Kurtain assigned me to work with Bill Mountford. Bill managed a super junior development program at Hopewell Valley. He taught me how to apply biomechanics to teaching tennis.[3]

Once I got that job, I taught all day and played all night. I loved this form of teaching and did it for six years.

While I was teaching at the club, along came Dana Bezar. Her mother and brother were taking lessons. Dana tagged along and watched from the sidelines. She was about 10 years old at the time and wanted to play tennis too. Dana's mom came to me to see if I could be of some help.

Here was the challenge. Dana was born as any other able-bodied person, but about the age of 2 she acquired an ailment that turned into pneumonia. She was at home when septic shock started to shut down her body's vital organs. The only way doctors could save Dana's life was to sever her arms below the elbow and

---

3   Bill Mountford later became the director of tennis at the International Tennis Hall of Fame and director of the USTA Billie Jean King National Tennis Center and the Lawn Tennis Association of Great Britain.

her legs below the knees. She made it through the surgery, but what would her prognosis be? How was she going to live her life? I can't imagine what it was like being a parent in that situation.

Dana rolled with the punches. She acquired four prosthetics—two arms and two legs—so she could function as other human beings. As for helping Dana learn to play tennis, I relished the challenge but had little knowledge of how to work with this special person—and certainly no experience.

I needed to do some fancy thinking. Australian players for years used the same grip for both the forehand and backhand, making changing grips unnecessary. If we could attach the tennis racket to the prosthetic in a position where she could strike a forehand and backhand using the one-grip system, it could work.

I used what was at my disposal: thick rubber bands and lots of athletic tape. After some trials and tribulations and lots of effort, we were able to fasten the racket to Dana's prosthetic in the correct position to hit the tennis ball, but after a few strikes of the ball, the racket would start to loosen and need to be re-taped. When it was hot, the tape lost its grip even faster. Not a very practical solution.

During my 10 years at Prince, I had established a rapport with a first-rate engineer and racket designer, Steve Davis. I reached out to this gentle, empathetic soul who responded compassionately to my request. Steve sicced me on his top machinist, Ed Hill. I taped the racket to Dana's prosthetic in the position we wanted it and gave it to Ed.

After a week or two, Ed came back with a gizmo that would clamp the racket onto the prosthetic. Ed and Steve came to the court for the fitting. It attached in the correct position and could be taken on and off in seconds. Bingo! A home run and a gift for life.

Dana loved hitting against the wall and practiced on her own. She served and hit underhand. She developed various strokes—topspin, flat, and slice off the forehand and backhand sides. Ninety-eight percent of recreational players can't do that. Dana can use these shots to play both singles and doubles. Her fight, determination, hope, belief, and tomboy attitude prevailed.

Dana Bezar skiing on Mount Snow

Dana in an exhibition match

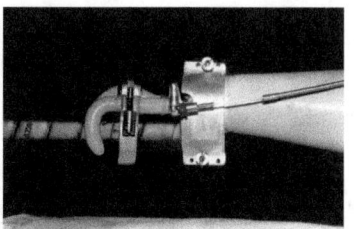

Dana's prosthesis

From left to right, I'm with Dana, Dana's mom, Andrea, and her brother Ian in 2022

Dana with Ed Hill (L) and Steve Davis (R), Prince machinist and Prince engineer who made it possible for Dana to play tennis

Ken Merritt, Dana, and me

Here I am with (L to R) Ian, Dana, and Andrea. We still play every week.

Dana has gone on to accomplish a lot in her young life. She went to college and finished her degree, and she still plays tennis. Once a week Dana, her brother, mother, and I play king of the court, otherwise known as Quink—short for queen and king. One person in the group goes to one side of the court and the three others to the other side. They alternate trying to take the one person down. To get to the other side, a total of four points must be achieved, and the server can't win more than two points in a row. The only rule that's different for Dana is that she's entitled to two bounces, and balls must be hit to where she has a chance to get her racket on them. She can place the ball anywhere on the court. Every week I look forward to playing with her.

After working with Dana for some time, I started thinking. If she could master the skills required by tennis, learning how to ski would be a piece of cake. But first I had to get her interested in the sport. We planned a trip to Mount Snow in Vermont, where I volunteered as a ski patroller. I wanted to give her a feel for the atmosphere. We started with a ride to the summit of Mount Snow on a snowmobile to visit my ski patrol buddies. She loved the cold and the thrill of movement. Now came the skiing part. To get her back to the bottom of the mountain we put her in a rescue sled, a toboggan, and gave her the ride of her lifetime. My ski buddies and I took off, making turns and skiing her down the mountain. We made it to the bottom, and Dana had the biggest smile. It made my day.

After this introduction to skiing, Dana was hooked. She wanted to learn to ski. Really ski. Dana and her family invested in ski equipment—boots, skis, and fancy ski wear. I talked to the experts in Mount Snow's adaptive ski program about working with Dana. They all recommended different variations of her coming down the mountain—in a sled, chair skis, skis without riggers, etc. They said it wasn't possible for her to ski like an able-bodied person. Dana and I would have nothing to do with anything but the real McCoy.

Her leg prosthetics have what look like real feet, so I knew putting her prosthetic in a boot was not going to be a problem. The problem was that prosthetics don't have the flexibility required for skiing. I must have rocks for brains. I had no idea how much I was asking her to do. Any activity, including walking, requires so much more energy for her than for an able-bodied person. Another problem was that boots and skis are heavy and riding the lift with that kind of weight could pull her prosthetics right off her legs. Another problem to solve. If we took her skis off before she got on the lift and put them back on at the top of the mountain it could work. We arranged with lift services to stop the lift before she got on and after she got off. We were in business.

We went to Ski Baba, a slope at Mount Snow where my three kids, years ago, had learned to ski. Dana would have the same experiences falling as any other novice skier. I quickly learned it was more devastating for her because of how much it hurt, so we had to minimize the number of times she fell. This is where I got tremendous help from the instructors in the handicapped program. They attached two tethers to Dana's skis (one to each ski) and skied behind her to control her speed. Now she could head down the mountain with confidence, and she would still be doing the skiing.

By the end of the weekend, Dana had skied down the slope more than 20 times in a row without falling. She is the only person in the world I know who skied with four prosthetics. She loved the experience and talks about it to this day.

Heaven – A House Near the River

After my divorce, I had to pay alimony and didn't have money for an apartment. I lived in a Ford Econoline 150 van for about six years. The van was better than any apartment. It had two wood-burning fireplaces, a refrigerator, a portable stove, a TV, a bed, and a beanbag chair located on a platform alongside the driver's seat. I had backup systems all over the place. I could travel to ski and play tennis. I even cooked a capon in one of the fireplaces located over the gas tank.

When Mary Ellen and I decided to get married, I asked her to look for a house with room for a tennis court. She came back in an hour with a big smile. The house she found was near the Delaware River, at a spot where people in the 1900s traveled from Trenton in horse and buggy to swim. It was nestled in the woods and had a big fireplace, a large picture window, and a floor plan I'll take to my grave. With one acre of land, there was room for a tennis court and a swimming pool. I'd just have to build them myself.

There is no place in the world I'd rather live. I live in the jungle but out of it. I'm in heaven. Thank you, Mary Ellen!

I built the tennis court with my own labor and some help. My friend and tennis buddy Stan Dlugosz, was a civil engineer, as well as an All-American soccer player, soccer coach, and tennis pro. He served as the surveying engineer for the tennis court I built on my property in 1986.

My neighbor Mike Hartmann, a funeral director who is going to bury me, had a chainsaw. We cut trees down, and I brought in a front-end loader for $2,000 to level the steep hilly land for the tennis court. (Mary Ellen reminds me that I was away at a clinic when the machine came to do its work, and that she supervised this part of the project!) From that point on, it was wheelbarrow, rake, and shovel.

My big blue Rube Goldberg van

Clearing ground for the Swamp: Tara (L) and Kyle (R), my helpers

Ken Merritt is standing behind Stan Dlugosz, who served as the engineer for the tennis court at the Swamp. Kyle is the little guy near them, and I'm pushing the wheelbarrow in the background.

Working on a stone wall I built at the Swamp

My dream come true! Autumn at the Swamp.

Digging for the Endless Pool®. At one point, I was so tired I could barely lift my shovel, so I enlisted my brother Donnie ("Pancho"), on the right, to help out!

I raked, built walls, and back filled. By this time, I had so many tennis trophies there was no room in the house for them. Most of them lie buried under the court.

I had no timetable for finishing the tennis court but was organized and planned the work. Every day, I'd peck away at one pile, stop, and gloat over the accomplishment. I found my self-esteem growing and my pace quickening. I couldn't wait for the next day to build more walls and to dig out big rocks and small stones. I had more help. Tara, my five-year old daughter, and Kyle, my three-year-old son, loved putting nails in the holes of tapes I laid out. They would nail the tapes down with toy hammers. I planted ivy to hold together the three-foot thick shale walls and tied the net posts to trees. I felt like Rube Goldberg, the legendary and ultimate problem solver. A year and a half after I started the project, I was in business.

The court is known as the Swamp, and I teach tennis and played tennis with my buddies there. When I began playing pro baseball in 1952, I was discouraged from ingesting soft drinks. The recommended alternative was thirst-quenching beer. I've been drinking it for over 60 years. To lower my expenses, I purchased one half-keg. I hid it in my bedroom till my wife directed me to move them elsewhere. My buddies found out about the stash, and I had new friends.

Joe Basco would play at the drop of a hat. He is consistent as hell and has an awesome return of serve. Jack Furlong, a wrong-armer, is a brilliant criminal trial attorney, articulate, author of *Crime Scene*. He can play with anyone and uses tennis as a release from his stress-laden work. Mike Cremeans, who had his own tennis camp, has power strokes and the uncanny ability to read cues and respond in the middle of a stroke. Mike Ehrenberg is talented and willing to grow his game. Scott Stoner would get his son Jordan out of bed for early morning workouts. Doug Potkay, Jason Bielski, and my son Kyle were All-American college players who were part of the group. When he was younger, Carl Bielski couldn't keep the ball in the court. He became far better player as a senior player: big strokes, more consistency. He's still a great player now. Jim Cryan would get up in the morning for a 10- to 15-mile bike ride and then play tennis with us. When I was younger, I used to own Scotty in four-hour matches, until I got older and then he owned me. Nancy, Scotty's wife, has classic traditional strokes, and a sneaky good game. Maddie Stoner, their daughter, was an All-American player on the powerful College of New Jersey team. Rick Strandskov had a win over John McEnroe in the juniors. Pete Stratton worked for four New Jersey governors. When he hit lines, I was history.

They came over on the pretense they were going to play tennis at the Swamp. They did play, and played so often they got quite good, and I got poorer.

◆————————— • —————————◆

When you're inculcated with anything at an early age, you often come back to it later in life. Pools, canals, rivers, oceans, and bays were all a huge part of my early development. Part of the Swamp, and partner to the tennis court, is the Endless Pool®. When I was 55 years old, I began work on it. I dug out the hole for the pool with a pick and shovel. The one mistake I made was that I dug it out a foot

PUTTING OUT FIRES, REALLY

I found myself in some unusual situations in my lifetime.

When I was in my 20s, I was driving by a home down the street from my parents on Abernethy Drive in Trenton where I was living at the time. Smoke was coming from the house. I stopped the car, ran into the house, and hollered. Two kids yelled back from the attic. They had been playing with matches and had started the fire.

I rushed them out of the house and called the police. (They were at home, I later learned, because they had lost their dad, and their mother was working at the State House.) When the team of firefighters arrived, I directed them to the fire in the attic. Some of the firefighters assembled all the furniture in the room to its center and covered it with a heavy canvas to prevent water damage. Another one quickly climbed the steps. He targeted the fire with his hose once he reached it. There was no water damage to that house. Later, I received a citation for my efforts. This experience taught me about the work of a professional firefighter unit and the importance of training and preparation.

My other crazy fire experience occurred about eight years later when I saw flames coming from a house near my home in Washington Crossing, Pennsylvania. I asked my wife to call 911 while I ran up the hill to see if I could help. I hollered, kicked in the door, and as the door banged open and a swoosh of air rushed in, the oxygen fed the fire. But the floor in the house was already almost gone. One more step and I would have been lost to the cellar. Thankfully, no one was home. Meanwhile, the firemen—all volunteers—arrived. I saw one on the back porch and one underneath the porch at the front of the house. It was inevitable that the porch would come down on him. One firefighter sprayed his hose at full strength through the front door I had just opened and knocked the other fireman off the back porch. I don't know that it was intentional. It was like a tragic comedy. A snowstorm had come through hours before, and the temperature was subfreezing with over a foot of fresh snow. The soaked fireman came around the house wet and frozen, with icicles on his helmet. That house burned to the ground, but no one died.

The difference I noticed in these two situations was in the training of the firefighters. The first group of firefighters were trained to respond in a way that overrode their central nervous system. Their actions were intentional and planned. Even though the second house probably couldn't have been saved, there was no chance at all because the firefighters were responding in the moment from their emotional brain. There was no apparent plan, no thought or training behind what they were doing.

I became fascinated by how different people reacted in emergencies, in life-threatening situations.

and a half. It was too deep! I had to fill it back up enough to satisfy engineering specs. (The pool was 9 x 13 feet.) Later I built an extra room on the house to enclose the pool. I love that pool so much I would have put it in before I'd put in a toilet.

Mount Snow and Ski Patrolling

Mount Snow is the largest mountain in southern Vermont. My buddy Stan Dlugosz had a home up there and was a volunteer on the mountain. He talked up the ski patrol, got me on board, and I was hooked. He scheduled his engineering classes so he'd be done teaching by Friday afternoon. When we both had growing families, after his last class was over, he'd pick up me, Mary Ellen, and the kids in his van. Then he'd drive to pick up his wife Nancy and their kids after she'd finished teaching at Princeton High School, and we'd all head up north to spend the weekend on the mountain, driving back on Sunday night. Stan, my tag-team buddy, never did it without me.

Over 40 years of my life were spent skiing at Mount Snow, 35 years as a ski patroller and 5 more as an ambassador. None of my other life experiences prepared me for what I faced as a volunteer at Mount Snow. Ski patrolling was the most pressure-packed experience I ever enjoyed. Every time I put my foot on the mountain I could be dealing with a life-threatening situation. I developed tremendous respect for first responders in other arenas whose own lives are at risk when they are on duty, whether soldiers, medical team units, firefighters, or police.

Each year prior to ski season Stan and I took a three-day refresher course to dry run a taste of what we might encounter in the coming year. It required so much study, I might just as well have gone back to college and gotten a Ph.D. We had to place the names of 128 trails in the appropriate places on the map. We had to know the trail cut-throughs to expedite transporting patients in sleds to First Aid and learn the hundreds of checkpoints necessary for sweep, closing the mountain for the day. We had to know floor plans of buildings on the mountain to expedite our trips to accidents, called "codes." We practiced scenarios on and off the trails, like navigating through woods and down embankments, assessing injured skiers, and using backboards, neck collars, oxygen, and traction splints. The golden hour, the critical time after a traumatic injury occurs, was always in the back of my mind. We had to be certified in CPR and understand the relationship of breathing and bleeding to codes for conscious and unconscious persons.

Skiing is physical to begin with. Ski patrolling meant skiing in all kinds of conditions: snow, sleet, rain, ice. It was especially demanding if you did the hat trick—brought three people down the mountain in one day. I was an adequate skier when I started but got better over time and brought some 350 people down the mountain without incident over my career. (Full-timers take that many skiers down in one year.)

Every call was an emergency. The code system was the only clue you had as to how serious an emergency it was. This is how a typical day on the mountain went. The Hill Chief would holler, for example, "Code ___. Who wants it?" Code 1 was not severe, and Code 3 was the most severe. It was always a rush—mentally and physically—to race to the scene of the accident because you never knew what you were getting into. You might get incorrect information about the location. You could fall or wipe somebody out with the trailing sled. You could blow by the scene.

I volunteered Stan and myself for everything. This day we caught it right. We found the accident, determined the guy had a broken leg, and put a splint on. We asked him how he felt. He said, "Fine, but it's the other leg that hurts." We splinted the other leg and let the doctor determine which one was broken.

There is a first aid station at the bottom of the mountain. After bringing someone down the mountain, you ski the sled into the doctor's office, move the injured person from the sled onto the cot, fill out the accident report, and return to the summit for more duty. This day, after trail closing, the doctor called me into his office to look at the x-ray. My patient had 17 breaks in the tibia and fibula. He had a spiral fracture.

Another time I was on a Code 2 with another ski patrol buddy. Code 2 requires a backboard and collars and possibly oxygen. This fellow did a face plant, and I was asked to ski him down. I got him down the mountain but learned he died in the helicopter on the way to the hospital. I was okay until I went through debriefing. The evaluation committee began questioning me, and that's when I got upset. I knew I'd done all I could.

Screw-ups were infrequent, but they occurred. One of the full-timers was free skiing and came upon a hat on the side of the trail. He picked it up, looked around, and saw a person well off the trail lying against a tree. He skied up to her, and realizing he couldn't do anything for her, raced to the bottom and called the accident into the summit. The Hill Chief sent a rescuer, who skied past the scene. The rescuer was followed by a sled, who missed the accident too. *Surely poles, skis, something will mark where the accident is,* I thought as I followed, skiing with an 80 lb.-trauma pack. All three of us met at the bottom of the mountain. All three of us missed this Code 3. The person who reported the accident had failed to mark the scene where a 20-year-old woman had hit a tree. She would have died anyway. It was so tragic.

Once a weather front came through extremely fast, and the mountain turned into an ice-skating rink. The Hill Chief asked me to locate and escort two skiers down the mountain. Time went by and the Hill Chief was anxious to know our status. I radioed that I was passing Coopers Junction and almost down with 17 skiers. Kelly Pawlak, President of the Mountain, radioed a message to me, "1215, you made my day." Those moments I was able to help people gave me so much satisfaction.

One day Stan and I were asked to break up a fight on the lower mountain. All we found were two kids playing and jumping over a mogul, so we played a joke on Ski Patrol at the summit. I got off the lift and entered the ski rescue building with a patch over my eye and my arm in a sling. The Hill Chief asked what happened. I told him I was okay, but Stan was hurting. Stan came in with his false teeth out and ketchup on his face. That didn't win us the easiest trail closing that day.

Trail closing in the month of December can be horrendous. If you are delayed closing the mountain, Ski Patrol skis down the mountain in pitch dark. Yet when you are a ski patroller, you also get first tracks, unblemished snow. One morning the mountain was closed because of high winds. Ski Patrol snowmobiled me to the top and dropped me off. Sixteen inches of powder with only God and me on the mountain. That was heaven.

One day, as Stan and I were nearing the end of our ski patrol years, I volunteered us for two codes. We were doing all the work while some young bucks in their 20s were enjoying the luxury of a warm summit building. Then I volunteered Stan and me for a third code, the hat trick. I should have done my homework on the trail conditions. The moguls were so high, deep, and treacherous on the Chute Trail I could have gotten Stan killed. We not only had to find the code but splint his arm and leg, load the 250-pounder in an 80-lb. sled, and wrestle him through the mogul field. It's the only time we ever had to use a belaying rope. Stan wasn't a happy camper, and we weren't finished yet. Chute is an expert trail on the north face, and the only ways out were by snowmobile or grooming cat. We lifted the loaded sled on the cat, transported the injured skier to Snow Dance, unloaded him again, skied him down the remainder of Snow Dance to First Aid, and again loaded him onto a cot. It felt like we were in the weightlifting business. After Stan and I went on our third code, Ski Patrol was chewed out unmercifully because two old men were doing all the work. That day, we were awarded the easiest closing trail.

I still liked pulling sleds, but Stan wanted to transfer from Ski Patrol to the Ambassador program. I agreed to serve the mountain in a different capacity—after all, we couldn't be separated. The ambassadors provide hospitality and guidance to skiers, greeting people as they arrive, guiding them to the trails, letting them know where the best skiing is, and saying good-bye as they left the mountain. This transition to Ambassador also made sense given that my social skills were now stronger than my first-aid skills. Hard to believe my progression! Jim Saulnier ran this program for a year before Stan and I signed on. (He returned to Ski Patrol because he missed pulling sleds.) This program would allow Stan and I to foster positivity throughout the mountain.

We had it all figured out: Stan and I would ski during the week and work the Ambassador program during the weekends.

This will be a cakewalk!

We couldn't wait.

Instead, we found ourselves taking on more and more responsibility, practically running the mountain by ourselves during the week. We knew the cut-throughs, the trails, and the conditions. We brought all our knowledge and skills from work-

Ski Patrolling

The role of ski patrollers is to promote ski safety, enforce area policies, and help the injured. Ski patrollers set up the mountain before it opens, provide avalanche control, and set up the equipment for the day. At the end of the day, they also conduct a sweep to clear the mountain.

The National Ski Patrol (NSP) was founded in 1938 and has over 31,000 members serving over 650 patrols in all 50 states and 10 countries. Some members are paid and others volunteer. The NSP serves the industry by providing education and accreditation to emergency care and safety service providers.

There is an inherent risk in skiing and snowboarding; therefore, a huge part of a patroller's day is serving as a trained first responder in medical emergencies. A CPR certification is usually required. Members are recognized by the red jackets with a white cross on the chest and one on the back.

ing Ski Patrol into the Ambassador program, sharing them with the volunteers and giving weekday skiers the best experience we could give them. Instead of skiing, we were stuck in the building at the top of the mountain, getting clobbered with phone calls and requests. We ended up doing whatever dirty work needed to be done. The ski patrol element we brought to the Ambassador program made us top dogs Monday through Friday. We ended up trading off Hill Chief responsibilities so one of us could ski.

One week, Pete MacDonald, who headed the program, was planning for a big event that was coming to Mount Snow. It was the X Games—a televised competition that was like an Olympic event. Stan and I told him to leave managing the event to us. He did and found it all ran like a clock. He told us he "was humbled" by all we did to support the mountain.

We still served as first responders on the mountain, assisting Ski Patrol when needed.

—————— • ——————

One day I had the opportunity to find a 10-year-old boy who had been separated from his panicking father and mother. Back home it's called Amber Alert. On the mountain it's called lost child. Every department is notified and has a thorough description—from skis to hat to skiing ability to where last seen, etc. Sure enough, I spotted this boy as he was starting to ski down River Run into the expert trails on the north face. I needed to intercept him.

"Hi, Old Buddy, what are you up to?" I asked him.

I could see he was confused and upset.

"I'm looking for my mother and father. They are lost."

"Let's go find them together."

We took One More Time, a fun trail that went over and through little hills and valleys. I instructed him to follow me. We reached out to touch low-hanging branches with our poles and traversed the trail and in and out of small moguls. I spotted a trail in the woods, and we took it. I could hear him giggling behind me. He was a good little skier.

When we reached the bottom of the mountain and arrived at the customer service building, he said to me, "Can we do it again?

"We have to find your parents."

He grabbed my hand, and I almost lost it.

We entered the building together, and I got as many hugs as the son got from his parents. The father wanted to give me a $50 bill. I said to the father, "My new buddy, your sensitive and delightful son, is all the reward I need."

—————— • ——————

I have treasured sharing this special place with friends and family. At one time,

Mount Snow owned the adjacent Haystack Mountain. Ski patrolling there was much less hectic than at Mount Snow. I had two young children and more opportunity to ski with them at Haystack, and I could do things at Haystack I could never do at Mount Snow. I did trail closing on a snowmobile without being certified. Kyle, my 10-year-old son, drove the snowmobile, took sleds to caches, slipped backboards under injured skiers, and learned about first aid. We got away with a lot of things we weren't authorized to do.

I also wanted to ski with my precious granddaughter Kyla. I knew everyone and everything about that mountain and the people who worked there and wanted to offer her an amazing experience. I taught her how to negotiate singles lift lines, manage six-person lifts, and learn the names of trails. During one run, we skied different trails by mistake. Then I came across her at the lift. She had come into it from one side, and I came in from the other. She had the biggest smile when she saw me. She was proud she skied from top to bottom by herself. I turned her loose at 10 years of age.

When my buddy Dave Haggerty came to ski, I served as his personal guide. We started at Mount Snow, rode lifts 11, 9, 18, 2, and 7, always staying ahead of the crowds. At noon, we went to Haystack to have lunch and ski that mountain the remainder of the day. Great memories.

Mount Snow became one of my loves. I have great recollections of listening to the fresh snow trickling through the branches among four inches of new snow, being transported by snowmobile to the top of the expert mountain to ski 2 feet of untracked powder to the bottom, and skiing with my son Kyle. After one of the most enjoyable skiing days I ever had on Mount Snow, I even expressed this love of the mountain in a letter to Kelly Pawlak, president of the mountain. Her response was, "What a great retell of your day. You made my day. When I'm 81, I hope I have the positive attitude that you always have."

The mountain and the Ski Patrol were my teachers. I learned amazing skills, worked with fascinating and knowledgeable people, and continued to grow and learn about myself and the human spirit. I have tremendous respect and admiration for my mountain buddies, who dedicated their lives to service. It has been a privilege to know them as patrollers and as quality human beings. Many hold highly regarded positions away from the mountain.

Sandy Safford, a prominent businessman, was my first ski patrol leader. His longevity and dedication impacted the Ski Patrol immensely. He led with old-fashioned values. His life lesson is to do what you want to do, not what you happen to get caught up doing. Bob Sparrow, a banker, was next. He had more than 100 volunteers under him, so many he had to weed them out. I remember vividly two tasks he assigned to Stan and me during training. One was to spread bales of hay. To accomplish this, I was in mud up to my knees with ski boots on. The other was to stop racers in aluminum canoes as they sped down the mountain by diving at them as they went by, catching them, and serving as drags, like a parachute on an airplane after it landed. One day it was lightning, thundering, snowing, raining, sleeting, partly sunny, windy, all at the same time, yet the legendary tag team of Stan and Marty would not quit.

Stephanie Conrad, the current Ski Patrol leader, is in charge of some 80-plus full-timers and volunteers—mostly men. Women *should* run the world!

Then there was Anne Bartlett, who went on to become a doctor and stayed with the Ski Patrol. She brought back medical knowledge greater than Ski Patrol was privy to. Bill Cohen has a Ph.D. and is a professor who loves to ski. Rescuing during the cold, snowy winter months bought him time to ponder a new path in life. Cindy Hassig, a physical therapist, was a feminist before it became a movement. She showed us how to lift people in and out of sleds. Ringo was a full-timer and a volunteer who owned and ran his own golf course. He counseled me that I needed only 3 golf clubs in my bag, not 14. (I'm down to 6.) Jimmy McDevitt (Silver Fox) and Bill Holmes should have gotten their degrees in cribbage. Silver Fox was admonished more than once for busting chops in not the politest of terms over the airwaves. But what I'll most remember about him was how he motivated Stan, a proud man, to get into a sled his last time on the mountain. Stan was so exhausted he couldn't stand up. He refused to be transported down the mountain until Silver Fox, on the pretense of going to another code, skied by with a sled and talked him into a ride.

Larry Cohen, a lawyer in the Albany area, could ski over the tops of moguls like I could ski on flat terrain. Dick Towsey had a heart attack but continued to pull sleds

With Stan Duglosz (L), my tag team partner on the mountain

With my granddaughter Kyla on Mount Snow

Bill Holmes and Jim McDevitt getting their PhDs in cribbage on top of Haystack. I'm lighting the candles.

I spent 35 years with my Ski Patrol buddies—lots of love and respect

into retirement. His daughter Cheryl regularly skied and raced down Ripcord, the steepest and most difficult trail on the mountain, all the way to the award stand. That's borderline crazy. Her husband, Kevin Delaney, was a university athletic director and a former college baseball coach. We had a lot in common.

Brian (Skip) Meaney was large in size and could hunt bear with a switch. He had a great sense of humor and kept the troops laughing. Steve "Mighty Mouse" Cohen was a male nurse who ran marathons. He could ski better than most. I could relate to him because of my size. Jim Saulnier ran a roofing business and continued to "bag and drag 'em" into retirement. Dan Smyers was the best dispatcher I ever had. He was prepared and thorough and ran the mountain weekends and holidays from the high chief's chair.

Dave Shuster was a little guy who for years worked all night making snow, then went on to learn the skills of rescue and climbed and cut trees in the summer. Grygles Gulch was named after Dave Grygles, who missed a turn and did an unforgettable yard sale. Dave Blake was an expert on lifts as well as Ski Patrol. He and other members of Ski Patrol took my son Kyle, at 15, under their wing. They taught Kyle skills of first aid and rescue that few people learn at his age. Never, in my 40 years on the mountain, did I ever cross the Ridge Trail connecting Haystack Mountain to Mount Snow. Dave rode Kyle across that trail and back on a snowmobile right after a blizzard. On one of these trips, Kyle was launched from the snowmobile headfirst into a huge snowdrift. Dave had to dig him out. All these challenging mountain experiences greatly enhanced Kyle's growth and confidence and helped him become the successful man he is today.

Two full-timers, J. C. Clark and Mike Piniewski, were the real backbone of Ski Patrol without the titles. They ran the mountain most of the time. J. C. Clark was a full-timer who banged nails in the off-season. He was up before the chickens to measure the snow depths on trails and to report snow conditions. Mike was a full-timer who liked to rock climb and was an expert on lift evacuation. I learned from him how to twist the evacuation line to dramatically reduce the speed which the person descended.

Volunteering for the Ski Patrol helped me realize that a team of exceptional people can accomplish what one person can't do alone—and the experience on the mountain helped me realize how much I learned from every person I encountered there and gave me the chance to help others and even save lives.

On Teaching Tennis

The beauty of teaching tennis is that it's both physically and mentally challenging. I love the game. While at Prince, I did promotional clinics throughout the world, but I considered it unethical to go into tennis clubs and impose my teaching techniques because they might be incompatible with those of the local pros.

After I retired, I taught tennis the way I wanted. I was the father of the Prince clinic system copied throughout the world. It's a system I have used for all age levels. I put the players in groups of six and introduce them to drills to reinforce the basics. No one sits out. It's a cardiovascular workout that's specific to tennis. The players get feedback throughout the drills, and they have fun. They cycle one another up, helping each other improve, as I introduce piles of different forehands, backhands, volleys, approach shots, overheads, tactics, serves, and strategies tailormade to each individual. (I might add that tennis legend Stan Smith recognizes 128 different serves.)

I have heard people say teaching tennis is boring. Not for me. I use tennis to teach positive attitude, goal setting, positive self-projection, dealing with failure, managing stress, resiliency, work ethic, and creativity. I teach life as much as tennis. The way I teach tennis, it is a curriculum for life. I'm a father confessor to many who come to the Swamp. They come for meaningful conversation about life and for the pleasure of being with one another as much as for the tennis, which provides the environment for this all to take place.

They have been with me forever and are experts at drills. They have gotten so good I tell them they should be on TV. Maureen Myers volunteers as the scheduler for a pool of 160 exceptional ladies who have come to my house for lessons over the course of a week for years. My ladies love her and what she does and so do I. She schedules the tennis lessons/workouts I give at my house every day and at the Bucks County Racquet Club and the Hopewell Valley Tennis Club in the winter from a pool of players. My interaction with the ladies provides me a social aspect of life that I relish. I find I learn from them as much they do from me. I tell my jealous buddies I service more than 160 women. I'll let it go at that.

At Christmastime, several of my ladies of the court, led by Kelly Kiefer, sent me a funny and creative poem, using the story "Twas the Night Before Christmas." Here are pieces of it, even incorporating two of my favorite curse words, "cheese and crackers." Gotta love these women and their creativity!

> 'Twas the night before tennis and all through the place,
> not a player was sleeping, not even what's her face.
> The racquets were hung by center court with care,
> in hopes that Saint Marty would soon be there.
>
> The sun on the court shone bright as can be.
> It gave the ball reflection of shots hard to see.
> When what to our wondering eyes should appear,
> but a limo and eight handsome players with beer!
> With their coach as the life of the spectacular party,
> we knew in a moment it must be Saint Marty!
>
> More rapid than topspin his team jumped out.
> He whistled and shouted and called them about.
> "Now Roger, now Rafa, now Novak, now Andy.
> On David, on Stan, on Tomas, and Randy!
> To world number one, to the top of the rank,
> now spring now split step, now run to the bank!
>
> He was dressed in Under Armour from head to toe,
> and his clothes were all sweaty from what we don't know.
> A bundle of shots he wrapped in a bow,
> they spun and they twisted like a seasoned pro.
>
> He sprang to his stool and gave his team a holler;
> at this point, the beer made him a wee bit taller.
> We heard him exclaim as they pulled out of sight,
> "Cheese and crackers to all and to all a good night!

Golf and Mountain View

My buddies kept talking to me about taking up this awesome sport. I put them off until I was 80. I'd fooled around with hitting a golf ball when I was in the minor leagues, but this was different. Once I committed to learning golf, I knew it would become a passion like so many other endeavors I have taken on. I now play year-round in all kinds of weather—rain, wind, heat, cold—two to three times a week. I love walking three to six miles, the exercise I get pushing my bag and cart, and the beauty of the course. I enjoy playing alone and with my buddies. All day long I have a happy face.

The Mountain View Golf Course is right down the street from home and is maintained by just five county employees who work their butts off. (By comparison, a U.S. Open course employs 50.) I hook my cart and golf bag to my 100-miles per gallon motorcycle with a bungee cord and drive it the mile and a half to the course. You can walk faster than I ride there. I love it.

The Mountain View course can challenge any player and is too challenging for most. I make it play the way I want it to play—and can make it play 200 different ways. I tee up my drives in fairways, in roughs, or anywhere so I can reach the greens in regulation. It's a great psychological lift. I try out new swings. I've even tried swinging the club like a baseball bat. Alone on Saturday mornings at 6 a.m. doing the back nine, I can take my time filling divots on the fairways, greens, and tees. An added advantage is I'm with the geese, squirrels, rabbits, foxes, an albino deer, and the rest of the herd. Sometimes I have my breakfast with them. A very simple, beautiful pleasure.

The Mountain View course is public, but I treat it like my own. I didn't build it like I built my tennis court and swimming pool, but I help maintain it. Besides fixing divots I use the golf cart with the picker-upper attached to gather balls up on the hitting range. I clean the balls, separating the gashed ones from those ready for another round on the range. I also gas, wash, and move carts. I've even volunteered to be a ranger. Everyone thinks I'm nuts because I offer my time. I tell them that people volunteer their services at hospitals. I just do it on a golf course. Helping has become a more routine habit as I age. Besides, the people who work at Mountain View are the nicest in the world. They call me the Mountain View mayor because I greet everyone.

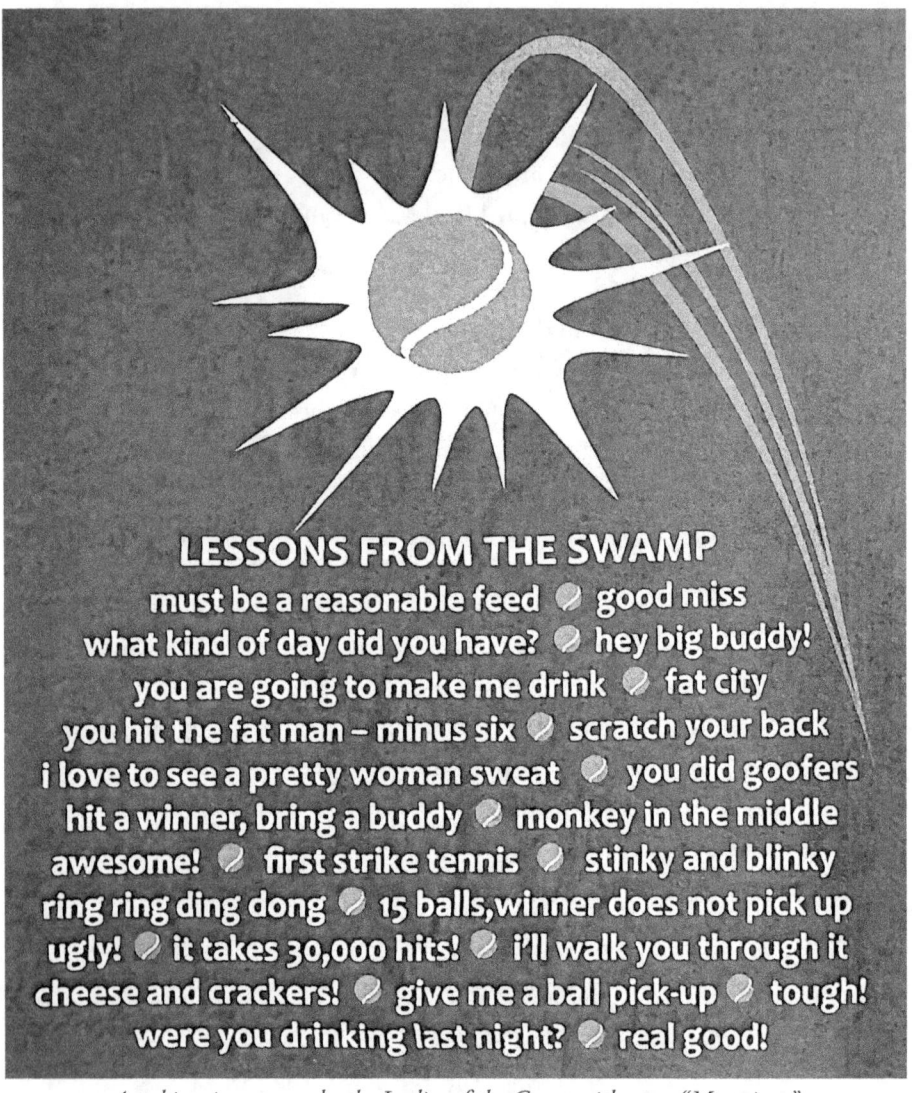

LESSONS FROM THE SWAMP

must be a reasonable feed ● good miss
what kind of day did you have? ● hey big buddy!
you are going to make me drink ● fat city
you hit the fat man – minus six ● scratch your back
i love to see a pretty woman sweat ● you did goofers
hit a winner, bring a buddy ● monkey in the middle
awesome! ● first strike tennis ● stinky and blinky
ring ring ding dong ● 15 balls, winner does not pick up
ugly! ● it takes 30,000 hits! ● i'll walk you through it
cheese and crackers! ● give me a ball pick-up ● tough!
were you drinking last night? ● real good!

A t-shirt given to me by the Ladies of the Court with some "Martyisms"

With some of the Ladies of the Court and Good Buddies, August 2022

*The Swamp even hosted a tennis combination tennis drill and baby shower
in the summer of 2022*

In the game of golf, I am still physically shortchanged. With my short arms and legs, I have no levers to give me added strength and at 89 years, no flexibility, so I'm still trying to make lemonade out of lemons. I'll never hit 16 of the 18 greens at Mountain View in regulation—I don't have enough power—but I hit my drives, fairway, woods, and approach shots straight as an arrow and with scoring consistency.

Bye to Good Buddies

After Stan, my best buddy of 50 years, up and died on me, Saint Nancy, his wife, asked me to speak at his funeral. Stan had a tremendous impact on my life. Even though we fought like cats and dogs—over how to get things done, over his wanting to be in charge—he was always the first one I'd tell if I came up with something new.

"Stosh, I've got a new wrinkle," I'd tell him.

He introduced me to tennis and skiing, and we enjoyed both activities together for 40 plus years. I can still feel him putting that big paw of his on my shoulder when we played doubles and hear him saying, "Good shot, Marty!"

The funeral was a celebration of his life and the most joyful memorial service I've been to. The day of the funeral, Greg Ferrone, a Ski Patrol buddy, and his wife, Jan, showed up to pay their respects. I was elated to see them and reminisce. I longed to see my mountain buddies at least one more time before I packed it in.

Greg and his wife invited me to stay at their house when I made the trip back to Mount Snow. Mary Ellen put me on an Amtrak train with more instructions than she would give a 2-year-old. I got off at Bridgeport. My son Kyle was there to pick me up and drive me to Vermont.

I hardly remember the drive, Kyle and I were so deeply engaged in conversation. Greg's beautiful Vermont house overlooked the mountain trails. When morning arrived, the sun came through the big picture window and warmed the house. It was the most spectacular view of Mount Snow I had ever seen. I could see the trails of the south and north faces of the mountain at the same time. *Hell, I don't need to ski*, I thought to myself. *Just sit there and relive the memories on each of the*

80 trails.

Pool table snow covered the mountain. The sky was Colorado blue. No wind to be had. The temperature, 0 to 15°F, yet it felt like a walk in the park on a summer day. Few of the full timers I knew were still working the mountain, so I had fun with the newbies. I took some runs with Greg, Kyle, and Bill Holmes, who flew in from South Carolina to see me.

Greg's son Jonathan drove in from New Jersey to be with us for dinner at Joe's, the hangout the locals, ski patrollers, and Ambassadors frequent. Then two more full-time buddies showed up—along with what seemed the whole valley. The place was packed like a can of sardines. Drinks were passed from the bartender across the room, like the drink was a conquering hero. I made a special effort to give my due to everyone—even when I had no idea who they were. The Ferrone's and the Devlin's closed the place, but not before enjoying a meal of salmon stuffed with crab meat and taking a call from Jim Salonier, who was vacationing in Florida.

The next morning, I barged into the Ambassadors' 7 a.m. meeting to see their leader, Pete MacDonald. Pete was the best mountain boss I ever had. Then I crashed a 9 a.m. meeting to see my volunteer buddies who ski patrol mostly on weekends. Even John Densmore, a previous patrol leader, showed up. Kyle met the people who remember him as "Little Man." I took a few glorious runs and had a bowl of clam chowder at Cousins restaurant, talking to everyone there whether I knew them or not. Then I had a leisurely ride back to Kyle's home in Connecticut. His mother would be proud of the effort Kyle made to keep his father safe so he wouldn't do anything dumb. He almost succeeded.

On the way home, Kyle stopped at a rest area off the Merritt Parkway. I had to relieve myself and took off for the facilities with untied boots. I did a face plant and yard sale at the same time. This, after skiing all those years and managing icy parking lots without incident.

It was one of the most enjoyable times with my son Kyle that I can remember and a special time with my mountain buddies.

When he was young, Kyle had extraordinary physical and mental talent but couldn't manage his behavior on the tennis court. Tennis is a game of skill and strategy and requires changing your approach when you're facing a challenging opponent. You can have all the talent in the world, but if your emotions overtake you such that you can't think on the tennis court, you go down the drain fast. When Kyle was young and I'd see this happening, I couldn't understand why he let his emotions get the best of him. I'd tell him what to do and got so wrapped up in his struggles I would get angry and upset. Lacking in emotional intelligence, I would leave in the middle of the match. I didn't realize at the time he was being hard on himself.

When he failed miserably in school, I came down on him hard too. He couldn't focus or control his emotions in academics, and I thought he didn't care or was being lazy. It wasn't until well into high school that we had a name and a reason for his struggles: Attention Deficit Hyperactivity Disorder, ADHD. Until then, neither the school nor Mary Ellen or I had any clue he had ADHD. I had no understanding of what he was dealing with. To this day, I squirm thinking about my attitude towards him.

Despite his struggles, Kyle was an All-American at Mercer County Community College, where he played tennis for Stan, who coached the team. Kyle's and my last trip to Mount Snow was so gratifying because of the mutual respect we had developed.

The Joys of Family and Grandparenting

When you're young and dumb and your wife is having a baby, you don't quite take things for granted, but you are so caught up in trying to make ends meet, you don't appreciate why women would ever want to have children. When you're in your 80s, you become more aware, sensitive, compassionate, and considerate about all things in life, especially family.

My daughter Tara was pregnant with her second child and her stomach was bigger than a basketball. She looked so uncomfortable. The baby was kicking the hell out of her. I was anxious. I took her to the hospital and stayed up all night with her. At nine o'clock in the morning, she was only three centimeters. I had to teach tennis, so I left. When I finished, I called Tara and Mary Ellen and heard the baby's first sounds right out of the womb. It was perfect timing. I slipped in nine holes of golf and then went to see the baby.

When I got to the hospital, Feisty hadn't even been cleaned up and she was nursing for one-and-a-half hours straight. Seeing her for the first time was a beautiful moment. Modern-day nursing procedures had her lying under the heat lamp naked as a jaybird, flailing her arms and legs and screaming to get the fluids out of her lungs. Scarlett's got Pop-Pop's lungs and I hope nothing else.

I was in another transition in my life, learning the joys of being a grandfather, but I still would never give up my workouts. The next morning, I was up at 6 to fix greens on the golf course and walk and play nine holes before Kyle's kids came over for their own workout prior to their three-hour car trip to Connecticut.

I left Kyle and Kyla, my 13-year-old granddaughter, at the golf course and drove home to take the other grandkids for a swim. I taught Rocky (Liam) how to hold his breath, and for two hours, his mother skyrocketed him into the pool, only for me to fish him out with Tuna Surprise, what I call Liana, my 18-month-old granddaughter, in my arms. As I dipped down to get Rocky, Liana would get dunked in the water, coming up for air giggling. A beautiful sound from a tyke who a few minutes before refused to get her head wet!

I fed the grandkids before their trip home to Connecticut and my tennis lesson. They hadn't reached the gas station down the street and were sound asleep.

Growing Old and Retirement

What a glorious time of life! Officially, I retired in 2003. Some people say I've been retired all my life. They're not too far wrong because every job I ever had was fun and I got paid for it—paid enough so I could really retire. I retired when my financial adviser told me I could make more money by not working. You figure that one out. But the power of retirement, and ultimate happiness, is having complete control of your life so you can do what you want when you want and continue to have a positive attitude toward whatever comes your way.

Retirement affords me the opportunity to keep my body fine-tuned with proper diet, sleep, weight control, and exercise. I golf, swim, and teach tennis—and I maintain my property, read, write, and enjoy my family. I love taking naps and watching CNN. I shovel snow from my tennis court, split and stack wood, and do exercises using light free weights and rubber bands. I sprint, run lines on the

Mary Ellen and I with our grandkids. From L to R, top row: Martin P. Devlin V ("Pat"), me, Mary Ellen, and Kyla; bottom row: Liam, Conrad, Scarlett, and Liana, celebrating Mary Ellen's birthday, Summer 2022

Martin Patrick Devlin V at about the age he wrote his essay on work ethic

Our daughter Tara with our grandkids Conrad and Scarlett

Our son Kyle and his family, from L, Diane holding Liana, Liam (front), and Kyla

tennis court, do suicide drills, and use the tennis ball machine to exercise all the major muscle groups. The neighbors must shake their heads watching an 89-year-old man running around like a chicken with its head cut off. I surely don't get bored. I cook all the meals at home, applying my mother's early cooking lessons and having learned the principles of cooking watching Rachel Ray's shows on television. I don't need recipes.

After all the traveling I did as a ballplayer and much later in life as an international tennis clinician, I never want to ride a bus, limo, train, boat, or plane again. I've been in all but two states, many cities in Canada, and all but a few countries in

Europe and South America. My choice of places to live is hands down where I live now, nestled on one acre of wooded bliss. I have my tennis court, my indoor swimming pool, my golf course, and my hole-in-the-wall house. The house was built around 1900. It's simple and magnificent at the same time—a fireplace, a beautiful view towards the river. It's the perfect environment for me. I spend most of my time in the kitchen, swimming pool, on the tennis court, and in the nearby gazebo. I have three wood-burning fireplaces. I have access to New York, Philadelphia, the seashore, the mountains, great universities, fabulous Revolutionary War history, and all four exciting seasons. There's no need to go anywhere else.

My hat trick these days is riding my motorcycle with golf clubs in tow up the street to play golf, teaching tennis in the afternoon, and taking a one-hour swim workout in my heated indoor endless pool at night.

Why do I still teach tennis? Because I love it. I play tennis and love the competitive action in singles and doubles. Most of my buddies are pushing up daisies, so I'm always playing down. I tape professional matches on television and watch and study trends. I enjoy the tactical game the most and make up my own drills to replicate a match.

I rate my day like reviewers rate restaurants and hotels, from one to five stars. One star is for working out every day with one physical activity. Two stars is for doing two activities in a day. Three stars is three activities a day. To get to four stars, a great meal after three activities. Five stars would include time with my wife. Add in regular get-togethers with family—brothers, my sister, spouses, kids, and grandkids—and the ratings are off the charts.

Life is good at 89. I am a very lucky man.

My father had high hopes for me that were different than mine. Eventually he told me how proud he was of me. "You did it your way," he said to me. I did. How indebted I am to my family for letting me loose. How happy I am that I followed my own path and have enjoyed my accomplishments and my life.

PART II – PRINCIPLES FOR LIFE

If there is one thing that makes you different from other animals, it is your ability to think. Humans don't just react to the world as it is: We reflect on the past, imagine what could be, and then plan ways to make our thoughts become reality. Our brain's advanced outer layer, or cortex, enables us to remember past events and predict the future consequences of our actions before we make decisions. We can think about thinking, and use language to exchange these thoughts with others.

—American Museum of Natural History brain exhibit

I was 26 years of age and had been physically active my whole life. I loved it, craved it, needed the physical, and still do. Then I went back to college. I had a hunger to learn. There I learned how the body works. Majoring in physical education, I took courses in anatomy, physiology, and kinesiology, which further fueled my interest in what makes us tick. I loved learning, became more confident in my ability to learn, and started to believe I was not such an idiot. I taught high school, developed an intramural program, became a tennis player, and ran clinics for Prince. As I accumulated life experiences, I developed emotional intelligence, bringing that piece more into my life, and I learned how to connect with people. Earlier on in my life I had been propelled by just my emotional brain and the physical. Later, I became aware of how I used both my emotional and thinking brain to be successful.

With experience in sales, marketing, public relations, public speaking, and as a professional athlete, I asked myself: Why not write a speech about my beliefs? "How to Be Successful," "How to Be a Winner." All the off-the-cuff presentations around the world I gave for Prince helped me feel very comfortable in front of people. The larger the audience, the more challenging and fun it was. I started making notes and putting them in my own words and many times in others' words. As I became more conscious of the principles that guided me, I used anything I came across that would explain and illustrate to others their importance.

No overhead, no inventory, no office. I just expressed what I knew to be true about how I succeeded, rehearsing and memorizing my speech on my guiding principles. These values were reinforced over and over by my own life experience, by the people I met, and what I read in books and articles and heard from other speakers.

Then I met Russell Fleishman, the director of fitness at Bristol-Myers Squibb. Russell read the presentation I had prepared for my launch into motivational speaking and gave me some more books to read. They were on the cutting edge of knowledge and research, and all were written by PhDs and MDs. Hell, I soon realized I was writing about the same things but in layman's language, and what I had to say came from my own principles and common sense. Unsubstantiated, but surely my beliefs and my experience.

The research Russell showed me reinforced what I have always known. That our minds and bodies work together, and one influences the other. This scientific research explained how thoughts and emotions have the power to change our DNA and our very chemical makeup.[4] The research told me what I knew to be true: by managing and directing our thoughts and emotions, we can move toward greater success and happiness.

I gave the presentation that constitutes the rest of this book eight times, start to finish, with lots of preparation but without a single note. I delivered it on the campuses of William & Mary, Harvard, University of Vermont, Trenton State College, twice at Rider, and at the Billie Jean King National Tennis Center. I still use segments of it every day, on and off the tennis court. The rest of this book conveys the essence of this talk.

---

4 Details can be found in *Molecules of Emotion: The Science Behind Mind–Body Medicine*, by Candace Pert, Ph.D., particularly drills down into the science of how our thoughts affect our health.

Our Basic Needs

The first time I became aware of the need to be liked occurred when Father Degnan, my grammar school boxing disciplinarian, was murdered. His boxing blows had helped me tolerate going to school. After he died, I needed to find a way to finish 12 years of school. The halo effect soon became the answer. If you're liked by the teachers by smiling, listening, not being disruptive, following directions, and being polite, you might be socially promoted. Damn, if that principle didn't work my entire life.

No matter what your IQ is or where you're from, everyone wants to be loved, admired, respected, acknowledged, cared for, and recognized. Everyone wants to be productive, mentally tough, a winner. Everyone wants to receive the accolades of other human beings. Everyone wants to be successful.

But what is success? Society has ways to measure success. Mainly it defines success by money and status. I wanted to make a living and enjoy my life, but for me it's never been about the money. When I made the transition from Rider to Prince, from the academic world to the business world, I could have gone after a higher paying position. I could have gotten involved in the typical life of a businessperson and dealt with endless meetings and social events. But keeping up with the Jones's has never been my goal. The simple, everyday pleasures of life are what make me happy, and this has been reinforced in me many times.

> **If you want to be successful, find out what the other guy doesn't want to do and do it.**

When I started with Prince, I knew I'd rather have less money and stay physical by being on a tennis court. The first job they talked to me about didn't fit. Then another opportunity came open and I became product manager for the ball machine. I loved figuring out how the ball machine worked and how to sell it. Soon I found myself conducting clinics across the country and around the world. Playing and teaching tennis was and is a joy. Even the president of Prince, back in 1980, said, "Ol' Buddy, you have the best job in the company." I believe I did.

Success is happiness and it comes in two forms—home runs and singles. Home runs are what most people and society associate with success. These kinds of successes only come once in a while. They are big ticket items. Three homes—one at the shore, one in the mountains, and one in the city—and all the amenities that go with each. Those who are swinging for the fences may see this as the way to be happy. I'm a singles hitter. I dislodge the common society-oriented definition of happiness—the visible signs of success—and instead notice the regular mundane miracles and small pleasures of life: the freshness of a shower, the warmth of a fire, a glass of beer, intimacy, the joy of my work and family. Happiness is right in front of me. Each season holds its delight, especially the fall with leaves turning color like a painter's palette—a burst of red, a dash of yellow, a splash of blue, a shade of gray, and streaks of muted green, and all the hues in between.

"Happiness is a present attitude, not a future condition," wrote self-help author Hugh Prather.

I advocate the simple pleasures of life. Having a tennis court and an indoor endless swimming pool at my home seems extravagant, but I personally participated in building them both using a wheelbarrow, a pick, a shovel, and a rake. They give me the simple pleasures of accomplishment, enjoyment, fun, and activity. Working with my own sweat and effort gave me pride, a sense of accomplishment, and it enhanced my enjoyment and fun. Neighbors and friends stop by the tennis court to play and visit. I've taken part in making my happiness and want to contribute to theirs.

I call myself an epicurean humanitarian. An epicurean because I love and pursue the pleasures of life. A humanitarian because I want to make other people's lives better.

How to be successful? How to be a winner? Some people need church, some people need other people, and some need wine, women, and song. I have my creed, which is nothing more than a set of principles. My principles aren't religious, but I believe in them and advocate them as fervently as a preacher. These principles helped raise my kids and still guide me today. I'd like to share them with you because they have expedited my journey to success. I believe they can help you in yours.

These principles are based on attitude toward myself, others, and the environment.

Chemicals and Our Emotional/Thinking Brains

Learning to manage and direct our behavior—learning to succeed—depends on how we manage the chemicals in our bodies. It's scientific. What we think and say to ourselves changes the chemical makeup in our bodies and our very DNA.

I focus on 12 main chemicals. These chemicals are controlled by the thinking part of our brain and our emotional brain. In terms of evolution, the thinking brain is very young and the emotional brain very old. They work separately and together and control our behavior.

Billions of atoms flow in and out of the brain a second. It is estimated that 60,000 thoughts go through our brain every day, and there are 700,000 ways to alter those chemicals to change everything from the fluency of our speech to the beat of our heart. It is so fascinating that the makeup of a thought is being studied at Princeton University.

In layman's terms, this is an example of how the two brains work.

Scenario #1
You're driving down the highway, a deer darts out in front of your car. You slam on the brakes. Whew! Your emotional brain took over.

Scenario #2
You're driving down the highway and you see a deer 100 yards ahead. Your thinking brain takes over. You slow down, you blink your lights, toot your horn, and, lo and behold, it moves on. Your thinking brain in action!

Scenario #3
You're a ski patroller near a lift when it goes down. People who drop from the lift are scattered all over and in bad shape. Loads of options. Triage! You think it out by using your thinking brain. (Your training helps you override the central nervous system.)

Scenario #4

You're playing tennis, you get a sitter at the net. Wow! A chance for an easy winner. You take a big swing. The ball hits the bottom of the net, and you lose a point. Your emotional brain took over.

When the deer ran out in front of your car (Scenario #1), your emotional brain saved you, your car, and the deer. When you see the deer down the road (Scenario #2), you have time to think and plan. You have more options to solve your problem (don't hit the deer that's down the road!). In Scenario 3, a ski patroller goes through training and has loads of experiences rescuing injured skiers. He manages the chemicals correctly, overrides the emotional brain, and knows to help the most critically injured skiers. In Scenario 4, when you see that ball and get excited, your chemicals were out of balance, and you let your emotion take over.

Now we don't know what thoughts are, but we do know that the body consists of axons, atoms, neurons, molecular compounds, and eight chemicals that deal with the brain and neurological system. These chemicals or electrical impulses travel along pathways (railroad tracks), myelin fibers, and jump gaps called synapses. They transmit messages to and from the brain. For instance, if you touch a hot stove, your emotional brain sends a message to take your hand away. Your thinking brain tells you not to do it again.

We have three chemicals that deal with sex: testosterone, progesterone, and estrogen. (I'm not messing with those three.)

The last chemical, made up of ligands, represents 95 percent of all 12 chemicals in your body and deals with the emotional brain. There are molecules known as peptides or bits of protein. They are like keys. When inserted into the bloodstream, they travel fast looking for locks or receptors. These receptors or locks are found on the outer walls of cells. And when the peptide or key finds the right receptor or lock, it quickly travels into the innards of the cell and changes our behavior at the rate of six trillion reactions in the cell a second. That's the emotional brain.

We know that working out the mind increases the number of pathways and strengthens the myelin fiber, so we have more options for making decisions. And working out physically brings more oxygen to the brain and improves our ability to think.

The central nervous system can manage seven bits of information (thoughts or emotions) at one time. It can tell the difference between one set of bits (thoughts or emotions) versus another in 1/18 of a second. Therefore, it is possible to process 126 bits per second, 7,560 a minute, half a million per hour, and 185 billion a lifetime (16 hours a day until the age of 70).

You need 40 bits of information per second to understand what a person is saying. If we are in the zone, it is conceivable that we can understand three people at one time.

Our ability to manage these thoughts and emotions determines our quality of life. Here's another way to look at it. The thinking brain is made up of 100 billion cells or neurons and they connect to 1,000 to 10,000 other cells, or a total of 100 billion elements. This means that, in each person's head, there are a trillion connections.

This is powerful information and cutting-edge research I couldn't possibly make up. Details can be found within the recommended readings listed in the Acknowledgments section at the end of this book. *The Molecules of Emotion* by Candace Pert, Ph.D. was very impactful to me. It gave me a better understanding of how the mind and body work together. I talk daily about how we use the thinking brain and the emotional brain, especially as they relate to tennis.

If the proportion of 12 chemicals is in balance, the behavior of an individual is good, but an imbalance of one chemical over another leads to unusual behavior and sometimes a conflict. Did you ever watch a tennis player who wants to win so much but his on-court behavior is atrocious? Until he calms down and puts his 12 chemicals in order, he likely won't win. We can control an imbalance of chemicals with drugs (I'm not endorsing drugs), or we can overcome this imbalance by being aware of it and using rationalization or thoughts to correct the imbalance. If the mix of chemicals is good, the soup is good.

The amazing connection between the mind and the body and the power of thoughts shows us the fantastic opportunity to change our life for the better.

My Principles

My principles are of utmost importance to me. I live them each day. I wake up every morning thinking about them, and I go to bed thinking about them. I preach them to everyone around me, especially in teaching tennis, which I continue to do seven days a week at age 89. These principles are rock solid and are behind everything I do. They are my creed, my religion. I believe fervently in them, practice them daily, and advocate for them as fervently as a preacher. These principles helped me raise my kids and helped me succeed on many levels.

The principles I use in my motivational speaking and teaching are what I call a curriculum for life. All the principles in this part of the book work together. When I think of my principles, I picture a pie with many slices, or principles, that make up the whole.

- Positive mental attitude
- Positive self-projection
- Work ethic
- Mental toughness
- Physical and mental exercise
- Stress and recovery

- Positive self-change
- Preparation
- Creativity and problem solving
- Integrity and honesty
- Goal setting
- Leadership and motivation

There they are. The principles that helped me succeed in my endeavors. I believe they can help you. Pick one and start working on it. You'll find worksheets on these principles at the back of this book. They will help you apply these principles to your life.

My voice has always been a big asset for me. I use it to connect and communicate to people. My tennis lessons are peppered with messages that convey my principles. Some of my ladies of the court call them "Martyisms." I speak them with intention and use them to motivate and instruct—to help people change. They are scattered throughout this section and more can be found at the end of this book. Read them aloud or to yourself. Use them. Let them sink into you until your brains leak out. They'll help get you moving from *can't* to *can*!

Positive Mental Attitude (PMA)

When I was in grade school, the Catholic nuns drilled in our heads that everything in life was black or white, right or wrong, good or bad, positive or negative. There was no gray area in between. Was it better to be positive or negative? To look at the glass and see it half-full or half-empty? For me it was a no-brainer. Despite the negativity around me growing up, early on I made up my mind that I was going to look at life as half full. The mindset that started during my school days was something I had to work at every day until, over time, having a positive mental attitude became a habit. I'm on automatic pilot now. No matter what's going on in the world and in spite of my low self-esteem as a kid, I look at the good side and love life. Being positive has made my life what it is, and I'm told this has rubbed off on countless other people.

If you need other reasons to be positive, look at the health benefits of looking at a glass as half full. Positive thoughts and emotions change your body chemistry and impact your happiness and health for the better. Happy people are healthier and easier to be around. Happy people love what they do, are highly motivated, less controlling, and are good team players. Cultivate happy people as friends and cultivate happiness in yourself.

Positivity is a powerful message and a powerful defense against negativity. It gives you self-belief. When you believe in yourself, you have the ability to change your circumstances for the better.

If one of the most important characteristics of a winner is a positive mental attitude, how do you develop a PMA? How do you make being positive a habit?

> **Positivity is like a spitball in baseball — don't worry; don't complain; hit the dry side.**

Change the messages you are giving yourself. These new messages can be delivered many ways: as affirmation, rationalization, self-talk, brainwashing, visualization, deception, focus, humor, perseverance. Brainwashing?! Deception?! …Sure! If you're convinced, absolutely convinced, that you can't do something, brainwash yourself, deceive yourself. Even if you don't believe in yourself, keep sending yourself positive messages. These messages will override the central nervous system and put you in the position to succeed.

I was surrounded by negativism growing up. The message I kept getting was that I was dumb and couldn't learn. I heard this at home and in school. At the time (and sometimes now), putting people down was how you elevated yourself. It was a way to stay top dog. These negative messages came from the church, the family, the school. This negativity wasn't always from bad intentions. There was a belief that you motivated someone by punishing and belittling them. That's how it was for all kids growing up then. I had to practice having a positive attitude. I had to work hard to overcome this negative message.

In some ways, society has changed, but negativism is still all around us. To develop a positive mental attitude, you first need to become aware of all the negativism that's out there and identify it for what it is.

Low Negativism

From the time we are born, we are blitzed and bombarded with negativism. The first words from our mothers' mouths were "No!" "Stop that!" "Get out of there!" and it's been that way ever since. Look at TV, read the newspaper, listen to the radio. Listen to our friends, especially when someone's back is turned. One person says, "Isn't she pretty!" Another person responds, "Yeah, but she's got bad wheels, a crooked nose, and buck teeth."

Ninety-five percent of all the information we receive on an average day is negative. The entire world is negative, and people carry this negativity with them and spread it around where they go. Walk around and you'll find people who are bored, moody, critical, uninterested, irritated, apathetic, nagging, irascible, peevish, cranky, bitching, complaining, moaning, and condemning. They hate their jobs, their marriages, you name it. They are burned out and watch life go by. They put themselves and others down. They are the albatross, the gloom and the doom.

This kind of negativity is low negativism. It is natural, contagious, and easy. It gets passed around like a disease and is so widespread and common we think it's normal. This kind of negativity is the everyday complaining, criticism, and name calling that leak into everything and everyone.

When I first joined the Ski Patrol at Mount Snow and someone got hurt, the dispatcher would often say, "There's a wreck out there. Who wants it?" Not a person, a *wreck*! Or "There's a turkey on Trail X." A *turkey*?! Turkeys don't fly very high, and if they look up in the sky with their mouths open during a rainstorm, they may drown. They are so stupid they must be taught how to eat. Fortunately, the Ski Patrol is now more professional and has stopped using these negative labels.

What if I told you that my oldest son Butch is as useless as a screen door on a submarine? He's a medical miracle, walking around with no brain and no guts. If he threw a ball, he couldn't hit the ocean. My second son Kyle is so ugly that when he was born, my wife didn't know which end to diaper. My wife used to hang chicken bones around his neck so the dog would play with him. My daughter is so dumb she couldn't pee out of a boat if the directions were written on her heels.

These extreme examples of "humor" show how negative thoughts and words are demoralizing and degrading, and will take anybody down—an organization, corporation, team, group, or individual. Why all this negativity? Most people don't have confidence or self-esteem, so they rag on others. People who are negative think they enhance themselves in the eyes of others, but knowledgeable people know better.

Trash talking is a form of negativity that surfaces as demeaning, degrading, relentless, and disrespectful. My Swamp tennis buddies are awesome—talented, funny, bright—but some of them like to trash talk to try to get into one another's heads, especially on critical points in a tennis match. They criticize their opponents' tactics and even criticize their teammates during play. When one player is serving for a game, set, or match, another player might remind them of the occasion their shot selection was not the best (though in harsher language!). My buddies won't admit it to each other, but this kind of behavior hurts feelings.

Trash talking can destroy relationships or damage them such that it takes them a long time to heal. At one point some members of the group were so critical of one another they refused to play or even talk to each other for two weeks. Eventually, they missed the tennis fun and came back to the Swamp.

HIGH NEGATIVISM

There is another kind of negativism. It's called high negativism and it's the worst. It's lower than low-mowed grass and uglier than homemade sin. What does high negativism look like? It's the fellow out there who is a mudslinging, dirt-wrestling, no-good, two-bit rabble rouser. He is belligerent, arrogant, vociferous, surly, egotistical, abusive, and obnoxious. He's vulgar, swears, uses obscene gestures, berates officials, intimidates opponents, bitches at the fans, and throws his racket. He is visibly upset, stressed out, hateful, anxious, confused, apathetic, and angry. This kind of negativity affects everyone around them. Even if this individual has cleared his head enough to play well, he's poisoned the whole atmosphere for opponents, fans, and officials.

Negativism affects all of us physically and mentally. Negative thoughts can wreak havoc on the immune system and cause disease. Thoughts of despair and hopelessness raise the risk of heart attacks. Psychological distress increases the chance of an early death. If we think we are old, we are likely to die younger. How negativism can affect us is powerful. Consider the following. Negative thoughts of depression can wreak havoc on the immune system and cause disease. Thoughts of despair and hopelessness can raise the risk of heart attacks. Thoughts of psychological distress can cause cancer and increase the death rate. If we think we are old, we are likely to die young and have certain early retirement. Fearful living shortens our lifespan. Being a loner raises our blood pressure and cholesterol levels. Negative thoughts disempower us by fear, panic, hostility, anger, accidents, ill health, unhappiness, and failure. All are harbingers and handmaidens of disaster.

NEGATIVISM AND FEAR

Another form of negativism is fear. Fearful living shortens our lifespan. What is fearful living? It is never getting out of our comfort zone to try anything new. We become frozen, afraid to make a change, no matter how big or small. Even on the tennis court you can see this. A grip or a serve may not be working, but a player resists changing what they're doing. People are afraid to take a risk and fail. Or when a change feels awkward or unnatural, they drop it.

Change is hard. It's easier to do what you've always done. This is especially true with big life changes. Going from 18 years at Rider to a position in the business world was scary and difficult. As a new product manager, I knew nothing about the business world at the time. Only that I loved tennis and that I had a wife and child to support. I had to learn marketing, sales, and R&D, research and development. I took another risk in leaving the athletic director position at Rider to teach tennis. There was a lot of negative talk about my leaving that job. Many people thought I was demeaning myself taking the teaching job, taking a step down. I didn't care. I have never been afraid of what people think. If you are, it limits you and what you can do.

THE COST OF NEGATIVISM

We pay a big price for negativism. Being negative is like carrying around a disease. It's contagious and isolates us from positive people. Positive people avoid negativity and people who are negative. Negative thoughts disempower us. We live by fear and in panic, harbor hostility and anger, encounter more accidents, ill health, unhappiness, and failure. Why in God's little acre would anyone in the world want to be negative considering all the research about how it can negatively affect one's life?

We don't choose to be negative out of the blue. We grew up with negativity, and we are bombarded all day long with it—from our friends, the media, etc., and this negativity gets to us. Those messages seep into our subconscious and start to take over without our even realizing it.

You may think you're positive, but listen to what you think and say throughout the day, both to yourself and to others. Pay attention to negative thoughts you hear inside your head and the negative words coming out of your mouth. You can change when you increase your awareness.

I see how much negativity becomes an ingrained habit. Some tennis players I've worked with are extremely negative. They go to the trouble of coming to practice but are always talking themselves down—"my serve sucks," "my backhand is a disaster," any self-demeaning comment you can imagine. While tennis players may think giving themselves these negative messages motivates them, in my experience it makes it harder for them to improve their game, not to speak of their mood or enjoyment of life.

Extreme negativity is hard to overcome. Someone who is extremely negative usually can't accept positive messages directly. When I teach, I continue to feed encouraging messages to other people on the court. Eventually these messages and new ways of thinking start to take hold.

Negativity is easy. Creating new habits requires acrobatic audacity. If you expect things to break your way, it is more likely they will. When you don't think you get any breaks, think again, and think differently! Embrace positivity and you are likely to live longer and be happier.

POSITIVITY: LOW AND HIGH

Just as there is low and high negativism, there is low positivism and high positivism. With low positivism you're relaxed, easygoing, pleasant company. You may be out of gas, lowly motivated, and looking to become reenergized. You may joke around, listen well to others, and have positive thoughts. What does low positivism look like for me? I may be enjoying a beer, sitting around and having a good conversation, talking to my neighbors who come by. It's pleasant and fun.

In low positivism, you take things as they come, roll with the punches. Low positivism is good unless that's the only kind of positivity you know. If you're stuck in low positivism, you may be content, but you won't get too far in life. To succeed, to be truly alive, there are times you have to put it in afterburn. Go from being a lamb to a lion. Take on the challenge. Switch into another gear.

When we're in high positive, we have a challenge in front of us that we are itching to take on, whether it's a tennis match or an assignment at work. We enjoy the battle and don't focus on the outcome. We banish all negativity and summon all our internal resources to be at our best.

In Venezuela, where I played winter league baseball in the Occidental League, I demonstrated unbridled enthusiasm. I was a clucking fury on the field. Baseball fans there gave me all kinds of nicknames: Cambeir (drunken wino), Babbling Idiot, El Torpedo. I was always (naturally) higher than a Georgia pine. The fans loved my positivity.

When I did tennis clinics for Prince all over Western Europe and in every state in the USA except Alaska and Wyoming, I impacted thousands of people by doing the clinics and being on TV and on the radio and in the newspapers. Dave Haggerty, who was the director of marketing and sales, awarded me a bonus because I was so high positive, so animated, so full of life—a good representative of the company.

The Dodgers gave me $4,000 to sign with them because in my tryout with them I was steely determined, intensely tenacious, persistent, had a blinding focus, and I hustled—all forms of high positivism. I had so much energy in my second spring training in Dodgertown, I played three games in one day. I was a whirling dervish from game 1 to game 3, and they let me play with the Dodgers, the big league club, when they played the Pittsburgh Pirates the next day. Walter O'Malley, owner of the Dodgers, was so impressed with my positivism he entrusted me with a date with his beautiful daughter. I must say I was bubbly under the skin on that date!

This high positive behavior helped me 1,000 times more in life than any skills I had. It helped me in public speaking, in jobs, and in my daily experience with people.

POSITIVE THOUGHTS

What we say to ourselves and to others matters. Every thought, every word affects how we feel. Thoughts and words can affect people positively or negatively. Negative words, whether in your mind or spoken by others, lead to negative thoughts that can disable you and prevent you from succeeding in life.

Positive thoughts are powerful weapons. They can biologically reduce our chronological age by 12 years. They can help us heal from an illness or injury and give us the desire, belief, and confidence to take on new tasks and responsibilities. Positive thoughts change the chemicals in our bodies, easing stress and enhancing our chances for success, happiness, well-being, and a good quality of life. Positivity gives us the ability to change our circumstances, to make our lives better and happier. That ability is called self-efficacy.

What if you don't feel positive? Faking positive thoughts can override negative thoughts. "Faking it" can put us in what performance psychologist Dr. James Loehr calls the ideal performance state, where your mind and body are performing at their peak. It is a direct result of positivity, along with planning, preparation, a fabulous work ethic, and a blinding focus.

Having a positive attitude requires courage, commitment, and the desire to change. It means not just thinking about changing but doing it. It's not, I'm going to work out, going to go on a diet, going to do more cardiovascular work, going to work on flexibility. You *are* working out, eating better, doing more aerobic and anaerobic work, and doing stretches.

Positive thoughts and positive emotions go hand in hand. You can change your emotional state, your feelings, and the molecules in your body by faking it with positive thinking. Some other ways to change your emotional state are drugs, grimacing, smiling, eating, and exercising. (I don't recommend drugs.)

Practicing a positive mental attitude is the most important thing we can do to improve our lives. It gives us the desire and belief to take on new tasks and responsibilities. A positive attitude helps give us the courage to face our fears. A positive attitude helps us take positive actions. Great writers call this self-efficacy, and it's a powerful ingredient to success.

HUMOR, A FORM OF POSITIVITY

Another form of positivity is having a sense of humor. Laughter adds years to our lives. It softens the inevitable blows in life and gives us bounce-back ability. It boosts the immune system, reduces stress, lowers blood pressure, and can even give us a sense of euphoria.

When I was working at Prince and came back to the office after conducting clinics, Smiley Bones and I would do crazy things to crack people up, to loosen things up at the office. We didn't care about making fools of ourselves. I believe humor lightened the mood and made people more creative. We would come into the building dressed up as Popeye and Olive Oil. Patti Haggerty developed the apparel line for Prince. We'd put on dresses, wigs, and makeup for Patti's skits at sales meetings. Once I crawled into work dressed up, incognito, with Kyle on my back. We took work seriously, but it was like creating a comedy routine, going into everybody's office to take the monotony of the day away.

When my father was diagnosed with a brain tumor, his options were to get it operated on, and possibly become a vegetable, or do nothing. My mother had Alzheimer's, and my father didn't want to take the chance of becoming a burden to his family, so he elected not to have surgery. My sister Trish and her husband took our parents into their home.

My brother Pancho and I agreed to bathe my father. We put a stool in the tub for him to sit down on. All three of us were butt naked in the tub, and Pancho and I worked him over. Throughout the process, we flung different discharges from my father at one another. My father was in pain from laughing so hard that we stopped. But then we would find another way to crack him up. He was super clean when we finished, but Pancho and I needed a shower! We Devlins have what some people would consider a distorted sense of humor—but we do have loads of humor.

Having a sense of humor and laughing balance the chemicals in our bodies. We become more resilient, and our mood and our immune system improve.

Positive Self-Projection

Another principle that is a key to success and happiness is positive self-projection. Positive self-projection is a form of self-marketing. When you are projecting yourself positively you are making yourself so attractive that people recognize you and are happy to see you. When you are friendly, relaxed, and smiling, people will see the way you carry yourself, notice what you do, and reflect it back to you. That's who this person is! Wow!

Walking into the room you want to radiate positivity. Use your facial muscles to smile. You want the room to light up. That's energizing for everyone around you. When you enter with a smile on your face, it lowers barriers, makes people feel good, and lets people know that you care about them. Make it a point to talk to everyone. This makes people feel important. Your energy will motivate and excite them.

I put into practice these behaviors whenever I see people. It was tough to do at first. It felt awkward and uncomfortable, but with lots of practice and guts, it has become automatic. If you don't project well, start by faking it. Doesn't feel natural to you? Keep at it. It gets easier. It is what you need to do, and it works.

Playing pro baseball reinforced for me the importance of positive self-projection. I was voted the most popular player many times when I was playing pro ball.

If you're going to influence others in a positive way, you need to learn how to be with other people. It took me years to tolerate being comfortable in a social environment. I used to feel that I didn't need society. For me society was about people telling me what I should do. Sometimes the advice I got was good. A lot of times it went against my grain. I suppose I was a nonconformist. I don't need society as much as most people, but I'm glad I was put in situations where I had to be social.

I've learned that being social does more than mold our behavior. Research has proven its importance for our health and happiness. While being a loner raises our blood pressure and cholesterol levels, being a social animal adds years to our lives. Being with other people in a positive way sends out cascades of hormones that regulate our physiological systems from our hearts to our immune systems. Good, close relationships buffer us from the challenges of getting old. Learning to be social has enhanced my life immensely.

My mother recognized the importance of learning how to interact positively with others. I never respected the phony social climbing I saw in my upper middle-class upbringing, but my mother wasn't completely off base.

I was lucky to have some good role models. When I was working for Prince, John Powless was the lightning bolt that hit me and lit up for me the power of positive self-projection. One afternoon, I flew into Madison, Wisconsin, to run a clinic at John's tennis center. He greeted me at the airport, and before we left, he had talked to everyone there—ticket agents, porters, fellow travelers, and custodians. He connected with everyone in a positive way. A year or two later, following his victory in the Philadelphia National Grass Court Championships, John walked across the tennis court, dropped his Prince bag visibly in the middle of the court, and accepted his award. He knew how to project himself and the company positively. I followed his example while giving tennis clinics all over the world. There's a little showmanship in this too!

What does positive self-projection look like?

It's a person who projects a positive self-concept, wants to talk to everyone, has good interpersonal skills, and makes everyone glad they talked to them. How do you do this? Maintain the basics. Be neat and well-groomed, appropriately dressed, and, because our expression is the most important thing we wear, smile. In a survey of over 500 people in all walks of life, a smile was deemed most important, and number two was eye contact. Energy was number three. Good energy is infectious. Posture, our shoulders back, is number four. Number five is integrity and honesty. To me there are a few more. Speak clearly so that you are heard. Use clear-cut and concise language. Be spontaneous and have a sense of humor. Display energy and enthusiasm. Be mentally calm and serene within yourself. Have good emotional control.

Want to know how powerful positive self-projection is? When I was playing pro baseball and then tennis, I always squinted. I have blue eyes and a light complexion, so I was especially sensitive to sunlight. My squinting led fans to believe I was always smiling. I could be dying inside, but that's not what they saw. I appeared to be happy and having fun. I also hustled and projected energy and enthusiasm. They appreciated this kind of behavior and picked up on it.

In sports I was known for extreme hustle. I have taken that intensity and applied it to connecting to people. I stand out for how I interact and do it differently than most people. I use my booming voice, one of my biggest assets, to connect to others. It has become one of my trademarks. It's gravelly, loud, clear, and unmistakable. People have to pay attention when they hear me. Sometimes it raises eyebrows. While most people like it, some are put off. You can't please everyone. I am a chatterbox too. My smile, energy, and being a chatterbox helped me connect to fans and has been an important ingredient for me in projecting myself positively. You may not have my voice and you may not be a chatterbox, but you have your own way of reaching out and connecting to others. Make them feel good about themselves and about life. I have received tons of feedback about how I have positively affected people, and it is gratifying and humbling to know that. It's something you can do too, whether you need to practice it or are already a top performer in this arena.

WOODY—POSITIVE SELF-PROJECTION MAVEN

For nine years I performed at Prince tennis clinics in 65 major cities. Over that time, I endured late nights and missed plane connections. One time, I pulled into a hotel at 3 a.m. I was whipped. I got my key, went to my room, and before my head hit the pillow, the alarm went off. I had to give a presentation at 7 a.m. Now I had to get fired up. I called down for breakfast and figured that by the time I finished my shower, it would be there. I was getting ready to jump in the shower when there was a knock on the door.

I hear, "Woody...room service. I've got your breakfast."

The minute I opened the door, I saw a smile bigger than heaven. He was sharper than a tack with lots of energy. Appearance? Clean, well groomed, big smile. He came bombing through the door.

"Good morning, Mr. Devlin. What a glorious day it is!"

He threw open the drapes, and sure enough it was.

"How about a nice cup of coffee? I brought you a whole container. Brewed it myself. I must apologize. I fished through the bananas but couldn't find any good enough for you, so I brought you some strawberries instead. I picked them myself."

This guy got me pumped up, and for his service and positivity and he got a big tip. I thought and talked about Woody all day long. The next day, he got flooded with calls for breakfast.

Work Ethic

We talk about work ethic often, but let's establish what it really means. Wikipedia describes it as…

> …*a set of moral principles a person uses in their job. People who possess a strong work ethic embody certain principles that guide their work behavior, leading them to produce high-quality work consistently such that the output motivates them to stay on track. A good work ethic fuels an individual's needs and goals. It is considered as a source of self-respect, satisfaction, and fulfillment.*

I couldn't have said it better. But what does a strong work ethic look like in real life?

When I was 14, I got my first job. I showed up for work at the Trenton Country Club and was asked to rake an entire gully of hay. I came back in two hours with the job completed. From an early age, I looked at the positive in work and saw it as an opportunity. I had a chance to do a job that was physical, no one was looking over my shoulder, and I got paid for it. I developed a work ethic early on and never stopped applying it in my life.

In baseball, I demonstrated my work ethic by hustling. Hustling is a form of work ethic I learned playing for my American Legion national championship coach Kelly Palumbo, who fostered it in his players. When I went to play for the Brooklyn Dodgers organization, he sent me a long telegram encouraging me to continue to hustle, knowing how important it was to success. I took it to heart and sprinted to first after I walked. When I was at bat, I ran out every ground ball, and I dove for balls playing the infield. In AAA baseball in Montreal, I didn't play much, but I'm convinced Clay Bryant, my manager, had me on the team because of my attitude and my hustle and how I encouraged my teammates from the dugout. At one of my stops in the minors I was told that the fans listening on the radio couldn't hear the broadcast of the game, only me!

Hustling got me a long way in tennis too. The three national championships I won had less to do with my skill than my hustle.

A blinding work ethic is how you overcome your shortcomings and other obstacles in the way of achieving what you desire, including the negativity of others. Whenever someone tells me I can't do something, I get even more focused and work even harder. At Rider, I was told I couldn't do what I'd planned for the intramural program, that I wouldn't be successful. Yet I achieved something I'm proud of, not only for myself but also for the students who participated in the program. When I was told I wouldn't be able to be a motivational speaker, I used this as motivation. I was even told I couldn't write a book! I use naysayers as fuel.

Hard work requires effort, but effort driven by passion is a joy and a challenge. Everything I have done in my life has been a passion for the occasion, not work. From day one I had that drive. I always gave 1,000 percent. I love being physical. Working hard is part of the fun. For me it's always been about the journey, not the triumph but the process of getting there. Where are most of the tennis trophies I won? Buried under the tennis court at the Swamp! I take pride in my accomplishments but don't dwell on them.

I have applied my work ethic to whatever challenge I've faced. When it came to building my tennis court, I decided I was not going to pay someone else to do it. I planned. I hauled rocks. I shoveled. I am still enjoying that court.

When faced with a challenge, I may have a smidgen of fear, but the fear never takes charge. A bit of fear was always in my mind when I was competing and stuck with me with every job I took—from promoting the ball machine at Prince to working at Rider College. Fear is based on having doubts. I had my share of them. *Maybe my arms are too short. My legs too stumpy. Maybe I can't learn. Won't be able to read.* A little fear can be a motivator if you don't let it take you over. When I ran the clinics for Prince, I always feared something would go wrong and I'd be unprepared. That made me prepare more and worked harder. I bought an extra generator to make sure that the ball machine would run if a power source wasn't available on the courts. Smiley Bones and I practiced our routine the night before at the hotel. I turned doubts, fear, and negative thoughts to positives by applying my work ethic.

I am driven by a desire to succeed, to figure things out, to solve problems, to work harder and more diligently than the people around me.

Earl Nightingale, the acclaimed motivational speaker and writer, said that if you want to be successful, you must surrender to the habits that others don't like to do. True as it sounds and simple as it seems, it's easier to adjust to the hardships of mediocrity than to adjust to the hardships of making your life better. Think about it. What are all the things you're going without by avoiding the things you don't like to do?

If you have a genuine interest in doing something, apply yourself to it. Overcome fear and a lack of confidence by creating new habits. Be persistent in making a change. Talk yourself out of the negative into the positive. Visualize what you want to do, how you want to be. Feel and see the change occurring as you make changes in your habits. The chemicals in your body will change. Over time, you will become comfortable with the new habit.

Work ethic manifests itself in different ways. When I was younger, I was being given a stress test on a treadmill when the doctor stopped administering the test. I already passed the test with flying colors, and he didn't want me to break the treadmill! I aced this test because I cross trained and continued to do the exercises my athletic coaches advocated long after I'd stopped playing. In the middle of the Covid-19 pandemic, I shifted my focus to what I could do. I continued to work out and completed projects around the house. This is another form of work ethic.

When I was employed by Prince, I met up with a world-class professional tennis player by the name of Steve Krulevitz. Steve was under a racket contract with the company and came by for a visit. While there, he expressed a desire to work out. I had developed an anaerobic fitness program to market the Prince ball machine, and he was delighted to give it a go. The workout consisted of hitting ten tennis balls corner to corner on a tennis court at high intensity punctuated by 6-second rest periods. The workout was supposed to be 30 minutes in duration. He went for 45. Since he wasn't using a heart monitor, I was afraid I'd kill him if we continued beyond that. No tennis workout could come close to the one I gave him. He took everything the machine could give. Only an unbeatable work ethic got him to that level. Work ethic and something more.

For 35 years I wondered how he had been able to go toe-to-toe with a machine and why the workout that was a killer for so many people was so easy for him. I finally called him and asked. He told me that while attending UCLA, he took a course where he learned to apply exercise physiology to sound principles of conditioning. To achieve an optimum heart rate, he monitored his heart. His workouts were specific to the activity and mostly anaerobic. He incorporated the concept of *stress and recovery with equal diligence*, doing a heavy workout one day and a light one the next. He also did some running workouts incorporating the Fartlek system—sprint until you're tired, slow your pace down till you feel nearly ready, then sprint again.

I got my answer. At the time few athletes applied scientific approaches to training. He beat the machine because *he was doing what other people were not doing.*[5]

When I coach my tennis players, the sessions run an hour and a half. I inspire them, and they inspire me. There is nonstop movement and nonstop focus. These women have come to work on their game, many for years, almost every week out of the year. That demonstrates a work ethic that can't be beat. That is perseverance. It is a form of work ethic essential to success in life.

Having perseverance means having a never-say-die mentality. It overcomes everything—sometimes even nature. Years ago, in Fargo, North Dakota, there was a big-time flood. I can still see this photo: a farmhouse sitting in what looked like the middle of an ocean surrounded by sandbags to keep the water out. Someone put those sandbags there. This came out of effort, grim determination, and perseverance. At Mount Snow where I ski patrolled, the snowmakers would lay down 4 trails, top to bottom, with only 130 more to go. Once the 134th trail was laid, along would come a rainstorm and wipe them all out. What would happen? They'd start all over again. That's perseverance.

Perseverance is a work ethic that never gives in. I told my kids that the difference between a big shot and a little shot is that a big shot is a little shot who keeps on shooting.

---

5   Steve is still involved in sports and has an academy in Baltimore where he runs tennis clinics and tennis and soccer camps, krulevitztennis.com.

Work and Passion

My grandson Patrick wrote an essay on the importance of a work ethic. His learning experience from one summer was a powerful one.

> Throughout my life, I have centered on academics rather than athletics. I always thought of myself more of an intellectual than an athlete. Within my family, that is a rather unusual trait, being that most of my family members played at least one sport, generally tennis, at a high level. I focused mostly on math. While my grandfather has never enjoyed math, or any other type of schoolwork, he has had a bigger impact on me and my pursuit of a career dealing with mathematics than anyone else.
>
> The summer after seventh grade, when I was too old for camp and too young to stay home alone, my mother decided it would be a good idea for me to go to my grandfather's house to work every other day for the entire summer. Up to that point, I had never been particularly close with my grandfather, despite the fact that he only lived 20 minutes away. Now my grandfather was far from an ordinary 72-year-old. As a professional tennis teacher, he had his own tennis court along with an infinite amount of work to do around the house. While he gave tennis lessons, I was instructed to split wood, clean the tennis court, move logs, as well as help him occasionally with a lesson.
>
> In the beginning, I spent most of my time working while he was watching and slacking off when he wasn't. Of course, he would catch me occasionally and laugh. My grandfather, being the upbeat person he is, hardly ever gets upset. He laughs his way through every situation and never gives up. So naturally, when he caught me sitting down on the job, he would laugh at me for being lazy rather than yell at me for not doing my work. Each time he would say the same thing: "Pat, how do you expect to keep a job if you're always sitting around? You have the worst work ethic I have ever seen." Although each time he said

it jokingly, the message began to stick. I began to work harder and became more focused on the job I was doing, working to complete the job instead of taking breaks. I remember one job above all the others. He told me to take a wheelbarrow, fill it with rocks from behind his house, and move it to the front driveway. Given that his house rests on an incredibly steep hill, there is absolutely no pavement on his property, and the tire of the wheelbarrow was flat, it was an extremely difficult job. As he sat and watched, I filled the wheelbarrow with rocks and proceeded to wrestle the wheelbarrow forward a few feet until it tipped over, losing everything it contained. Again and again, he watched me repeat the same process until I finally got the wheelbarrow to the front driveway. Of course, my grandfather laughed and laughed and cracked jokes the entire way (he still enjoys telling stories of my failed effort at family gatherings), but I will never forget what he told me. "Even though you let the wheelbarrow drop every few feet, you still eventually got it to the front. Now I would have tried to do things a little differently, but the point remains the same, you didn't give up. That's the meaning of work ethic." To this day, I remember his words clearly, and the message will stick throughout my entire life.

I started to see that he truly lived what he preached, and that his was the absolute epitome of work ethic. I learned that at age 36, he began playing tennis and, within 15 years, he was ranked number 1 in the nation and number 10 in the world in the 45-and-over division. I began to give some validity to his nonsensical rants about work ethic and saw him as an incredible, truly unique person, rather than a crazy old man (of course, it is still certain that he is a crazy old man). In the summer I spent with him, I saw something unlike anything that I have seen before: a complete desire to do things to the fullest, no matter how difficult or frustrating they may be. Although his lessons were primarily around tennis and other physical work, the message remains the same for anything and everything that I choose to do. Within me, he instilled a desire to complete what I started, no matter what difficulties come along with it. While I don't want to be my grandfather, I aspire to be just like him, doing things to the fullest and, most importantly, doing what I love.

— *Martin P. "Patrick" Devlin V*

I nearly cried when my grandson showed this story to me. He wrote it for one of his college classes 15 years after this occurred. No one—not me, not even his mother or father—knew the impact this summer had on him until then.

You never know the effect you have on other people.

Physical and Mental Exercise

To be successful, one must be a good animal. That's what a doctor told me in my 20s. Think about this as it relates to another part of the natural world, a tree. A tree must transpire (breathe) and needs to be copiously refreshed by wind, frost, and rain or it becomes barren. Wind strengthens a tree's root system and helps the tree grow and become more resilient. Some trees blossom only after they have been exposed to the cold for a period of time. The human body needs excitement and movement. Movement is life. Rest or rust. Use it or lose it.

Don't get me wrong. I like my beer, but I work out every day. Regular physical and mental activity are a narcotic for me. Where did this come from and how did it manifest itself and why? I believe my love for the physical to be genetic in nature. Maybe my need for adrenalin was disproportionately high. I never even knew about ADHD growing up and hadn't heard of it until my second son was diagnosed with it in high school. He may have inherited from me.

My environment also greatly influenced my desire to be physical. My naps as a baby were spent snuggled in the baby carriage on the front porch, even in mid-winter. In preschool, I spent most of my time outside. My mother had three boys and a girl and the sole responsibility of raising us. When my father came home from work, my mother assumed the role of a good wife. That's the way it was in the 1930s. With no time to herself, her respite was sending us out to play regardless of the weather. Parents considered their kids playing outdoors as a form of wholesome neglect, and a hardy environment was not considered overly dangerous. We lived out in the sticks with little vehicular traffic. Mom only had to worry about one slow-moving train, two canals, and a river.

The vigorous, physical lifestyle began for me at such a young age and was so addictive that inactivity felt like an almost impossible restriction. Sitting in a classroom for years in grammar school with no physical outlet felt like a sentence worse than death. It only intensified my desire to be physically active. Running through backyards in the darkness made me feel powerful. Trees, bushes, clotheslines, and houses went by so fast I felt I could outrun a hunted deer. Leaping off a monkey swing over the canal to execute a somersault, a back flip, a twisting move required strength. I loved the challenge of fighting the current to get back to shore for another try. Inventing a new dive, dreaming up a new challenge, required imagination and stimulated my creativity.

Sometimes I took what some consider unconventional paths to get the exercise I needed. One day, my first wife and I, along with our son, Butch, were planning to visit my parents, who lived six miles south from us in Trenton. I needed a workout, so I told my wife I'd meet them at my parents' house in an hour. She and Butch dropped me off at the Washington Crossing Bridge on the Pennsylvania side.

I jumped in the river wearing my bathing suit and a reasonably good pair of sneakers to fend off any obstacles I might encounter. No life jacket or buddy system for me that day.

Two hours into the swim and I hadn't even reached the treacherous Scudder Falls rapids. If you know anything about rapids, they are swift-moving waters rolling over a tremendous number of rocks. Most of the rocks were smooth but, they were also hard, as all rocks are, and dotted all over the river. Any object, including me, would be at the mercy of the rapids and the rocks.

I had a game plan. I would float on my back feet first to fend off the rocks. The first rock I encountered flipped me over, and I went through the rest of the rapids on my stomach, my head and hands leading the way. I made it through Scudder Falls, but it turned out I had two more hours of swim time ahead of me. In the meantime, my family and the police were frantically searching for me. When darkness set in, the search was put off until morning.

I eventually made it back to my parents' house that night with a shredded swimsuit and scraped, bruised, toes sticking out of now-beat-up sneakers. (One of my Don Quixote moments!) Everyone was happy they didn't have to pay for a funeral but mad at me for causing them such anxiety. I had miscalculated how long that swim would take and was in the doghouse. But it was a great workout.

Later in life, surfing in Hawaii offered another beautiful, life-enhancing physical challenge. My pregnant wife Mary Ellen and our toddler accompanied me on the trip while I was conducting tennis clinics. A day off enabled me to try "board surfing" at Waikiki Beach. I rented a surfboard so big it could hold a sumo wrestler. Initially, I was defeated in my effort to stand up—I blamed the waves for being too small to catch. I paddled out again and again to try and catch a wave. The waves were getting bigger.

I got 'em now! I thought.

Paddling that giant of a surfboard through and over a rapid sequence of bigger and bigger waves was exhausting to my arms and shoulders. When I finally managed to get myself upright and riding a wave, the wave appeared to suck in all the water in front of it, exposing body-ripping coral that had my name on it. Seeing my family on shore observing my efforts, I was reminded of my responsibilities. Bailout time! All day long, I searched for a wave with no coral in front of it but found not one. My arms and shoulders were so weary from paddling, I honestly felt it would be easier to roll off the surfboard and drown than paddle one more stroke. What a workout and humbling experience.

You would think my unsuccessful efforts to master surfing would discourage me from trying snowboarding. But I am always finding new ways to get a workout. Haystack Mountain, part of Mount Snow in Vermont, was where I thought I would become the next Shaun White, the king of snowboarding. At 65 years of age, I couldn't afford to get hurt so I borrowed my wife's operating room medical smock and placed under it two giant pillows to cover the front and back sides of my body and soften the inevitable body slam blows. Then I put on ice hockey shoulder pads, elbow, wrist and knee pads, and a helmet. A sight to behold and another beautiful physical endeavor that required optimum balance, agility, quickness, and effort. I had my first concussion getting off the lift. My attempted turns on the bunny hill resulted in shattering falls. Standing up after falling on snow on an incline is tough without a snowboard. Try this with your feet anchored to a board! Two hours into the experience, I hadn't had one successful run and was feeling as if I'd been in the boxing ring with Mohammad Ali. Even this less-than-successful endeavor reinforced to me that physical challenges have so many positive benefits. They cause euphoric highs, reduce stress, retard aging, combat depression and jet lag, and help you think young and enjoy the pleasures of life.

My emotional brain told me from the time I was born that physical activity was high on my priority list. The need for mental exercise kicked in for me later.

The older we get, the more we need to seek out a healthy level of both physical and mental stress or we will die. Mental exercise causes more pathways, train tracks, routes, or axons to develop in our brain so we have more options for making decisions. These pathways proliferate like roots of a growing tree.

Until 2018, it was said that mental and physical activity prolongs our lives only one to three years. That was so sad to me. I *knew* the incredible benefits of keeping active. New research says that now it's seven to nine years. Now I'm happier than a pig in mud. My emotional brain and my thinking brain tell me that I will continue to be a good animal till the day I die.

Stress and Recovery with Equal Diligence

In the 1980s, stress was considered a dirty word. Dr. Jim Loehr opened my eyes big time when I read his book *Stress for Success*. To summarize Loehr's message, stress is our body responding to demands on it. We can't escape it.

Everyone seems to have a negative view of stress, but without a certain amount of it, we sit on our couches and die. First, we need to understand that stress does not have one flavor. There are two. There is good stress and bad stress: *eustress* is good stress. *Distress* is bad stress. Eustress is the positive stress necessary stimulus for all growth. It goes toe to toe with the devil. It's stress that is challenge, excitement, competition. We can train for it and deepen our capacity for it.

Contrary to what society thinks, stress can be good for us. It makes us psychologically and physically hardy—as long as we plug in the missing link: recovery. Let me illustrate it this way. The mountains go up and down. The waves of the ocean go up and down. The stock market goes up and down. A pearl diver goes up and down. The heartbeat of a tennis player goes up and down. If you plotted mountains, waves, the stock market, pearl diver, and tennis player on a piece of paper, the graph would look like a yo-yo. The "up" is the stress and the "down" is the recovery. When this up/down pattern occurs, it is good stress. For example, you work for 90 minutes, then take 15 to 20 minutes off.

But what happens when you have your foot on the pedal all the time? When you have no rest? This stress is linear. Unlike the up-and-down pattern of stress and recovery, this stress is nonstop, constant, relentless. This is bad stress. It is *distress*. No rest or recovery breeds disharmony, disarray, disorder, energy depletion, and burnout. It is equal to smoking one pack of cigarettes a day or a 20 percent increase in the hardening of the arteries every four years. This kind of stress can kill. People who suffer from this most are the corporate athletes—those who begin work at daybreak, skip lunch, and work late 365 days a year.

We need to build in recovery from stress. If our stress is physical, recovery should be passive. If our stress is passive, our recovery should be active. I teach tennis all day, so naps, reading, and cooking are ways I recover. If you are in the office or cooped up inside all day, you need to get moving. Play tennis, take a walk, go to the gym, or do whatever activity you love to counter all that time spent not moving your body. With periods of rest and recovery, stress is manageable, making it less of a malady.

The concept of stress and recovery applies at any age, but when you're young, you're more likely to be too dumb to recognize the need for it. When I was a student teacher, teaching PE classes was easy for me, but preparing health classes took time and energy. So did coaching wrestling and golf and assisting with the baseball team. On top of that, I was officiating, going to class at night to earn a master's degree. I had to study, take exams, and have some family time. Being something of a local sports celebrity, I was also in demand on the banquet circuit. One night, I stood up to walk to the podium and crashed to the floor. I earned a nice ride to the hospital in an ambulance. I had no recollection of that experience until after the EMTs juiced me up with an IV. The diagnosis? I was exhausted. I had failed to balance mental and emotional demands with my need for the physical. When I saw my doctor, he emphasized that I was a physical animal. I learned that when I get my workout in first, I can tolerate anything. *Stress and recovery with equal diligence!*

In my opinion, Roger Federer, was the best tennis player who ever lived. He was light years ahead of his contemporaries in the way he manages stress. Periodically, he withdrew from playing tennis to recharge his brain and body. He was the first to do so in this era, and fabulous results occurred. He still competed at an age when most players were packing it in.

Stress can be good for us as long as we build in recovery time. As we deal with mental, physical, social, and emotional stress our immune cells respond and become robust and vigilant, protecting us from illness and giving us the energy to respond to life's challenges. Physical stress also increases our mental capacity. When we work out, the mind develops more pathways, or railroad tracks. Neural axons are laid down and we have more options for making decisions. If stress is periodic, it strengthens us. It may cause discomfort because we are pushing ourselves to do what we haven't done in the past. But that is how we grow. By learning to tolerate and increase the discomfort zone, we constantly cycle upward and can move through greater and greater challenges. Getting through challenges enhances confidence, self-esteem, and character. It's like keeping high-test gasoline in our cars. When we don't exercise, we weaken our immune system and can atrophy.

Retirees, take note! It gets harder to push yourself when you are older, but I do it anyway. I know the benefits of continuing to challenge myself. At 89, if I work my body excessively hard one day at skiing, swimming, tennis, or working around the house, I cool it. I back off and rest the next day. If I work my mind excessively hard by writing this book or engaging in some other mental or nonphysical activity, I work out physically to recover the correct balance. What stress and recovery with equal diligence and in equal amounts looks like varies with the individual. Each of us has a different makeup. Everyone needs to find his or her own optimum balance.

While I'm exercising, I make sure to have recovery time. I manage the intensity and frequency of my workouts by incorporating equal amounts of exercise and rest. Fartlek training, the system Steven Krulevitz adopted, is ideal for this. Both my body and my mind, my thinking brain, tell me what to do to ensure optimal well-being.

I also don't do the same exercise or activity over and over. No one activity exercises and satisfies all the muscle groups of the body, so I incorporate cross training. Running quickly up and down the hill of my driveway works the power and braking muscles of the front, back, inside, and outside of my legs because I run the hill forward, backward, sideways, shuffling, and karaoke. This gives me a dynamic warmup. Tennis emphasizes speed, power, quickness, agility, and balance and works the legs, the arms, shoulders, and back. Resistance bands strengthen my upper back and upper front muscles as well as the muscles that shrug the shoulder. Free weights work the shoulder girdle. Shoveling snow works the biceps and lower back. Riding a bicycle strengthens the muscles that support the knees. Skiing works the quads and balance. Playing golf and pushing a loaded golf cart for 18 holes—at my local golf course, this is six miles—keep my legs strong and areas of the body flexible.

Drilling six people on a tennis court works my neck muscles as I follow the flight of the ball. Interacting with tennis players through coaching keeps my mind sharp. So does cooking, reading, writing, teaching, and learning. Swimming and exercising in my pool provide the most complete of my cross-training activities. It's fantastic for keeping optimum range of motion and building endurance. The way I exercise is not boring and is reasonably thorough and complete. When you find an exercise that you love to do, do it. Add in variety, your own form of cross training.

Both aerobic and anaerobic exercise are necessary for optimum health. Aerobic exercise taxes the heart and lungs over a long period of time. It builds endurance by improving the efficiency of the cardiovascular system so that you can run or swim for longer periods of time. Aerobic exercise builds lung capacity and trains your body to use oxygen more efficiently. Anaerobic exercise is intense exercise in short bursts. Your body can't keep up with how much oxygen it needs so this exercise burns fat while building muscle.

One of my ladies works out at the gym before she comes for her tennis lesson. She's in her 60s and can run the drills without getting tired. Her footwork is good too. That extra work helps.

Think about the activities you do to keep your body and mind in shape. What are you doing now? Would you like to be more successful? Then ask yourself: What can you do to challenge yourself? Are you allowing for recovery? How can you stress yourself in a positive way?

Creativity and Problem Solving

Everyone is born creative. My granddaughter Kyla is a wonderful example. She lived with Mary Ellen, Kyle, and me for the first five years of her life, and, boy, did she let it all hang out! She charmed the ladies that take tennis lessons from me with her energy and spirit. Look at what kids do, how they act. They have boundless imagination, and if you ask them a question you may get an answer you never heard or thought of before.

Most people get creativity knocked out of them at an early age, through school or by adapting to family or other social expectations. They conform with what is expected of them. Once you lose track of your creativity, it becomes easier to go along with how things are, even if you're not happy or satisfied with your life. When you go along with how things are rather than enduring the discomfort of change, you may find yourself feeling trapped in your circumstances. You may have convinced yourself that you're satisfied with your life, even if you don't feel a sense of fulfillment or aliveness. You may lack confidence in yourself. When you try something new or go about something in a new way, an element of failure may lurk in your mind. You may lack passion or awareness and go along sleepwalking through life.

We're all creatures of habit, which makes it hard to change. But we all have the capacity to change and grow. Along with conformity, laziness, and fear, we have that superpower called creativity. It's free and available to all of us. It is my belief that success and happiness are possible only when we embrace change, and change is possible only when we live creatively and with courage.

Creativity and problem solving work hand in hand. Creativity is how we come up with new approaches, new ways of thinking. It comes from using our imagination to see something that doesn't already exist or to see how to improve what's already there. Applying creativity to a problem is called problem solving. While creativity comes from our left brain, problem solving is the right brain at work, the brain that orders things logically into steps and stages, that tells you how to get from A to Z.

I've been creative and a problem solver my whole life. At 10 years of age, I wanted a baseball glove. It was soon after the Depression and my parents weren't about to buy me one. Sports were not so highly valued at the time, and a glove was seen as something frivolous. I decided to make one. I got some thick cloth, put my hand down on it, and traced the outlines of my fingers—I did this twice. Before sewing the pieces together completely, I put in some extra cloth as padding. I improvised. Making this glove for myself gave me confidence that I could do things. Over and again in my life, when I applied creativity to a problem, my world opened up.

Being creative and a problem solver has been an escape for me. I enjoy it. It's fun. I like to build and make things, and then tweak them to make them better. When I achieve something, even one simple thing, I gloat over

The mind is like a parachute; it doesn't work unless it's open.

what I've done. That pile of rocks I've moved today? Fantastic! Creativity and confidence are necessary to a strong spirit.

All my life I have challenged assumptions and looked for ways to improve. When I couldn't master the backhand, I learned to play tennis both right- and left-handed.

When I was younger, I had all the energy in the world. As I get older, I'm motivated to change how I do things to save time and conserve energy. Instead of taking my truck to the golf course, I now hook my golf cart with clubs to a motorcycle using a bungee cord. It's a fast, easy, and fun way to transport them that saves me the time, effort, and energy of lifting my clubs in and out of my truck. My tennis court is beautiful and surrounded by trees. Every day in the fall I need to get it ready before teaching lessons. I found a systematic way to efficiently blow leaves and debris off the court that saves me steps. Finding a way to tee up a golf ball in the dead of winter on frozen ground at the exact height required soul searching. My mind is always working to see how I can make things easier and how I can improve the space around me.

Benny, one of the golf clerks at Mountain View, the course near my house, once said to me that I'd have made a good engineer. (Too bad I didn't have the math!) I suppose he's right. Everything I do is trying to solve a problem and to make things better.

I have taken those opportunities when they come up. Jim Orange, a well-known senior tennis player and a businessman, had a colorful, combative personality on the court and was one of the nicest guys you'll meet off the court. He had acquired a tennis club, a yacht, the sister ship of the presidential yacht, *Sequoia*, and two airplanes. One was a Skymaster, a push-and-pull airplane used in the Vietnam War that had no toilet and held four people. He and his wife Carol talked my future wife Mary Ellen and I into flying with them across the United States to play in the USTA 45-and-over national championships in California.

There were some barriers to flying across the country. Jim wasn't certified to fly instruments, which meant he was allowed to fly through clouds only when he saw daylight, a hole in clouds. If we were flying above the clouds, he needed to know the weather and cloud cover at the next pitstop. Jim's airplane wasn't equipped with oxygen, so he wasn't allowed to fly it above 10,000 feet. Without oxygen, we'd pass out if we went any higher, so we headed south to avoid the mountains in the west-central part of the country.

We left on Thanksgiving Day. Our first stop was McComb, Mississippi. We needed gas and had to pee. As Jim started in for the landing. He pushed a button to lower the wheels of the airplane, but they didn't go down. Then he asked me to help him manually pump them down. We did a fly-by and the ground controller confirmed that the wheels were down. A good start. But we had no guarantee they were locked.

By now it was dark. There were lots of flashing rescue lights on the ground below. Ambulances. Fire trucks. Not too reassuring. The second time we approached the airport we landed, and the wheels held. How do I know? I'm here to write about it.

We'd barely started our journey and, once on the ground, we learned we'd blown a solenoid. It would take days to get a new one and we had to get to California for a tournament. Priorities are priorities. We had every engineer in McComb working to solve the problem. They were all huddled around the plane trying to figure out how to repair it. They got the solenoid working, but it overheated when left on. I was off to the side, thinking about the problem. *What if we plugged it in during takeoff, unplugged it when flying so it wouldn't overheat, and plugged it in to land?* I proposed this, we tried it, and it worked. Can you imagine flying across the country like this? We got the solenoid replaced while we played the nationals.

———————————— · ————————————

Nick Saviano, a former national tennis coach, noted that if you emulate what everyone else does you, you're always playing catch up. If you're doing what the other guy says to do, you're behind the curve. Go beyond that. Find a way to get the results you want. Tap into your native abilities. Imitating someone works only to an extent. Don't limit yourself. Search for other ways to solve the problem and get the results you want. Ask yourself if are you looking at what is, or at what is possible?

That doesn't mean you have to start from scratch. Use what's there and adapt it to make it work for you. Throughout my presentations, in my teaching, and in this part of the book, I take quotes and use them to make my point. I have used what's there. When I worked for Prince, I would go to the R&D department and talk to the engineers to see what I could learn from them. I'd also pick the minds of dealers and get feedback from them on the equipment. I have an attitude of always improving by building on what others know.

In solving any problem, look at every aspect of it, including the difficulty of the task. Keep an open mind. Consider how long it will take and ask yourself, "Do I have the time?" It's more fun when you're not rushed. When you decide to take on the problem, commit to it. Figure out the order in which you are going to do things and prioritize. Make it easy on yourself and consider economizing your moves. After every step, stop and admire what you just did. Then consider what your next step is rather than jumping into the next thing spontaneously, without thought. When you have completed the ultimate task and solved the problem, gloat over your accomplishment and reflect on how you could've made what you've done easier and better. Even when looking at others' accomplishments, think of how you might be able to improve on their outcomes. That's a look into an engineer's mind. That's how you can think like an engineer without being an engineer. I've done it this way all my life.

If opportunity doesn't knock, build a door. When I was at Rider College, I talked the administration into renting the tennis courts to the public during my 3 months off and hiring me to administer the program. This gave me a 12-month job and the college derived revenue from the courts.

Being creative also means challenging assumptions. Years ago, I saw a guy teaching a topspin volley. That was taboo at the time. Now everybody is doing it. Ditto with taking the ball on the rise and hitting swinging volleys. All professional tennis players are doing now what used to be considered incorrect or improper. I may have been the first in this area to teach playing in no man's land. I taught how to hit five or six different forehands and to leave the ground for power. Leaving the ground to hit a ball?! That was considered bad form. Now everyone does it. Many people focused so much on "proper form" they didn't see how leaving the ground increased power.

I've thought out of the box my entire life. I couldn't hit with power in baseball or in tennis, so I had to learn to control the bat so I could hit the ball where I wanted. Think about your own limitations. How can you think differently about them? How can you change something to help you get beyond where you come up short? Consider the talents you have and how you can use them to your advantage. I was shy and introverted but had a powerful voice. I used my voice to be noticed and to connect to others.

Whatever I learn in one area of my life, I try it out in another. I applied principles I learned in baseball to tennis and in tennis to golf. I've even used a baseball swing to hit a golf ball. I try out different things. My buddies ask me about my "new wrinkle." I am always seeking to learn and improve.

———————— • ————————

Making a future you want depends on living with purpose, planning, and being creative with the opportunities presented to you. Tori Baxter was in charge of player development for Prince. Her job was to work at the grass-roots level with the junior program and get the promising kids tied to the Prince brand. She identified the up-and-comers early on, talked to them, got them free rackets, and sent them birthday cards. She cared about these kids and became like a second mother to them. Creativity, combined with a work ethic, can't be beat. She had 56 percent of the national juniors playing with a Prince racket.

I derive a great deal of satisfaction solving problems. When I was 12 years old, I was a little bored and needed something to do. I surveyed our driveway. It needed something so I lined it with bricks. My mother was happy with how it looked, and I had the satisfaction of improving what was around me. As I get older, new problems around the house take more of my energy and the tasks required to solve them seem larger and more difficult to complete. Often the answer is to plan better.

Let me give you an example: It's Thanksgiving Day. My son Kyle and I are preparing a turkey. It's too early to put it in the oven and there's no room in the refrigerator, so we elect to put it outside. It's a cold, blustery day. We have a one-story house. My wife Mary Ellen was sitting in a "sucky" chair looking out the window. Kyle was in the middle room watching TV. Tara was taking shower number 40, 41, or 42. I was doing the dishes (that's how screwed up our house was!). Suddenly, I heard Mary Ellen scream. A big wind had come along and lifted an umbrella to the roof of the house. It sounded like Santa and his reindeer had arrived. I looked out the window and watched the umbrella fall off the roof and spear the turkey. Now we had a bruised turkey, but we ate the turkey anyway.

What do you learn from this or any other screw up? First of all, take responsibility for it. Then, plan and organize better. As they say, never assume anything because *assume* will make an ass out of you and me. Always anticipate and troubleshoot.

I now prefer fun problems like golf, tennis, swimming, skiing, and cooking.

If you feel your creativity was lost somewhere along the way, find it. Try something new. Take a problem and find a way to solve it. Make it fun.

Integrity and Honesty

The nuns and my old man taught me this principle: The quickest way to success is integrity and honesty. Life is about character values. Some are obvious and others implied. To me, they are the staff of life. Just like the Ten Commandments, you need to follow them.

My father and grandfather, both great attorneys, prosecutors, and judges, one a confidant and adviser to Woodrow Wilson, often said they could make a million great decisions in the court of law, and no one would remember one of them. But one shady deal and their reputation would be destroyed.

When I was playing the tennis legend Harry Hoffman in a Middle States–sanctioned tennis tournament. I was playing his "out" balls as good. Finally, he caught one of my tennis balls, stopped play, and said, "Marty, I want the game to be played the way it's supposed to be played." When I played out balls as good, I was saying that I'll beat you in spite of the advantage I gave you. For the remainder of that match, I called them correctly. This was a man of character and integrity.

My reputation of being fair with my calls followed me the rest of my life. It made tennis fun, and I built good relationships with my opponents, who often became friends. A side benefit was that my opponents also gave me the benefit of the doubt on their calls!

Failure and Resiliency

The more sports you play and the more teams you play on, the more opportunities you have for failure. The first time I failed in organized sports I was captain of my junior high school basketball team. We didn't win much. I hated the feeling of not winning, and it motivated me to work harder to succeed.

But sometimes you work hard and fail anyway, or you suffer an illness or defeat. Failure, problems, and stress give us opportunities to learn resilience. Coming back after you've failed or been knocked down is part of the equation for being successful. During the two years I was in the Army, I was seriously ill twice. I contracted spinal meningitis and then hepatitis. I came back from both.

I had one failure that was particularly traumatic. It's called divorce. It shook up my whole world and what I believed about the church I was raised in. In the settlement I gave my ex-wife the house on the river I loved so much. I had no place to live. I had to brainstorm, daydream, think backward, and preside over innovation.

I used my money to buy a van—a six-cylinder Ford 150 Econoline—in my favorite color, blue. The interior had only two seats. On the passenger side was a sliding door and, in the back, a door that could be opened on one side or both sides. I paneled the walls and floor with wood. I stapled a fluffy, cozy blue and red rug to the walls and linoleum to the floor. I took out the passenger seat and replaced it with a platform six inches off the floor and put a comfy brown bean bag chair on it. (Seat belts were not required back then.)

Behind the driver's seat, I installed a Franklin wood-burning stove. I exited the fumes through the roof by way of a chimney. Alongside the fireplace and on the floor, I installed a heater. I put the refrigerator on top of the heater. Both were fired by propane gas. On the other side of the heater/refrigerator unit, I built a long seat that reached to the very end of the van and folded out into a bed.

Across from my seat/bed and above the gas tank, I built another 6-inch platform and mounted my second Franklin stove, securing it with car buckles and guide-wire. My amenities were a TV, an electric heater, and a round cooler to hold beer and sit on. I had electricity from the car engine, wood to keep me warm, and propane for a portable four-burner stove to cook my meals. Two chimneys, two wood-burning stoves, and it still passed motor vehicle inspection!

I had a home.

Now where to park it?

There was a parking area at Rider designated for athletic staff. My parking space was so close to the gym I could roll out of bed and land in my office.

My office was in a large equipment room in the very back corner of the gym where we stored and dispensed intramural equipment. I had a desk, a telephone, and a shower in that room. I had six bins to lock up the equipment so it wouldn't walk.

They were so big I could put a baby elephant in each of them. I used one of them for my personal equipment— clothes, etc.

The power cord from my van just happened to fit through a hole in the bottom of the building's exterior the size of a sewer pipe in a house. I connected it to an electrical outlet in the office. Diagonally across the gym was the varsity equipment room, which housed a commercial washer and dryer. Next door was the cafeteria.

I had other amenities. The weight room was on the other end of the gym. I never used it. The mobile partition that divided the gym in half allowed me to play handball and develop my left hand for tennis. I made the gym floor into a tennis court. I'd bring my buddies in when the gym was available on weekends so we could do battle. If the gym wasn't available, I had access to the outdoor courts. In the winter I'd shovel the outdoor tennis court, which was a shuffleboard-throw away from my parked van.

Buying and outfitting my van gave me a focus for my energy after my divorce, and it was a way to re-create my life. I was also taking action to deal with the huge change in my life, going from being married to divorced.

Resiliency, that bounce-back-ability, means that you don't stay stuck. You redefine your life and reframe it. Resiliency is a powerful ingredient to success in life. Each day we face challenges that require resiliency and courage. I do not have the same physical body I did at 50 or even 60. Resiliency requires effort to keep up my daily regimen of exercises.

There was this gentleman who failed on a regular basis. He ran for the state legislature and lost. He spent 17 years paying off the debts of his business partner. He ran for Congress and lost. His fiancé died. He had a nervous breakdown. Three years later, he was elected to Congress. Two years later he lost his bid for reelection. He ran for vice president of the United States and lost. The gentleman was Abraham Lincoln, who became one of our greatest presidents.

Some people have a problem with failure. I don't. I see failure as a challenge and an opportunity. Responding to failure builds resiliency and confidence.

My son Kyle competed in open tennis tournaments. In one big tournament, he faced a professional who had played in the U.S. Open. Kyle won the first set 6–3 and was up 3–2 in the second. He lost 6–3 in the third. Kyle was only 10 years old. In great attempts, it can be glorious to fail!

What are the qualities and attributes of people who are resilient? They have self-esteem and self-discipline and are responsible. Resilient people understand their strengths and weaknesses. They keep an open mind, are good listeners, have lots of interests, and love life. They are somewhat independent, have friends, and they are able to change.

One more thing to know about resiliency. Play helps us be resilient. It gives us an opportunity to be creative and approach life with a sense of humor. Play allows the mind to flow freely. Play breaks down rigidity and teaches us to respond to disruptive experiences, to adapt to and recover from change. All my life I've been paid to play. This has helped me because my work is play and play is my work. If you have a playful attitude towards your work and your life, you will become more resilient and find it easier to change. This is becoming increasingly important because the world around us is chaotic and changing more quickly all the time.

Positive Self-Change

I wasn't always aware of it, but one of my strengths is an ability to change. Many friends and acquaintances who watched me play tennis matches over the years commented that I won a match because I changed my game in the middle of it. All I knew at the time was that I didn't want to lose. Sometimes necessity is the mother of invention.

I was playing a national senior tennis tournament in Salt Lake City and the match wasn't going well. In the middle of this losing endeavor, I switched from using a one-handed left-handed forehand to a two-handed backhand. I had never hit a two-handed backhand in competition before. Not too bright, but I was willing to try something new to see if I could turn the match around. It didn't work, but I wasn't about to go down without trying something new.

People are typically comfortable in their own arena and doing what is familiar. They may not like their situation or their performance, but they don't want to go through the process of change and push through areas of discomfort, which is necessary to grow. If you're too fearful a change won't bring the desired result, then focus on the process, not the result. What do you have to lose? If you're going down the tubes with the approach you are taking, take a new tack. I have gone from using 39-inch-long tennis rackets to pee-wee length rackets, from 10-lb. string tensions to 60-lb., from extremely head-heavy rackets to extremely head-light rackets. I've experimented with different kinds of strings. I started to play in no man's land when I lost some of my speed and had more trouble getting to the net and back to the baseline. It was considered unconventional at best, but it worked for me.

I've always embraced change. I went from being an extreme introvert to an extrovert. I held many different jobs. I went from hating school to loving it. (It only took me 30 years to get there!) I left Duke University to become a professional baseball player. That change was a happy one. In pro ball I learned to play nine positions. I went from eight years of playing professional baseball to managing a Los Angeles Dodgers farm team. A week after I received a letter from Uncle Sam saying I could lose my GI benefits, I decided to go back to college. Goodbye baseball and managing. I coached golf and wrestling, sports I didn't know. I accepted a position at Rider College where I developed the intramural program and later coached the tennis team. I left to take a job with Prince, then went back to Rider in a new role. I traveled for eight years playing pro baseball. Then I stayed put in New Jersey for 30 years for work and education. When I was hired by Prince, it was back to traveling again, this time for 10 years.

I make small changes every day, honing my skills in golf and tennis. My buddies always chuckle when they ask me what's new. I've been fortunate enough to make changes along the way as circumstances arose and as I saw opportunities. One of the extraordinary changes was when, at 17 years old, my son Kyle became a father out of wedlock and he and his young daughter came to live with me and my wife for a time. The mother did not wish to further the relationship with Kyle, but he refused to bail out on his responsibility of having a child. He took his case to court to get custody of his child. He had no lawyer and pleaded his own case. The court ruled in his favor. I was proud of him.

Kyle came to live with us because he had to provide for himself and his daughter. I had already raised two families and was going for number three. This little tyke was beautiful in looks and spirit. She had little fear and was embraced by my 160 ladies of the court. At 6 years of age, she could enthrall adults with mature conversation. What a great, pleasurable, and challenging change that was.

Some things you can change, others you can't. Take, for instance, my long list of physical deficiencies. I make the best of what I have and appreciate what they do for me. For instance, my little feet get me skiing around a mountain. I'm equally proficient playing right-handed or left-handed. I can still shoulder my grandkids. I haven't figured out what my big butt and long waist do, but I have an idea.

Too often I find people struggle with change. They focus on what they perceive as their deficiencies, on what they can't change, and don't apply themselves to working on what's in their control. When I was with the Dodgers, the organization set goals for the players, managers, coaches, and teams from the minors to the major leagues. The goal was to finish toward the top of the standings. Why not go for first place? That was the hope, but the Dodger executives were a smart bunch. They knew that there were circumstances beyond anyone's control that could affect the outcome of a season—injuries, the level of competition. They focused on effort and the process of improving as individuals, as a team, and as an organization. With that as the focus, the outcome was more than likely to be a good one.

As a tennis coach, I often see how reluctant people are to move out of their comfort zone and make a change. As soon as they fail, they get discouraged and revert to old habits. Developing new habits requires a strong work ethic, persistence, and belief. You need to use your thinking brain to override your emotional brain. To change, you need courage, commitment, and desire. Work and persistence are necessary since adopting a new behavior usually takes six months to a year. Change is disruptive, but the effort to change is worth it.

Preparation

Many challenges in life require preparation. This applies if you're a student facing an exam, a lawyer facing a trial, a businessperson working on a sales pitch, an athlete before a big game. All these situations require preparation.

Preparation is where it all comes together—positivity, work ethic, managing stress, employing tactics like rationalization, learning to control your emotions and focus on the process, and using your thinking brain to process information quickly and respond with awareness to the situation. There are 700,000 ways you can change everything, from the beat of your heart to the fluency of your speech.

What does preparation look like? This example speaks mainly to tennis players, but it can be applied to many challenges in life. Preparation starts with focusing on the process, not the result. Preparation is not just making tough shots; it's using your mind to get information that will give you an edge on your opponent. Don't take anything for granted. Study your opponent, the patterns in their game, their weaknesses and strengths. Prepare, train, observe, think. Do the work others don't want to do.

I was not as physically gifted as many of the people I played against. That motivated me to work harder, to be more alert, more prepared. I focused on fitness and nutrition. During the match, I made sure that I eliminated distractions and stayed in the moment. I sought to cultivate that ideal performance state where I was prepared physically and mentally and was calm and confident. This started with preparation.

Getting ready for a tournament, or even just a match at the local club, I looked at the ball. Who made it—Penn, Wilson, Dunlop, or Prince? They all play differently on the same surface. The naps are different. The cores are different. The air pressures are different.

Examine the surface. There are four surfaces—grass, clay, hard, rubberized—at the four grand slams, not to mention all the other annual tournaments. At the U.S. Open, the center court plays differently than the satellite courts in the same complex.

How about the location of the sun or the effect of indoor lighting or lights outside in the evening?

What are the conditions? Consider the wind and the direction from which it is coming. Is it swirling? Topspin may be indicated on one side of the court and slice on the other, or you may choose to aim for the center and let the wind work the ball. How about humidity? I watched Ken Wilson never miss a ball on a hot, humid night. Then a weather front came through, and the next night and he couldn't hit a ball in the court. The humidity had lifted, the temperature rose, and the ball was dryer and lighter. The ball flew off his racket and he couldn't control it. What's the temperature? I was playing in Europe and couldn't get the ball to the service line. When I got off the plane in the United States it was 100 degrees, and the balls were jumping over the fence. Altitude also plays a factor. Tennis in New Jersey plays differently than in the mountains of Vermont, and in Vermont differently than in Colorado, Arizona differently than in California.

Consider your opponent. Look at the draw sheet, find out who your opponent is, and learn all you can about their style of play, foot speed, whether they are a wrong-armer or right-handed. What's your opponent's mental acuity and how physical are they? Is your opponent a shot maker or a grinder?

How about yourself? How do you feel? Look at any signals and messages to gain insight into your feelings so you can communicate them to yourself and be better prepared.

Be aware of all these things. Put them in your computer and out comes the printout. Given all these factors, formulate a game plan. Visualize, practice, and memorize that plan. Drill it into your head until your brains leak out and you are ready to execute it. For instance, decide in advance if you are going to make your first strike with placement or power. Spin. Angle. Depth. Touch. Disguise. Ugliness of shot. Keep away. Perimeter hitting. No man's land. Shorten your stroke for placement. Drop shots. Move back to gain time to lengthen your stroke for power. Get to the net. Think about what tactics will give you an advantage. Take time away from your opponent however you can.

Often the match doesn't go as planned and you must either adjust or abort your original game plan, so always have a backup plan. Have that in your back pocket so that you are not left empty handed or empty headed. Prepare for many possibilities so that in the middle of the match you can start the visualization process over with the same or a new game plan.

In working with Prince, I also focused on preparation. When Smiley Bones and I traveled across the country to conduct clinics we had to deal with unexpected situations. Bad weather, lack of access to electrical outlets, changes in scheduling. I believed in having a Plan A, B, C, and D.

Preparation and positivity are key to everything. If you're scared to make a fool of yourself, use that as motivation to prepare like a crazy person. When I was competing, I played like I was afraid—afraid to lose.

Mental Toughness

I see myself as a winner. This is key to being mentally tough. If you see yourself as a winner and have done all you can to prepare yourself, you will perform like a winner. You may have to deceive yourself and rationalize to eliminate any doubts you have. In tennis or another sport rationalize that your opponent has two arms and two legs, the same as you. Tell yourself that with the right game plan and execution, you can do it. Affirm to yourself that you can win—or at the very least that you are going to give 100 percent.

Brainwash yourself that you love the battle, and that you love to compete. For instance, you're in the third-set tiebreak. Tell yourself it wouldn't be any fun to win or lose 6–0, 6–0. But this, this is fun! This is what it's all about. Picture 60,000 people in the stands and $100,000 on the line but you don't need it. Lie big time. Be a good actor. Self-deception works.

To be mentally tough, you also have to control your emotions. Rationalize that you are in a war and it's not going to do you any good to get upset or nervous. Look at problems as opportunities to succeed. Maintain your composure and your dignity. Continue to try the hardest when the cards are stacked against you and love every minute of it. Treat triumph and disaster as two imposters. Remain mentally calm and serene within yourself. Relax and breathe slowly. This will have a calming effect on you. Be positive and optimistic.

Have rituals. They bring balance, harmony, poise, symmetry, simplicity, and order to our lives. Ever watch a tennis player pluck her strings and wonder why? There are 10,000 people in the stands and if she looks up, she can be easily distracted. Plucking the strings buys her time, quiet time, so the chemicals can be put in order, and she can recover her heart rate and perform better. This kind of ritual is a signal to you that it's time to visualize and mentally rehearse your game plan so you are prepared to execute.

If you're not feeling confident or if you are getting fatigued, don't let anyone see it. Fake good body language, keep self-deceiving, and override the central nervous system by being a good actor. I found that smiling sends a positive, uplifting message to your brain and frustrates your opponent. Frowning sends yourself a negative message and encourages your opponent. It's tough enough to play the game without an albatross around your neck. Classify the balls you hit inches out as great misses. Stay positive.

The deeper you're into a match, the more you need to keep your physical and mental energy up. Become even more alert and aware. Capture the moment and be on it like a dime. Know where your feet, hands, and the court are. Be into the game so much you could be naked and oblivious to it. When you are there, you are in a zone. You are laser focused, imperturbable. Nothing else matters.

Remind yourself that hustle won't cost you anything. Good sweat has no odor. Run the hardest when you feel the worst—after all, nobody ever drowned in sweat.

Handle distractions. Keep those demons out of your head. Paralyze their resistance with persistence. Focus on getting one more ball back. And one more. Then one more. Time and patience are the strongest of warriors. Be tremendously focused on your game plan. Get into the process and not the outcome. It's the antidote to anxiety.

If you find yourself losing focus, become more focused. Get your energy up. Before you know it, you're mentally stronger.

Be like Rasputin—fueled by passion and drive, you ward off dying. Tell yourself it's going to be a gut-wrenching performance. A volcanic eruption is going to occur. Get fired up. It's easier to temper a fire than to build one.

Be aware that fatigue makes cowards of us. Mental toughness is managing physical fatigue with positive self-talk. Have a big heart and lots of grit. When you feel like you're starting to droop like a flower in a drought, you can fool your body and change your body chemistry by thinking positively, remaining confident, and maintaining good body language. Before you know it that flower is looking up toward the sun.

Fear and anxiety inhibit performance. Eliminate them. Learn to enjoy the struggle. Change your focus and your thought process. When you're on a tennis court playing a match, focus on the process, on each point. Harden your attitude. If you find yourself not performing well, don't panic. Treat it as a problem to solve. Focus on the basics of what you have to do. Get a ball back. Get the first ball in. Anticipate what your opponent will do. Expect the weak ball. Short ball. Looping balls. Look for cues.

Choking happens when fear and anxiety get the best of you and get in the way of your performance. It starts with doubting yourself, worrying about what other people think, worrying about the outcome. First your muscle groups tighten up. You feel tired. These physical changes then lead to negative thoughts. You think about being tired and it goes downhill from there. You feel worse physically and listen to a stream of negative messages you are giving yourself. If you're choking, it means you care about how you're performing—which is good—but learn to deal with fear so that you can achieve what you desire.

Tanking is another way of dealing with pressure. Tanking is giving in, losing on purpose, and it occurs in sports and other areas of life. You quit, pack it in. Tanking is having an attitude of indifference. When you tank you don't even try. You won't have to deal with fear at all if you are indifferent to how you perform. But who wants to spend time and energy doing something they don't care about? Don't tank. Don't take yourself out of the game.

There are many ways to deal with your emotions under pressure. Do what works for you. One of the greatest competitors who ever lived was flamboyant, cocky, aggressive, vivacious, fearless, and showy. His mother taught him to channel his passion into a remarkable emotional response under stress, a response he learned to thoroughly enjoy and thrive on. He got the crowd fired up. No time for pancake performances because he pulled himself up with his bootstraps. That was Jimmy Connors.

Ever watch a duck on water? So serene on top, but the feet under the water are churning away 60 miles an hour. That was Mr. Iceman. He won six French Opens and five Wimbledons. You never knew whether he won or lost a point, game, or match. He managed his emotions by keeping cool. That was Bjorn Borg.

Another great competitor was Mr. October, a baseball player for the Yankees who performed brilliantly in the postseason, hitting a flurry of home runs. When asked how he did it, he said he would remind himself to stay within himself. In pressure situations, his hotshot pitching opponents would try to take it up a notch. "They made more mistakes and I hit more home runs with insulting ease." This was Reggie Jackson.

What about an example of a guy who *never* had his chemicals in order as far as his on-court behavior is concerned? His attitude was negative, unfair, and unsportsmanlike. He was amazingly talented and that's how he compiled many grand slam titles and rose to the top of the men's tennis rankings. Many say that his behavior fired him up to perform better, but I see it as disruptive to himself and to his opponents. He could have performed even better if he managed his chemicals better. That was John McEnroe.

My game plan is to bring my mental toughness into play well in advance of going onto the court and to evaluate it constantly while on the court. I tell myself I can do it, especially with the correct plan. I focus so that I'm oblivious to any and all distractions. When I block out distractions, I can't be nervous. I get my physical and mental energy up. I remind myself that I crave the battle. I harness my emotions as they arise and measure my success success by the effort I give.

Mental toughness requires situational awareness. Look at all the signals and messages to gain insight into your thoughts and feelings and those of others. Absorb everything so you can adequately respond.

Some people call it being in the flow, others the zone. This occurs when you have eliminated all distractions by having a blinding focus on the process. Be oblivious to the outside world. You've lost all self-consciousness when action and awareness come together. Focus on your game plan and not the outcome. The outcome is just the motivator. If you get the process right, you will surely realize the outcome.

Here is one way I taught a group of ladies in a tennis lesson about mental toughness. I told them that mental toughness is being focused on a point like you are engaged in reading a compelling book or watching an intriguing movie. As they were playing a point, I walked across the court and lowered my pants. Pandemonium transpired and I admonished them for being distracted. I'd made my point. My lady tennis players will always remember mental toughness.

I'm proud that people perceive me as being mentally tough, both on and off the field or court. Playing sports was my crucible, it was where I got my PhD in mental toughness.

While I was in the Army I was hospitalized with spinal meningitis. The illness was often fatal, but as far as I was concerned, I just had an illness like the mumps, the chicken pox, or the measles. Being in the hospital gave me more time to dream of the day I'd get out of the Army and back to playing pro baseball. I walked away with nary a single affliction.

Going through a divorce was much tougher for me than nearly dying. I was a good ole Catholic boy who served Mass as an altar boy, who received more than his share of the sacraments, who believed in marriage for life, and who was aware of the stigma attached to divorce at that time. Picking myself up and moving on required mental toughness.

Tennis is a difficult game without any excess baggage, any major distractions. How do you do it knowing your father is dying? At the 45-and-over senior tennis tournament I used my dying father to motivate me. I rationalized that his dying wish for me was to win, and I couldn't let him down. I affirmed to myself that if he had the courage to die, the least I could do is put out more focus and energy than I have ever given in a tennis match. Personal feelings can sometimes be a factor in how you play, but it wasn't going to be for me, not in this tournament. I'd better have the courage to leave my efforts 100 percent on the tennis court. I won the tournament and my first gold ball. I couldn't tell you the scores of the matches. The only score I could tell you: it was one for the old man.

The mental part of performance cannot be overrated. An extreme example of its importance was when a CEO of a major corporation came to me. Although a strong leader in business, he would cave in during tennis matches. After seeing him play, I soon realized that his problem wasn't skill, technique, strength, or endurance. He had a wicked backhand, could outthink his opponent, and had a strong serve. The trouble was psychological. In talking to him, I found out that growing up he yielded to his mother's wishes and sought to please her instead of himself. It translated to the tennis court in that he collapsed when competing. Once he became aware of this and changed his focus to the process of playing tennis, the problem was solved.

How do you develop mental toughness? Whether on the athletic field or court or in your job or family, you must practice. You must give yourself positive messages. You must convince yourself that failure is not an option. Maybe your job is on the line. You are in the tar pit and under pressure to perform. You tell yourself you have to be as smart as a day is long. You want to feel that you are dealing in the currency of life and death. You want to know that you must win. You must be tremendously focused.

Years ago, I asked the great sports psychologist, Jim Loehr, what mental toughness was. He responded, "Marty, you ain't got much to work with but you are mentally tough. No one begins playing tennis at the age of 36 years, wins three national tennis titles on three different surfaces, six silver balls, and becomes number 1 in the nation and 10th in the world without being mentally tough."

That was a great compliment. He never really did tell me what mental toughness was. I realized I didn't look good doing anything, and for that reason, I couldn't stand looking at pictures of myself. So I started to look at my athletic achievements and realized I did manage to achieve a lot. As a high school diver with zero flexibility, I responded to the pressure of being 99 percent naked on the diving board with judges and spectators checking me out and somehow became an All-American. I was an All-City football player at a mere 135 pounds and played both defense and offense. As the quarterback, I had the added pressure of calling the plays. I enjoyed the luxury of getting my head kicked in blocking for 250-lb. backs.

I played in the Brooklyn Dodgers organization, which got the name from dodging trolleys in Brooklyn. Somewhere along the line, I must have been hit by one. In eight years in the organization, I demonstrated unbridled power. I hit four home runs in those eight years, and two of the homers were inside the park. They couldn't find a position for me to play, so I played all nine and was always in the lineup. At 29 years of age, I managed the Orlando Dodgers, a team made up of kids not much younger than me.

In over 35 years as a ski patroller, I helped rescue over 350 people. There is pressure racing to the scene, hoping you don't take out the skiers you're weaving through on the way. Pressure to quickly evaluate the injury, pack the injured person carefully in the sled, and get them down the mountain.

Simply put, all these achievements required mental toughness. But mental toughness doesn't just relate to sports, a lot of things in life require mental toughness. Think about your achievements, about when you have shown mental toughness in your life, about when you had pressure and still performed. It may have been when you took the SATs in high school and went on to graduate from college, when you earned a master's degree and a PhD, or when you landed a good job in the business world.

Growing old requires mental toughness. Some of my buddies are retired and older than Methuselah. Some are couch potatoes. I tell them, "Get off your duff!" Staying active when you're slowing down benefits both your mind and your body.

My buddy Pat Danahy spent fifty-three years on ski patrol at Mount Snow, and when he wasn't free skiing or cutting brush, I would catch him doing 360s in front of a lift line of people. Another buddy on rescue, John Metcalf, was 75 years young. He had an artificial hip, a busted-up knee, and he still ski raced.

At the age of 65, my good friend Stan Dlugosz had an artificial hip and a fused ankle. He wasn't supposed to ski or play tennis. One summer in Philadelphia, he kicked my butt in a grass court tennis match. Ken Wilson, my doubles partner, beat Bobby Riggs some 20 years ago. Ken was playing the best tennis of his life at 79.

Before he died, John McGrath went for his seventh national tennis title at 80.

The late Dodo Cheney was 82 years young, had 130 national titles, and was still counting. She died at 98. When my neighbor Joe was 87, he helped me split wood all winter. Joe said that he and I will never die because God's got enough trouble up there without him and me in the mix.

I have another buddy, Roald Flater from Denver. He took up flying at 60. Now he ferries airplanes across the country for major corporations. Sometimes he takes his bride, 20 years his junior, with him as his co-pilot. A few summers ago, he sailed across the Baltic Sea, 375 miles in a boat about the size of your bed.

We all have different challenges in sports and life. Developing mental toughness will help immensely in performing well in all realms.

Goal Setting

I was asked many times in high school and college, "What are your goals?" At the time I had no clue what my teachers meant. The question was too abstract for me. Most of my goals were derived from my emotional brain. I didn't so much think about my goals as felt them. I grew up running, jumping, and swimming. Being physically active was as important as life to me. I felt a need to take every opportunity to play sports. It gave me a direction for my all my energy. Later I started to think about how I could continue to be physical. Only then did my mind kick in. I thought about where being physical could take me and thought about how I could make a living by playing baseball. My body directed my mind to what I wanted to do. Those goals grew out of what I felt.

How I approach goals has been at the heart of what I have achieved in life and what makes me who I am. Let me drill down to explain what I believe has made me roll or tick. It's very gratifying and satisfying to understand and be able to articulate this. Here goes!

It's a fact that we all have 12 important chemicals in our bodies It's a fact that 8 of the chemicals affect the neurological system or thinking brain and 3 of those chemicals affect our desire for sex. It's a fact that the balance of these 12 chemicals determines the quality of our life.

It's a fact in terms of evolution that the emotional brain is very old. It's a fact that the thinking brain very young in terms of evolution. It's a fact that, today, that the two brains are struggling to work together and separately.

I believe people are mini-models of the process of evolution. Some people are more developed in some areas and less in others. My mental development was very slow. The balance of chemicals in my body determined how important physical exercise was to me. My thinking brain only told me the options of the physical available to me at that time: football, diving, baseball, etc. Indeed limited by today's standards!

My feelings were the catalyst to my 89 years of a glorious life. The strong feelings I experienced after working out and being physically active were addictive, euphoric, narcotic, lowered stress, suppressed pain, and enhanced my confidence and self-esteem.

That is how I could understand goal setting—it was instinctive, and it was visual. My goals related to something I felt and the positive feedback or response I had mentally or physically. My goals also related to something I saw. For example, I could visualize moving a pile of dirt or building part of a wall as working toward the goal of constructing a tennis court. My goals were concrete, not abstract. Not too many or too unrealistic or too difficult—and they weren't going away until I accomplished them. The beauty of building my own tennis court has been the enjoyment it has brought my friends and me and a sense of accomplishment for the fruits of my labor.

Not understanding big, abstract goals didn't get in the way of my dreaming big. Those big dreams led some people to consider my goals unrealistic. I didn't think of them that way. Some might consider my goals unusual, but to me they were certainly achievable. I envisioned a retaining wall for my first house on the Delaware River. This required mining the river for rocks, loading and unloading 500 railroad ties, and building walls and steps to terrace the land to the river's edge. With the help of friends, I cleared my one-acre property of two-foot diameter trees to build my dream tennis court. These were goals I knew I could achieve over time.

Looking back, I can now see that my overall goal in life has been to try to make everything I see or touch better. With that as my purpose, I've moved from one thing to the next. I've done it all my life that way and continue to do so while I have continued to enjoy the drug of physical activity. However, the need for the physical has gradually been usurped by the mental.

I'll try to explain this through my experience at Prince, selling the ball machine. When Jim Baugh asked me to leave 18 glorious years as director of intramural athletics at Rider College to become product manager of the Prince ball machine, I knew nothing about the business world, but I sensed I needed a change. I had a passion for playing tennis, and this new opportunity would allow me to be associated with a leading company in the game I loved.

If your goal is to be top dog in your endeavor, you need to become an expert. In my case, it meant learning everything about the ball machine, from building it to marketing it. As soon as I got the job, I was off to the assembly line to understand what made the ball machine work. I began using my mind.

> **Someone without goals is like a ship without a rudder. Everyone needs a carrot on a stick.**

I had lots of questions for the engineers. If it breaks down on an outing, how do I fix it? Next, I needed to know how it performed, so I took it out and used it on a tennis court. The machine was good, but I asked myself, *how could it be better?* Prince engineers told me a variable speed would allow me to increase and decrease the flow rate of tennis balls.

Your goals can develop as you learn more about your endeavor if you are curious and driven to constantly improve. At Prince, I asked myself questions. *How could I increase the value of the machine by developing programs to make it more versatile and valuable? How about starting by incorporating jogging on a tennis court and hitting balls at the same time? Two hundred balls programmed corner to corner equals a mile run. Now design a chart to record the results.*

Tennis is an anaerobic game—30-second bursts of exercise followed by rest periods. To mimic that, hit 10 balls at 3-second intervals with a 6-second rest by letting 2 balls go by. Do this for 20 minutes at a reasonably high heart rate. Now we have a program specific to the activity of tennis.

How about comparing your progress from when you first use the machine to later? Now let's make this even more fun. Mark off sections of a singles court with a point value for each section and add up the results. Call the game "Beat the Prince." How about a simple drill program for one or more people? You can accomplish 80 drills with three machine settings and three formations. I kept making the value of the machine better.

Now how do you sell it? Sam McCleery, a Prince employee with lots of vision, told me the formula is "make people aware, try, buy, and repeat to buy." No better way than to start by conducting local clinics on six courts at a time—ideally with 6 people on each court, using 6 ball machines. In 1½ hours, 36 people have now used the ball machine.

The wheels in my head kept turning. Why not incorporate the entire Prince line of products—strings, bags, rackets, t-shirts, hats, wristbands, shoes, clothing, etc.—in my efforts to sell the ball machine? As part of the clinic, place these products on one of the courts for people to see. Put Prince tennis rackets in their hands. Answer questions about the products and encourage the participants to hit balls at Prince t-shirts laid out on the court. If they hit a t-shirt, they keep it. It was great marketing to have 36 people at a clinic walking around making others aware of the Prince name. Make it a show. Add music to the clinic and have smoke coming out of the ball machine. Have me come out to address the audience dressed as a prince or a king.

Let's take the clinic throughout the United States. To make Prince clinics more financially successful, plan a full day: have participants, usually women, start at 9 a.m., followed by teaching pro sessions at noon, juniors at 3, and working people at 7 p.m. This made for a long and productive day. Why not take the clinics internationally? So we did! What developed at Prince did not come from preconceived ideas or long-term goals, I was just trying to make everything better one step at a time. My mind just moved from one goal to the next.

Now, later in life, I know what having goals means. In addition to daily goals, I now have longer range goals, even at 89. I use my thinking brain to set these future-looking goals, which I pursue every day, pecking away at them in just the way I built my tennis court. I find as I grow older that my mental brain is flourishing.

I see it in the kind of goals I pursue, which include reading and writing, things I struggled with early on in my life. What a natural, beautiful metamorphosis!

Knowing what you want out of life is very important, so you know where to direct your energy and effort. Without any idea of what you want, you drift or get pulled from one thing to the next. Everyone needs long-range goals to get through short-range frustration and failure. The loftier the goals, the higher the risk and the greater the glory.

I understand the need to dream big and to pursue passion. That is what I advocate to others. Whatever you do, make your goals your dreams, and enjoy the ride by gloating over your accomplishments along the way.

Leadership and Motivation

Which came first, the chicken or the egg? Does the motivator become a good leader, or a good leader become a good motivator? One must understand the qualities of motivation and leadership. They go together. Once the characteristics of both are understood, they can be managed.

Zig Zeigler, American author and motivational speaker, said, "You can get everything out of life you want if you help enough people get what they want." It's an interesting paradox. Leading people is a both a selfish and unselfish act. During the first 30 years of my life, the only people I may have motivated were my teammates, and I did it by being a physical animal. My emotional brain guided me in this very selfish act. I needed my workout, and I had to make the team in order to get it. I needed to go beyond this to motivate and have an impact on others.

I learned that before you can motivate anyone, you must first lower barriers between yourself and others. You may have loads of knowledge to share, but people don't care how much you know until they know how much you care. Former New York Yankee skipper Joe Torre said it best: "Without trust, you cannot commit. Trust must be earned." Once people come to trust you, they will commit. They will listen to you and what you have to offer them. Trust is the highest form of motivation.

To develop trust, you need a high emotional IQ. The words that best describe emotional IQ are awareness, intuition, sensitivity, listening to your instincts, knowing your feelings and the feelings of others, insightfulness, relating, compassion, and empathy. All require calm and receptiveness. You develop a high emotional IQ by establishing a rapport with others by receiving and sending signals through words, the sound of your voice, your body language, common sense, and emotions. Lovemaking at its best is an act of mutual empathy and high emotional IQ.

Here's another way to think about it. Author Stephen Covey describes relationships with others as like having an emotional bank account. We can make deposits or withdrawals. If you have a high emotional IQ, you will make lots of deposits. Deposits come in the form of courtesy, attention, kindness, concern, patience, honesty, love, and generosity. They include keeping commitments, caring about others, and helping them succeed. By being sincere and clarifying expectations you attend to little things. All these are deposits into the emotional bank account that build trust. Withdrawals come in the form of hollering, being degrading, relentlessly disrespectful, negatively humorous, unkind, hurting feelings, demeaning others, judging, and bullying. These negative behaviors hurt and can even destroy your relationships. You want to keep building your emotional bank account with others while staying away from making withdrawals.

The three main positive motivators and energy producers are showing you care, being positive, and creating an outside attacker. You can use these strategies to motivate yourself, your family, and people at work, especially if you're in charge.

CONVEY AN ATTITUDE OF CARING

Throughout the eight years I played in the Brooklyn/Los Angeles baseball organization, Pee Wee Reese, the perennial shortstop of the Dodgers and future Hall of Famer, would come into spring training and show 32 other shortstops how to take his job by working with them, showing them how to improve. At the time, I figured he was not too bright. Now I realized he surrendered to an attitude of caring. What was most important to him, even more important than keeping his job, was sharing his knowledge and helping others. As it turns out, he never did lose his job. Don "Popeye" Zimmer couldn't take Pee Wee's job because he got hit in the head too many times with a baseball. The great Jackie Robinson couldn't

EMOTIONAL IQ AT ITS BEST

This story is one of the most exceptional examples of emotional IQ or emotional intelligence. It was a story I read that I never forgot.

The late Terry Dobson was one of the first Americans to study the martial art Aikido in Japan. It was 1950. He was riding home on the train in Japan when a huge bellicose, belligerent, bewildered, begrimed drunken laborer boarded the train, staggering, cursing, and swinging at everything in sight. He belted a woman with a 1-year-old baby and sent her flying. Everyone stampeded to the rear of the train. Terry, the martial arts expert, knew this could be a bona fide opportunity to use his skills.

As he got up from his seat, the drunk roared at him "Ah, a foreigner who needs to learn some Japanese manners."

With that came an earsplitting, oddly joyous, friendly voice, that shouted out a Japanese version of "Hey, Ol' Buddy."

The drunk spun around to see a 70-year-old man with a big smile dressed in a kimono waving him over.

"What the hell do you want?" asked the drunk.

"What are you drinking?" said the old man. "It smells like sake to me, and I love sake. As a matter of fact, me and the missus, she just turned 76, you know, we warm some sake up every night, go out to the garden, sit under a persimmon tree, and enjoy the fruits of our labor. I'll bet you have a wonderful wife."

No," said the drunk. "My wife just died. I lost my job, and my kids want nothing to do with me. I am ashamed of myself.

"Cheese and Crackers," said the old man. "I need to have a drink on that one. May I join you?"

The last thing Terry saw as he left the train was the drunk lying across the lap of the old man crying like a baby and the little old man drinking his sake. Emotional intelligence at its best.

do it, so they moved him to second base. Junior Gilliam, Charlie Neal, Dick Tracewski, Bobby Dolan, Jack Spears, Billy Cox, Bobby Morgan, Rocky Bridges, Bob Lillis, and Marty Devlin couldn't do it. When Pee Wee retired, the Dodgers still had a difficult time filling his shoes. Pee Wee conveyed an attitude of caring and was an example of positivity in action.

POSITIVITY

Of all the motivating ploys I've used, two of them helped me raise my third child. From the time Kyle was born, I made it a habit and practice of searching for things he did well and complimenting him. Sometimes those compliments were flowing as fast as the Delaware River. There could be as many as 100 times a day. If he didn't pee in the refrigerator, I complimented him. When he hugged his mother or cleaned his teeth, a compliment was forthcoming. With such positive reinforcement his self-esteem and confidence soared. I also treated him like an adult, someone I respected and cared about, and gave him lots of responsibility.

CREATE AN OUTSIDE "ATTACKER"

If you want to make a group more cohesive, allow them to be attacked by an outside source. Here is a motivating ploy I use often while teaching tennis. I have six people on the court and lined up on the baseline. I'm the bad guy, the outside source. Here are the rules. Everyone in the group lines up. I start feeding them balls. Each time through the line, everyone must use perfect technique: elbow in front of the nose, tip of the racket to the back of the fence, catch the racket with the other hand at the throat, shuffle back and keep the feet moving while in line. We go through the line five times. I am threatening them by looking for something they are doing wrong. If anyone does goofers, we start over. I'm the bad guy, and the group gets more cohesive as a result.

The year was 1941. Adolf Hitler was running rampage all over Europe. He captured Czechoslovakia and Poland, was nibbling at Russia, and had all of France. The only reason he didn't yet have England was the English Channel and bad weather. People in the U.S. were in a mood of isolationism, not wanting to get involved after fighting in a war some twenty-plus years earlier. President Roosevelt, the only one with any sense, couldn't motivate the people to support Churchill, the Prime Minister of England. Some historians say he deliberately ticked the

Japanese off by freezing their financial assets in the U.S., among other things. The Japanese then bombed Pearl Harbor. What did the people of the U.S. do? They left their cats, dogs, elephants, churches, husbands, and wives to go to war. What did 9/11 do to the people of the world? Brought them together. These are extreme examples, but if you want to make a group of people more cohesive, allow that group to be attacked by an outside force.

QUALITIES OF A GOOD LEADER

Leadership is not domination of people but the art of persuading people to work toward a common goal. It requires tapping into our deepest senses of meaning and awareness. A leader works to tap into the emotions of people by smoothly bringing them together and gaining their trust. That is being a connector. We become a maven because we have loads of information and knowledge to pass on to them and a sender when we empower them to achieve their goals. You can motivate and lead others only when you have their respect, which comes from having great character values.

Good leaders have a positive attitude that they pass on to others. They project extremely well, have a strong work ethic, manage stress calmly, deal with failure, love what they do, have fun, and crave new ideas and challenges. Good leaders are mentally tough. They accept Mr. Murphy as their best buddy and don't get upset when things go wrong.

Successful leaders have excellent emotional intelligence. Leaders with emotional intelligence are 80 percent more effective than those who have high IQs but are devoid of emotional intelligence.

You may have loads of information and knowledge to pass on, but before others can accept it, you need to connect to their emotions and gain their trust. Only then will they recognize you as a maven, as someone they'll listen to because you've drawn out their own passion.

Good leaders motivate people to believe in themselves. They don't so much tell people what they need to do as help them discover what they already know, uncover what's inside of them. This requires the leader tapping into their deepest sense of meaning and awareness. It means allowing people to be creative, not holding their hands or telling them exactly how to do something. If you do that, you inhibit them from finding their own solutions.

Good leaders set goals and empower others to set their own goals. I believe these goals should be individual and depend on how much each person can take in. My tennis lessons are a working laboratory. I seek to understand the psychology—the thinking, motivation, and emotions—of each of the players I work with. I provide ideas that I believe will improve a player's game and deliver them in a way that allows the player to choose what might be useful to them. I don't tell a player what they should and shouldn't be doing. My goal is not to dictate but to provide feedback and to encourage, guide, and cultivate positivity.

Leadership to me is about creating a positive atmosphere and giving ideas that help people solve a problem in their game and be the best they can be. When someone has a sense that I care about them, this emotional connection motivates them and helps them improve. In a group session, everyone feels it and feeds off this positive connection.

Leadership is also being a sender. Once you have their trust, give them lots of knowledge and a game plan. Put tears in their eyes and fire in their bellies. When I was playing or leading clinics, I had the ability to communicate through my body language and energy. Audiences always went away excited and more knowledgeable because that energy meant that they felt awake and alive and were paying attention. I communicate this same body language and energy when leading a session. I want them to feel their own energy and passion and think, "Man, I'm psyched!" Send them off excited about their game, about themselves, wanting to come back for more.

People learn more by a leader's example than by a leader's words. I set that example by working hard and being willing to do what I ask of others. When I coached the Rider tennis team, I ran the cross-country course with the players and worked as hard and long on the court as they did. This was motivating to them. Steve Diamond, who I coached at Rider, said he knew he could not do any less than his coach.

I play golf at nearby Mountain View Golf Course and help out by cleaning the carts, making sure the divots are fixed, and doing whatever else needs to be done to keep the golf course in good shape. I want the course to be a nice place to play and seek to demonstrate leadership through my example. After a time, the young county employees who work there began to take notice of how I went about things. My friendly attitude and the care I showed toward the golf course had begun to rub off on them.

Good leaders accept new ideas, endorse change, and are flexible. They don't let their egos get in the way. They listen well, especially to their own instincts. They mind getting their hands dirty, but they do it anyway. They pick up the secretary's phone, work on the production line, clean the toilets. They don't talk the walk, they walk the talk. They lead from the front. Take another position, draw fire, duck, and fire back. All of this is good for your morale as a leader as well as others' morale.

As a leader it is tempting to try to control things, but leadership requires letting go of the reins a little to get others involved and engaged. When I was coaching tennis at Rider, the players had their own system of enforcing discipline. Much better that it came from them than from me. As a leader you want to set up conditions for this to happen.

When I was director of the intramural program at Rider College, I set up a student council to run it. I had to keep my own ego in check for the good of the program and for the development of the students. I wanted the program to succeed and knew that could only happen if the students were involved in running it. As I saw it, my job was to plan, share my vision, be positive, show good energy, and motivate and support the students and the program. At the first meeting with the students, I greeted them at the door with a big smile, a firm handshake, good eye contact, and a friendly voice. I was appropriately dressed, neat, well groomed, and displayed lots of energy. I talked to everyone and made them glad they talked to me. I used humor and clear-cut, concise language. I conveyed an air of confidence, a confidence of purpose. I projected success without flaunting it. I was assertive in a nice way. I had a positive attitude and made it clear I was there for them.

I let them know that as members of the intramural council, they would be the governing body. Students would do their own coaching and officiating. I would support them by designing the football and soccer fields and an archery range.

Intramural bylaws, rules for each sport, and officiating guidelines were passed out. Rosters were due back in the intramural office within a week. I sent them back to their fraternities and dormitories all fired up.

I was a connector, a maven, and a sender. That's motivation and leadership.

Leaders in political positions have a difficult task. They often have to make tough decisions and move forward without having everyone on board. Dave Haggerty, President of the International Tennis Federation, had the insight and courage to revise the Davis Cup format. This change had been discussed for years, but no one had the fortitude to implement it. His principles supporting the change were rock solid, yet he faced opposition. He was booed on the court just after the announcement. That hurt. In many situations, you can't please everyone. Leaders have to be courageous enough to do what they believe is right.

When you are in a position to lead, don't think so much about what you want as what others want. People who come for tennis lessons are looking to improve their tennis and have a good time. When someone pays for a tennis lesson, I want them to have a sense of satisfaction and a positive experience. I demonstrate my commitment to them—I show up on time, have good body language, and constantly interact with them and give them attention. This is how to develop others' trust in you and what you are doing and to show that you care. This is how you show leadership.

In the business world, 68 percent of customers stop doing business with a company if they perceive that the company doesn't care about them. Even if there's a problem, 70 percent of customers will do business again if that problem is resolved, 95 percent if it's resolved on the spot. Ninety-six percent of customers never complain; they just take their business elsewhere.

How to Lead and Motivate

Here are two examples of motivating ploys that show how to motivate your people at work or your family. They both imply an attitude of caring.

My boss at Prince was charismatic and radiated leadership. One day he called me into an attractive, comfortable conference room. Music was playing in the background and visual aids were all around. In the corner were some snacks. Some big shots were milling around. My boss was excited, enthusiastic, and positive. He complimented me in front of everyone and told me he was giving me a raise and an extra week's vacation. Then we examined the company's goals and my goals for the tennis clinics, and he started to challenge assumptions.

"Marty, why are you planning on holding tennis clinics in Alaska in the winter?"

Not too bright, I thought to myself.

"What about the $80,000 worth of company prizes?"

Was he concerned that I was indiscriminately giving them away? My stress level began to rise, but I still listened.

"What can we do differently?" he asked me.

We brainstormed. Plug music into the clinics and choreograph them.

"How can we give Prince a bigger bang for the buck?"

He left me with this question and sent me back to the solitude of my office to visualize how I might pull it off. Later that day he came by to pick me up to play tennis, have a beer, dinner, and go to a movie.

This experience reinforced for me what positive leadership looked like. Instead of treating me like an angry father, he dealt with me as if he were my big brother. He motivated me without being cruel and abusive. He didn't make winning an ugly obsession. He didn't raise his voice. He made it clear that he wouldn't punish me for mistakes. He just required that I learn from them. He made the meeting an exercise in creativity, challenge, and learning. He laid out his expectations for me and made sure I understood them, but even before doing this, he had established a relationship with me. Without that relationship, without my sensing his attitude of caring, I might have resisted or rebelled.

When I got home that night, my morale was good. There was no sense of entitlement. As I saw it, I had a job to do. In a year's time, my boss gave me the responsibility for conducting clinics throughout the United States and Europe.

Another example of leadership, or stewardship, occurred when Mary Ellen and I were both working and raising a family. There were lots of jobs around the house, and we needed some help from the kids to get them done. Out came the blackboard and chalk. We listed the responsibilities: mortgage, insurance, car payments, utilities, cooking, laundry, dishes, house cleaning, tennis courts, ivy, and pool.

At first there were no takers except Mom and Dad. Mary Ellen and I had a real monopoly on the opportunities. Kyle must have felt guilty because he ended up volunteering to maintain the clay court, the ivy, and the pool. Terrific!

We first needed clarity and a mutual understanding of what the job required, so I came up with a mission statement: the court was to be firm and smooth, the ivy neat, and the pool clean. I showed Kyle a variety of tools and how to use them, but I left it to him to determine how to get the job done.

He could use a sickle, shears, clippers, or weed whacker for the ivy. For the clay court he had at his disposal a shovel, roller, wheelbarrow, rake, line cleaner, dragging broom, and water hose. *Firm and smooth* was part of our mission statement. The pool was to be drinking-water clean. He could use a long pole skimmer, vacuum hose cleaner, and chemicals. I showed him what a good job was and what I expected of him and warned him of the pitfalls—unharvested growth of ivy, deer tracks on the court, debris from trees, and algae and critters in the pool. I made sure he understood the psychological and financial rewards of doing a good job.

I gave him a certain amount of flexibility in his schedule and allowed him to be as creative as he wanted to get the job done. The challenge was going to be in managing and supervising himself. He needed to be a self-starter. Once a week, we would measure his progress together.

The first week was disastrous. Mice in the pool, deer tracks on the court, ivy like a shaggy dog. After that, I directed his every move and stayed over him, pointing out what he did right and wrong.

Then I gave him one more chance to take ownership. I volunteered to help, but this time he was the boss. He asked me to get the mice out of the pool—he was afraid of them—and I agreed to do it. That built his trust and solidified the deal between us. From that point on, you could have drunk the water from the pool, and the ivy was cascading beautifully, Wimbledon style, all over the property. I could have entertained the U.S. president and his Cabinet. Andre Agassi and Steffi Graf could have played on the court. Kyle did the job far better than I could have imagined. That's stewardship.

The greatest motivator I use in leading is conveying an attitude of caring. I want to help people succeed. I get a kick out of it. It's not a feather in my cap so much as theirs. I gave Kyle the tools to succeed, I help my tennis ladies improve by teaching them and enjoying seeing their progress.

This is where I've changed. Earlier in my life I led by setting an example of hustling and working hard. When I was player–manager of the Orlando Dodgers, I gave my players the baseball information and knowledge they would need to succeed, but I didn't have that attitude of caring that I do now.

Caring is the secret sauce of leadership.

My Principles in a Nutshell

Why have I achieved success? It's pleasure that motivates me. Yes, pleasure. Sometimes fear of failure, but more often the pleasure of achieving a goal, of improving what is around me. I may gloat for a short time after I've achieved something. I think that's necessary and valuable. But If I'm bored by not being active or after I've gloated on what I accomplished for a short time, I want to move onto the next pleasurable experience of life.

What supports that next pleasurable experience, what makes it happen is goal-setting. If someone asked me when I was young what my goals were, I'd have been tongue tied. Yet I felt something moving me from one experience to the next and believe I sensed my goals. Those experiences were mostly epicurean and pleasurable, which further fueled my desire to achieve and succeed.

Achieving goals holds a joy and completeness that cannot be duplicated by anything else. It is powerful. It is indeed as beautiful and necessary to a strong spirit as striving is to a healthy character.

If goal setting—moving from one experience to the next—underpins succeeding in life, the other principles support that movement. Listing the principles underlying success in a logical order reveals both a progression and reinforces to me that all of these principles are interrelated and intertwined. You can start with any principle because focusing on one area leads to success in another.

My mind says attitude is most important. Someone once told me that ATTI-TUDE = 100%.[6] That's what I believe and how I've lived. Everything in life starts with attitude. A positive attitude moves you to action because of your belief in yourself and others. Positive self-projection is number two because we are always dealing with people. Positive self-projection gives others a good feeling about you and often about themselves, which leads to a positive environment and positive interactions with others.

Work ethic is how you apply yourself to a particular challenge. Earl Nightingale identified it as the number one ingredient for success. I can't dispute his ordering. Hustle, a form of work ethic, was my trademark. My work ethic helped make up for deficiencies, where I was lacking in talent. I know my work ethic helped me succeed and gave me opportunities that wouldn't have come my way without it.

Problem solving is a priority because problems occur in work and life that can lead to failure and stress. Only by using creativity and your ability to solve problems can you overcome failure and learn to deal in a positive way with stress. Stress tests you. It challenges you. When you stare it down, when you overcome it, when you turn it toward achieving your goals you develop *resilience*.

Dealing with change, goal setting, creativity, mental toughness, motivation, leadership—they all serve as ingredients for success.

Change is all around us. It's in the air we breathe. If we try to hide from it and if

---

6   How do you get to 100%? A is the 1st number in the alphabet, T the 20th, etc. Add
    them up and you have 100.

we do not change, we will get left behind. We will stagnate and grow old in spirit. Change leads to growth.

Mental toughness is what we require when we are challenged, when we face the specter of failure. Mental toughness is related to positive mental attitude in that it requires an all-consuming belief in ourselves and our ability to perform under stress, to overcome obstacles, to not give in to others who may question our abilities or even in to our own questioning of our abilities. Motivation is just what it sounds like. It's what moves us. For me, my motivation was mainly my desire to achieve my goals. I loved competing with myself and others, and I loved the pleasure of achieving goals. There was also a part of me that was fearful, afraid of losing. That was and is a motivator for me as well. I believe you should use whatever motivation works for you to be successful, to achieve your goals and dreams.

Leadership brings us to how we deal with others. Beyond the necessity of positive self-projection, I believe real leaders help others achieve their goals. They may have special knowledge, experience, or expertise they want to convey to those they are leading. How you do that may differ from others' approaches. But it all comes down to leading in a positive manner, with an attitude of caring. You may use humor to lead, or you may become the "enemy" so that those you are leading coalesce. There are many ways, but I believe leadership is most effective when not exercised through fear or by exerting power, but by finding a way to influence others to make positive changes.

Final Thoughts

The Big Bang Theory suggests that our world came together after a tremendous explosion. There is no logic to it. According to J. H. Holmes, the world is not hostile, not friendly, but indifferent. According to Mihaly Csikszentmihalyi, the author of *Flow*, it's chaotic. According to Marty Devlin, it is like a round of golf. You try logically to connect and hold together as you go from one hole to another. It's called coherence, and it demands that you remain healthy by continually taxing the immune system through optimum emotional, mental, physical and social stress. No matter how bad the round is, maintain a positive attitude so you can continue to have the desire, belief, and confidence to take on new holes, rounds, and tournaments. This is self-efficacy. This is what makes for a successful, challenging, and pleasurable life.

There is a myriad of techniques to change your game and your life to play at a higher level. Bring action and awareness together by way of total concentration on the game and the game plan. Look at all the signals and messages inside and outside of you to gain insight into your feelings so you can impact, empower, connect, and move yourself and others in a nice way. It's called emotional intelligence.

When you have lost all self-consciousness, you are enjoying the process of living. This total mind–body experience is called flow. Flow is the ultimate everyday experience, and it's achievable.

I hope to be sending you, Reader, away fired up with lots of knowledge.

Remember, be hard as a diamond, flexible as a willow, smooth as glass, slick as ice, and empty as space.

As a great Chinese teacher said long ago: Be careful of your thoughts because they become words. Be careful of your words because they become sentences. Be careful of your sentences because they become paragraphs. Be careful of your paragraphs because they become your actions. Be careful of your actions because they become habits. Be careful of your habits because they become your character. Be careful of your character because that becomes your destiny. Destiny is a matter of choice, not a matter of chance.

I would like the following to be my legacy: *Every person should be judged by the content of their character. The highest and richest bequest a person can leave behind is a good example. Class is like a submarine; it doesn't take long to surface, and it's easily recognized. It's nice to be important but more important to be nice.* I would also like to be remembered as an ethical humanitarian, a motivator, and a teacher.

Of all the things I've learned in life, most important is that life is a habit or a series of habits, and people only remember that which they are reminded of. Since life is a habit, change your habits, make them better. Good, better, best, never let it rest until your good gets better and the better gets best. New habits begin as notions. Thought begets habit. What you think is what you believe. Visualize it. Drill it in your head until your brains leak out. Go from cobwebs to cables. Practice, practice, practice, relentless repetition. The beauty of it is that you are in control of yourself. Make these new habits and keep them. Surrender to them. Discipline is a regimen.

Life is preparing, working hard, and establishing habits that become you.

Establishing success is a lifelong process. With ordinary talent and extraordinary effort, all things are attainable. If for some reason you haven't changed, begin today. It's not where you start, it's where you finish. Happy birthday—it's the first day of the rest of your life. Look good, feel good, project well. There is a giant sleeping in you. Just wake that giant up and you will achieve beyond your wildest dreams. Pat yourself on your back and say I love you and the echo will come back to you. You need it and deserve it. The magic of believing will work if you believe in you. Be the captain of your ship and the master of your destiny.

May you draw on the spirit of those who have gone before you, and may your lives continue to influence those who come after you.

> If a man has talent and doesn't use it, he has failed.
> If he has talent and uses only half of it, he has partly failed.
> If he has talent and learns somehow to use the whole of it,
> he has gloriously succeeded and won a satisfaction few men
> ever know.
>
> —*Thomas C. Wolfe*

MARTYISMS

What are Martyisms? They are verbal expressions, proverbs, and sayings that express my principles, my creed. I live them and say them whenever I feel the occasion is appropriate. They have business world accuracy. They expedited my journey to success. They helped guide me in raising my kids. I use them in tennis and model them as best I can in how I live.

Many are my own creation; others I have embraced and made my own because they express what I believe. They provide motivation and inspiration to me, and I hope will inspire, instruct, motivate you, and make you laugh.

On the Tennis Court

I bombard my ladies of the court with these Martyisms during tennis drills.

Comments on Shots

You're going to make me drink!—my response to a player making the same mistake.

You've forever captured in my heart—my response to a great shot or other great move.

I'll marry you!—I say this to the "ladies of the court" who make a Don Quixote shot or who finally "get it."

It's an annulment—missing an easy shot.

We are going to renew our marriage vows—if you make the third shot.

It takes 30,000 hits to groove a stroke.

If you don't risk it, no biscuit.

Fat City—a set up to a put-away shot.

First Strike Tennis (also, First Punch, First Hit) — taking control of the point or forcing an error through shot discrimination and shot selection, using, for example, a perimeter shot, particular kind of serve, drop shot, power, spin, slice, touch, choosing when to hit a soft shot or a hard shot, an excessively low shot, a shot out of the hitting pocket, a ball that is difficult for your opponent to manage.

You have more shots than they have on TV.

More shots, more options.

Were you drinking last night?

More Favorites

Stinky and Blinky—names I called kids when I taught them; I used this "teasing" to break down barriers.

Goofer—a mistake.

You did goofers!

Cheese and Crackers!—said in response to a goofer.

Frog-strangling rain—a downpour.

Ambushed by bladder—announcing a bathroom break.

Uglier than homemade sin—a tennis shot that's "nasty," well placed, and hard to return.

Stir the blood—get warmed up (also, Go to swearin').

My game sucks like a no. 9 vacuum cleaner!

I'm so out of shape I couldn't make a rocking chair go.

My bell was hit so hard I lost my dental work!

Give your partner some empathy and undying support.

You could run a pork chop past a wolf—run fast.

Run like a scalded dog—run fast.

You need the patience of Job.

I smell a bagel. A big fat 0.

On Your Brain and Your Emotions

Drill it into your head till your brains leak out.

Use your thinking brain.

Your emotional brain did you in.

You have diarrhea of mouth and constipation of thought.

More Martyisms

Greetings

Hey, Ol' Buddy—how I say hello to almost everybody.

Hey, Big Buddy—another way I say hello.

On Enjoying Life

Every day is a day of festivities, pageantry, reverie, and splendor.

Life is delicious. Take a bite out of it!

I don't want to die, I'm already in heaven.

On Aging and Play

Continue to play with the psychological makeup of an elephant and the emotional stability of a rhino who skipped breakfast and misplaced lunch.

Working out—all kinds of exercise—delays the aging process. It puts more life in your years and more years in your life.

Live your life, not your age.

On Peak Performance

Focus on the process as the antidote to anxiety.

Be like Rasputin—fueled by passion and drive to ward off dying.

Stir the blood!

It's a gut-wrenching performance.

A volcanic eruption is going to occur—it's easier to temper a fire than build one.

Have a big heart and lots of grit.

Manage the 12 chemicals with the process of thought.

No time for pancake performances.

The mental is to the physical as 4 is to 1.

Crave the battle rather than the outcome.

Override the central nervous system.

Don't be flaky like a biscuit, be like dough and rise to the top.

Look at all the signals and messages like a portrait painter who caters to brush-mark detail.

Life Advice

Rituals give balance, harmony, poise, symmetry, simplicity, and order to our lives.

Be a good actor.

Routine loses motivation and is the devil's workshop.

Get rid of the albatross. Those distractions bring you down.

Smile, you have 15 facial muscles—use them.

Laugh when they get you and laugh when you get them.

It's nice to be important, but it's more important to be nice.

Be gentle, bold, noble, generous, frugal, and liberal.

Class is like a submarine; it doesn't take long to surface and it's easily recognizable.

Inspiration, Advice, and Motivation

These sayings line up with the principles in Part II of my memoir. Use them for motivation and inspiration!

On Success

Success is the courage to meet failure and not be defeated.

For pleasing methods, look for a loser; for pleasing results, look for a winner.

If you want to be successful, find out what the other guy doesn't want to do and do it.

If you're willing to work at it like a colony of ants, you will be successful.

Adopt a Positive Mental Attitude

Attitude is a little thing that makes a big difference.

Positive thoughts add seven years to our lives, five to our marriages—add to that exercise, especially tennis, and it's seven to nine years.

Positivity is like a spitball in baseball. Don't worry, don't complain, hit the dry side.

Count our blessings every day and we'll never have time for anything else.

There is beauty in everything, but not everyone sees it.

Rationalize. Change your body language. Pick up your head and smile.

Combat Negativity

Pessimists make opportunities difficult. Optimists make difficulties opportunities.

Anyone who flies into a rage always makes a bad landing.

If you're hard on yourself for mistakes, force yourself to think another way.

Fear creates its own prison of negativity, a fence made up of cannots.

Learn to Change

Pay attention to your thoughts, the sound of your voice, your language, your energy, and your body language. All of these will either sabotage or support the change you are trying to make.

The world is moving so rapidly that the one who is thinking about change is overtaken by the one who has changed.

Keep pace with the rising sun.

Practice Positive Self-Projection

Look like a winner, even if you don't feel like one.

Project on the outside what you would like to feel on the inside. Your central nervous system has no clue whether you are faking it or not.

When a happy, smiling person enters a room, it's like a candle being lit.

Meeting a happy, optimistic person is like uncorking a bottle of champagne.

You have 1,692 opportunities every day to project in a very positive way.

Be like a hedgehog at a urinal, stand tall on your toes.

Toot your horn!

A Work Ethic Is Essential

If you're not out there practicing, someone else is.

Work at your objectives every day, like an alley cat in a fish market.

With ordinary talent and extraordinary effort, all things are attainable.

A work ethic is a positive attitude put into action.

Idleness is the holiday of fools and the devil's workshop.

Hustle. It won't cost you anything.

Nobody every drowned in sweat.

Work like a one-armed paper hanger, like a one-legged man in a butt-kicking contest.

Stress and Recovery with Equal Diligence

Stress is the stimulus for growth. It goes toe to toe with the devil.

All work and no play make John or Jill a dull boy or girl.

Everyone needs and deserves some leisure time. Get out of the kitchen. Smell the flowers under the door. Recover.

Physical and Mental Exercise

If you don't have time for exercise, sooner or later you'll have to find time for illness.

Movement equals life, too much rest equals rust.

We have to keep moving like a bull with gas.

Creativity

You don't have to be smart or rich to be creative.

The mind is like a parachute: it doesn't work unless it's open.

Get excited.

Imagination rules the world and travels faster than the speed of light.

Fire the right side of the body to fire the left side of the brain.

Look for a new approach.

Challenge assumptions.

Think backwards.

Preside over innovation.

Brainstorm.

Daydream.

Embrace Change

Change is permanently a part of life—like death, taxes, winning, and fun.

The world is changing faster than a centipede with athlete's foot, like sauerkraut going through me, like crap through a goose.

There are 700,000 ways you can alter 12 chemicals in your body to change everything from the fluency of your speech to the beat of your heart.

Change requires pushing through feelings of discomfort at critical moments.

I'm not too old to change: I can change my attitude toward life. I can be more positive. I can learn to project better.

Life Is Problem Solving

Life is made up of obstacles, impediments, boundaries, limitations, adversities, frustrations, inequities, and setbacks.

Most people have more problems than I have shower water on my fanny.

If you think you're free of problems, Mr. Murphy and his law are going to get you because he is just waiting in the wings for something to happen.

Look at problems as opportunities to succeed.

Attack tough problems first.

Coherence is how you logically connect and hold things together as you go from one problem to another.

Luck follows those who try hard to solve their problems.

Life is like a round of golf. You get out of one hole, and you go to the next.

Overcome Failure with Resiliency

Most success is built on failure; you are never beaten till you think you are.

Failure is a test, an opportunity to try again more intelligently.

Recover the fumble and start over.

Sometimes in great attempts it's glorious to fail.

A kite rises against the wind and not with it.

Every day a little rain must fall.

Sometimes a kick in the butt is one step shy of a pat on the back.

A person is never beaten till they think they are.

Things work out best for those who make the best of the way things work out.

Show intelligence and class in the face of defeat.

Failure sharpens your intensity and humbles your vanity.

Failure is nothing more than a cozy piece of hell. Gosh grief, it can be a sacred wound.

Failing begins when you're born and is a big part of life.

Mental Toughness

Try the hardest when the cards are stacked against you—and love every minute of it.

Mental toughness requires situational awareness.

Put yourself on the line every day.

Mental toughness is character in action.

Discipline and a consistent ritual will become a habit if practiced regularly.

Mental toughness is managing 12 chemicals in your body using your thoughts and emotions.

Concentrate with a blinding focus so that you are oblivious to any internal or external factors.

Mental toughness means you don't even consider losing.

Be so mentally tough you could run through a blooming 10 acres, a field of onions, and handle a garlic milkshake. Hell, you could eat the rear end of a skunk. You're tougher than Woody Woodpecker's lips.

Set Goals and Dream Big

Don't belittle your ambition.

Part of setting a goal is finding a way to reach it.

Moving toward your goals is an expression of freedom.

Achieving goals has a joy and a discreet purity to it.

Pursuing goals is necessary to a strong spirit.

How do you plan on reaching your goals? Inch by inch is a cinch, yard by yard is hard.

How do you eat an elephant? One bite at a time.

How do you run a marathon? One step at a time.

How do you build a tennis court? One shovelful at a time.

If your goals are too high, unrealistic, or too many, be damned organized or efficient or failure is likely to marry you.

Don't wait for the ship to come in. Swim out to it.

Aim for the moon, and if you miss, you won't hit your foot, but you may become one of the stars.

Don't look up the stairway, climb it.

Great people are dreamers who have time restraints. They budget their time and prioritize.

Look for competition. You'll never realize your potential until you've been challenged. There is no testimony without a test. Without a struggle, there is no progress.

Action may bring happiness, but there is no happiness without action.

Without goals, you acquire a disease called malingering: you become bored, depressed, and despondent because of lack of activity and lack of direction.

Some of the most absurd aspirations lead to extraordinary accomplishment.

You cannot discover new oceans unless you lose sight of the shore.

Whether or not you achieve your goal, you will at least have the satisfaction of knowing where you are going.

No one can predict how high you can soar, not even you, till you spread your wings.

A person without goals is like a ship without a rudder.

Leadership and Motivation

Good leaders impact, empower, connect, and move others to do the same.

Leaders are like eagles—they don't flock—you find them one at a time.

The pace of the leader determines the rate of the pack.

People learn more by a leader's example than by a leader's words.

Avoid putting yourself before others and you can be a leader.

Leadership is all about caring, showing that you care and want the people you lead to improve.

Avoid putting yourself before others, and you could be a leader among men.

Great people are not afraid to share.

A person wrapped up in themselves is a small bundle.

POSTSCRIPT

My brother Donnie, who worked in the Mercer County school system, was able to check the records and told me that what I was told and what I had believed for years wasn't true: I didn't have an 80 IQ.

WORKSHEETS

While you can look at each principle, all of them are all interrelated. Every principle is interwoven with all of the other Principles. There are many that apply to more than one dimension.

These Worksheets are based on the worksheets I developed with Russell Fleischman, used for presentations to large groups. They have been modified and expanded for the book.

They are meant to provoke thought and help you achieve success and happiness in life.

Positive Mental Attitude (PMA)

Everyone has had an experience where they fall into the negative attitude trap. Yet some people remain in a negative state, fluctuating between high and low negative. Negativity places stress on the body and is associated with poor health.

How frequently do you find yourself in the high or low negative during the day?

Take a look at these traits to help you see where you are and where you want to improve.

High and Low Negative

HIGH NEGATIVE	LOW NEGATIVE
• Belligerent	• Bored
• Arrogant	• Moody
• Vociferous	• Cranky
• Surly	• Critical
• Egotistical	• Uninterested
• Beguiling	• Irritated
• Obnoxious	• Apathetic
• Vulgar	• Nagging
• Swearing	• Irascible
• Obscene Gestures	• Peevish
• Disrespectful	• Bitching
• Intimidating	• Complaining
• Visibly Upset	• Moaning
• Stressed Out	• Condemning
• Hateful	• Bored
• Anxious	• Moody
• Apathetic	• Cranky
• Angry	• Critical
• Confused	• Uninterested
	• Irritated

Identify Your Traits

HIGH NEGATIVE

LOW NEGATIVE

WHICH OF THESE ATTITUDES DO YOU WANT TO LESSEN THEIR HOLD ON YOU?

High and Low Positive

Two different characteristics comprise a positive attitude: high positive and low positive. It is nearly impossible to maintain high positive all the time, so shifting to low positive is important for balance. How often are you in positive vs. negative? high positive vs. low positive?

HIGH POSITIVE	**LOW POSITIVE**
Unbridled Enthusiasm	Pleasant Company
Fearless Sense of Energy	Low Degree of Motivation
Assertive	Out of Gas
Lots of Grit	Nice and Weary
Handle Distractions	Listening Well
On It Like a Dime	Positive Thoughts
Capture the Moment	Re-energizing
Aware of a Critical Moment	Easy Going
Alert	Joking Around
Prickly as a Thorn	Relaxed
Enhanced Physical and Mental Energy	
Hardened Attitude	
Change Focus and Thought	
Vivacious	
Blinding Focus	
Steely Determination	
Intensely Tenacious	
Persistent	
Bubbling under the Skin	
Showing off	
A Clucking Fury	
A Whirling Dervish	

Identify Your Traits

HIGH POSITIVE

LOW POSITIVE

WHICH OF THESE ATTITUDES DO YOU WANT TO STRENGTHEN?

Positive Self-Projection

Have you ever known a person who had a certain presence when they entered a room? Think about what you recognize about them.

Certain traits define a person with a high level of positive self-projection.

- Emotional Control
- Appropriate Attire
- Well Groomed
- Neat
- Make People Glad to Talk to You
- Happy
- Cheerful
- Optimistic
- Smiling
- Make Eye-to-Eye Contact
- Answer with Conviction
- Caring
- Positive Attitude
- Assertive
- Air of Success

- Firm Handshake
- Air of Confidence
- Charisma
- Project Success without Flaunting
- Confidence of Purpose
- Calm (Stoic) Demeanor
- Radiate Leadership
- Talk to Everyone
- Be Spontaneous
- Good Voice
- Clear-Cut, Concise Language
- Project Infectious Energy
- Enthusiastic
- Sense of Humor
- Good Posture

**WHAT TRAITS OF POSITIVE SELF-PROJECTION DO YOU HAVE?
(ASK A TRUSTED FRIEND IF YOU NEED HELP WITH THIS).**

WHAT TRAITS DO YOU WANT TO DEVELOP?

**SET UP PRACTICE SITUATIONS FOR YOURSELF SO THAT YOU CAN WORK ON DEVELOPING
POSITIVE SELF-PROJECTION. WRITE THEM DOWN AND THEN COME BACK TO THEM TO
CHECK YOUR EFFORT. REMEMBER TO STAY IN THE PROCESS RATHER THAN FOCUSING ON
THE RESULT!**

Work Ethic

It's far easier to adjust to the hardships of mediocrity than to adjust to making. your life better one. Choosing a better life over mediocrity requires having a strong work ethic. Below are some of the essential elements of having a work ethic that can't be beat.

- Effort
- Initiative
- Thoroughness
- Anticipation
- Hustle (pertains to both the physical and the mental)
- Self-Starter

- Drive (pushed forward by passion)
- Neatness (that is, not being sloppy)
- Positive Attitude
- Anticipation
- Preparation

WHICH OF THE IMPORTANT ELEMENTS OF A STRONG WORK ETHIC DO YOU HAVE?

WHAT DO YOU WANT TO WORK ON?

WRITE DOWN EXAMPLES OF:

- When you demonstrated a strong work ethic
- When you would have benefited from strengthening your work ethic

HOW CAN YOU ADD SOME OF THESE ELEMENTS OF WORK ETHIC TO MEET A CHALLENGE YOU'RE FACING NOW OR IN THE FUTURE?

Physical Fitness, Mental Exercise, and Recovery

To maintain your energy and achieve what you want to in your life, you need to a get enough and the right mix of physical and mental exercise. You need to get enough sleep and practice other forms of self-care. Use this worksheet to identify areas of strength and areas you want to improve.

Some people keep their noses to the grindstone all the time and think that this is hard work that will lead them to success. It will do the opposite. They will experience burnout and are likely to get sick. Make sure to add in Recovery. It is the missing link.

Balance your need for the physical and the mental. And be sure that you are enjoying your life and having fun!

NOTE: To be successful, you will need be able to change your habits. Become aware of how you make changes—a few do it quickly; for most people it is a slower process. Be patient and persistent and you will succeed! Remember, inch by inch is a cinch, yard by yard is hard.

These are your guidelines to a good healthy day. Have the right mix of exercise, sleep, and other forms of self-care. Adjust your expectations based on your physical limitations and your doctor's recommendations.

Physical Fitness

- Cardiovascular Fitness
- Flexibility
- Strength
- Balance
- Agility
- Hand–Eye Coordination
- Speed
- Body Composition

- Well-Balanced Low-Fat Diet
- Low Sugar and Low Carbohydrates
- Appropriate-Sized Portions
- Proper Vitamin and Nutrient Supplement
- Appropriate Alcohol Consumption
- Regular Exercise
- Have Fun!

Elements of Effective Sleep

- Quantity (7–8 hrs.)
- Quality (REM sleep)
- Naps (20–30 minutes)

Self-Care (Add other forms of Self-Care important to you)

- Self-Screening for Health Concerns
- Periodic Doctor Appointments and Exams
- Proper Daily Sunscreen Application
- No Tobacco, Vaping, or Drugs

Mental Exercise and Recovery

(Add other forms of Mental Exercise and Recovery important to you)

- Reading
- Cooking
- Watching TV
- Contemplating or Meditating
- Napping
- Relaxing
- Writing
- Reflecting on the Day's Accomplishments
- Dreaming and Visualizing
- Eating
- Sipping a Beer before Dinner (if you're not an alcoholic!)
- Sitting Still, Appreciating and Admiring Nature

Physical Fitness

- Do you consider yourself physically fit? In what areas (look at the list)?

- What areas do you want to improve? Identify one or two to focus on to improve.

Mental Exercise

- What forms of mental exercise and self-care do you practice?

- Are you consistent, or could you improve your consistency?

- Are there others that you'd like to add in to improve your daily life?

Recovery

- Do you have the appropriate balance of the physical and the mental in your daily life?

- If not, what changes will you make to get your life in better balance?

Stress and Recovery with Equal Diligence

It is important to know that stress is part of daily life and that not all stress is bad. You want to know the difference between Eustress (Good Stress) and Distress (Negative Stress).

Positive Stress

Positive Stress, or Eustress, is the stimulus of life. It is "Good Stress." This stress is stimulus for growth. Stress in the form of physical exercise strengthens your immune system. It pumps blood and oxygen to the brain. Good Stress is periodic (for example, 90 minutes working, a 20-minute break). Remember, stress and recovery with equal diligence.

Positive Stress is:

- Competition
- Challenge
- Energy
- Focus

To be successful dealing with stress:

- Attack It
- Love It
- Control It—don't let it control you

Negative Stress

Negative Stress is the opposite of Good Stress. Negative Stress is never stopping. When you are experiencing Distress, it's often because you have not allowed for enough time for Recovery. Negative Stress is characterized by:

- Burn Out—low energy, little enthusiasm
- Poor Performance
- Anxiety
- Physical Distress
- Mental Distress

ASK YOURSELF: AM I EXPERIENCING GOOD OR BAD STRESS IN MY LIFE? IN WHAT AREAS?

COULD I ELIMINATE NEGATIVE STRESS WITH BETTER PREPARATION? BY ADDING IN RECOVERY? MORE EXERCISE? MORE REST? (FOR IDEAS, SEE THE WORKSHEET PHYSICAL FITNESS, MENTAL EXERCISE, AND RECOVERY)

WHAT ELSE COULD I BE DOING DIFFERENTLY TO TURN INCREASE POSITIVE STRESS?

Creativity

Everyone is creative. Your ability to be creative isn't limited by your economic or social background. You don't have to be smart or get good grades to be creative. You can use Creativity to solve problems and make your life more fun! Here are ways to exercise your creativity, ways to be creative.

- **Re-Engineer Conceptual Blocks**—whatever you can't seem to master, find a way to practice it differently

- **Look for a New Approach**—experiment!

- **Segment the Problem**—take it a piece at a time

- **Challenge Assumptions**—don't let society's expectations and assumptions limit you; challenge them, you know what they say about assume (it makes an ass out of you and me!)

- **Think Backwards**—start with what you want to achieve and work backward

- **Preside over Innovation**—challenge everything; look for a way to make something better

- **Brainstorm & Daydream**—use visualization to find a new way of doing something

- **Eliminate Conceptual Barriers**

- **Start Over, Try Again!**

Use your own Creativity to add other ways to the list of ideas and to become a more creative problem solver!

Identify some challenges you are facing and pick one or two approaches above to exercise your Creativity. To start, focus on one challenge at a time. (For more on Creativity, see the worksheet Failure and Problem Solving.)

CHALLENGE	WAYS TO EXERCISE MY CREATIVITY

Integrity, Honesty, and Character Values

Why are there just three characteristics for Integrity and Honesty? Integrity and Honesty are simple to understand, but if you fail to put them into practice in your life, they are difficult to recover. My father would tell me that he could try many, many cases in court, but if he were dishonest once, he would lose his reputation for integrity in an instant.

- Openness
- Consistency
- Honesty

I also believe that Character Values are of utmost importance. If you have Character Values, you are likely to be a person of high integrity. People with high Character Values are:

- Industrious
- Responsible
- Prompt
- Caring
- Kind
- Sense of Humor
- Thoughtful
- Fair

- Trustworthy
- Courageous
- Unselfish
- Persistent
- Disciplined
- Concerned
- Nonviolent
- Passionate

ASK YOURSELF: AM I ACTING WITH INTEGRITY IN MY PERSONAL AND WORK LIFE? IDENTIFY ANY AREAS WHERE YOU NEED TO ACT WITH MORE INTEGRITY.

(Come back to this often and ask yourself how you are doing.)

ASSESS YOURSELF ON YOUR CHARACTER VALUES.

WHICH OF THESE CHARACTER VALUES DO YOU DEMONSTRATE EVERY DAY?

WHICH OF THESE CAN YOU IMPROVE ON?
(START BY PICKING ONE OR TWO TO FOCUS ON.)

Failure and Problem Solving

Failure and problems are a part of life—just like Mr. Murphy, you can't avoid them. With belief in your self-efficacy, by taking responsibility and continuing to work at solving problems, failure becomes an opportunity to grow.

As you deal with failure and problems, there are things you can do to take control of your life and turn chaos to order.

- Take Responsibility
- Refine Planning and Organizing Habits
- Never Assume Anything
- Anticipate
- Troubleshoot
- View Problems as Opportunities to Succeed
- Show Intelligence and Class in the Face of Defeat
- Maintain Composure and Dignity
- Seek Challenges and Opportunities

- Work Hard to Solve Your Problems
- Adjust Your Performance
- Collect Ideas and Evaluate Them
- Attach Tough Problems First
- Learn from Problems and Failures
- Accept Mr. Murphy—life is chaos, things will go wrong!
- Build Character
- Reflect on Opportunities and Respond More Intelligently
- Realize Failure Is a Step to Success

Problem Solving

WHAT OF THESE APPROACHES DO YOU USE IN SOLVING PROBLEMS?

WHAT NEW APPROACHES DO YOU WANT TO TRY OUT?

LIST A FEW PROBLEMS YOU ARE FACING.

What approaches can you use to solve them? Problem Solving and Creativity are married to each other. To look for other approaches, check out the Creativity worksheet.

PROBLEM	APPROACHES TO SOLVING
1.	
2.	
3.	

Failure

WRITE DOWN A FEW TIMES IN YOUR LIFE YOU FEEL YOU HAVE FAILED. THEN START THINKING ABOUT THEM DIFFERENTLY.

WHAT HAVE YOU LEARNED FROM THESE FAILURES?

DID THIS FAILURE LEAD TO ANY GROWTH FOR YOU?

HOW CAN YOU LEARN FROM FAILURE TO DO THINGS DIFFERENTLY NOW?

Mental Toughness

One of the greatest compliments I received was being described as mentally tough. Mental Toughness is character in action revealed in how you perform. In sports, you succeed by being mentally stronger than your opponent (remember, the mental is to the physical as 4 is to 1). But Mental Toughness applies to everything in life, and people of every age and in any discipline need Mental Toughness. It is key to responding to change and challenge.

Mental Toughness is a state of mind supported by the physical. When you are mentally tough, you can get into "the flow." This is a biochemical state where you are focused, and all distractions have dissolved. This state can be acquired and is available to every one of us.

Individuals with high levels of Mental Toughness exhibit many of the characteristics and use the techniques listed below.

- All Day Long—no time off from being mentally tough!
- Applies to Mental and Physical Activity
- Mental Discipline
- Emotional Stability
- Self-Discipline
- Consistent Habits
- Ability to Control the Central Nervous System
- Manage Well under Pressure
- All-Around Recovery
- Attacking Opportunities to Control and Stimulate Your Life
- Align and Regulate the 12 Key Chemicals
- Having a Mental Game Plan

- Awareness
- Affirmations
- Rationalization
- Emotional Control
- Mental Calmness
- Acting (as if)—related to Positive Self-Projection and very important!
- High Physical and Mental Energy
- Alertness
- Courage
- Capturing the Moment
- Focus and Concentration
- On It Like a Dime
- Handle Distraction
- Resistance and Persistence
- Gut-Wrenching Performance

- Big Heart and Lots of Grit
- A Volcanic Eruption
- Embrace Competition, Stress, and Challenges
- Get into State of Flow

- Good Attitude
- A Problem Solver
- Focus on Process, Not the Result
- Preparation

WHAT IS MENTAL TOUGHNESS, AND HOW CAN IT BENEFIT YOU IN YOUR LIFE?

WHERE HAVE YOU EXHIBITED MENTAL TOUGHNESS? WHICH APPROACHES AND ATTITUDES DO YOU USE?

WHICH CHARACTERISTICS OF MENTAL TOUGHNESS DO YOU WANT TO DEVELOP? PICK A SPECIFIC AREA OR PROBLEM IN YOUR LIFE THAT CAN BENEFIT FROM BEING MORE MENTALLY TOUGH.

Goal Setting

I can't overemphasize the importance of having goals. Without goals it is difficult, nearly impossible to advance. When you don't have goals, you become bored, depressed, despondent, lack direction, lack energy.

When setting goals, make sure your goals reflect who you are and what you enjoy. For me, goal setting starts with the pleasurable. I start setting goals by dreaming of what I want. I don't like doing everything I have to do to achieve a goal. But sometimes I have to do things I don't like to get to where I want to go. I know there will be a reward at the end.

Achieving goals holds a joy and discreet pleasure that cannot be duplicated!

These are descriptions of what setting a goal and pursuing it will give you. What grabs you from this list? Are you fired up yet to set goals?

- Expression of Freedom
- Challenges the Spirit
- Positive Magnet
- Provides Energy
- Gives Inner Drive
- Gives Direction
- Gives Meaning

- Gives Purpose to Life
- Increases Motivation
- Enhances Confidence
- Helps One Achieve
- Helps One Be Happy
- Rewarding
- Enhances Self-Esteem

When setting a goal, there are four things you need to ask yourself:

WHAT WILL THE GOAL DO FOR YOU?

DO YOU HAVE TOO MANY GOALS? (IF YOU HAVE A LOT OF GOALS, YOU'D BETTER BE ORGANIZED AND SUPER PREPARED.)

ARE YOUR GOALS REALISTIC? (YOU'LL GET DEPRESSED AND LACK ENERGY IF THEY AREN'T.)

WHAT ARE YOUR LONG-RANGE GOALS? (IT'S VERY IMPORTANT TO HAVE LONG-RANGE GOALS!)

PLEASE ANSWER THE FOLLOWING QUESTIONS:

I have goals

☐ Yes   ☐ No

What are my goals?

What will happen when I achieve my goals?

Do I have too many goals? If yes, what are my two or three priority goals?

As you think about each of your goals, if you don't feel some purpose, freedom, energy, etc., consider changing your goals.

As you focus on a current goal, think of how each of the motivators listed above come into play.

Positive Self-Change

There are tremendous rewards to making a change. Positive self-change opens up possibilities. If you can change how you do things, you will have more options for making decisions. It's true on the tennis court and in your personal life and work life. Whenever you feel stuck, consider making a change. If you're not sure how to do it, check out the Creativity and Problem Solving worksheet.

Change doesn't feel natural. You will have to go beyond your comfort zone and be willing to practice a new behavior to make it happen and make it a habit.

A few people can change quickly without ever thinking about it. They instantly feel the benefits, or they love the excitement of change. For most people, change is difficult. If they change at all, they do it more slowly and think about it before making a change. In James Prochaska's book, *Changing for Good*, he lays out six steps to change: (1) precontemplation, (2) contemplation, (3) preparation, (4) change, (5) maintenance of change, and (6) termination of change (because the change has become a habit). You can learn more by reading his book.

Change is necessary for growth. If you open up to learning something new, you'll go far.

Characteristics of Positive Self-Change

- Persistence
- Ability to Handle Failure
- Flexibility
- Understanding That There's No Right or Wrong Way
- Willingness to Try
- Recognition of the Need to Repeat and Practice New Behavior

- Effort
- Commitment
- Desire
- Being a Visionary — seeing the rewards for change as positive motivation
- Going after What Grabs You

CHECK OFF THE CHARACTERISTICS OF POSITIVE SELF-CHANGE YOU ALREADY HAVE.

WRITE DOWN THE ONES WOULD YOU LIKE TO DEVELOP.

Barriers to Positive Self-Change

- Resistance
- Personality—when you define yourself too rigidly, it's harder
- Background—if you grew up in difficult circumstance you may have to make more of an effort to change, but you can do it!
- Fear (that something will go wrong, that you will fail)
- Attachment to Routine—to change you need to get out of your comfort zone

WHAT ARE YOUR BARRIERS TO CHANGE?

HOW CAN YOU LOWER THESE BARRIERS?

Incentives to Positive Self-Change

- Never Bored
- Challenged
- Energized
- Seeing Payoff down the Road
- Fun of Change — make it fun!

WHEN YOU MAKE A CHANGE, WHAT EXCITES YOU ABOUT IT? WHAT ARE YOUR INCENTIVES TO CHANGE?

WHAT ONE TO TWO AREAS OF YOUR LIFE WOULD YOU LIKE TO CHANGE?

WHAT IS HOLDING YOU BACK? FEAR, COMPLACENCY, WANTING TO STAY IN YOUR COMFORT ZONE, SOMETHING ELSE?

LIST THE REWARDS FOR MAKING A CHANGE.

CHECK BACK EACH WEEK TO SEE HOW YOU ARE DOING AT MAKING THE CHANGES, BIG OR SMALL.

Emotional Intelligence and the E-Bank

Emotional Intelligence

Daniel Goleman popularized the idea of Emotional Intelligence. You may be brilliant and intelligent, you may have a sharp mind, but it doesn't mean you are intelligent in dealing with other people. Emotional Intelligence is the ability to connect to other people, bringing your heart into your relationships with others. Emotion Intelligence is critical to success. It is important for leaders and for everyone.

The characteristics of Emotional Intelligence are:

- Empathy
- Awareness
- Sensitivity
- Listening

- Relating
- Compassion
- Paying Attention to Gut Feelings

The E-Bank

The concept of the E-Bank was developed by Stephen Covey. It helps you think about how to improve your relationships with others (friends, boyfriends, girlfriends, husbands, wives, colleagues, etc.). You want to make deposits whenever you can and avoid withdrawals.

E-Bank Deposits

- Courtesy
- Kindness
- Honesty
- Love
- Understanding
- Keep Commitments
- Treat Everyone Equally
- Sincerity
- Clarify Expectations
- Attending to Little Things (e.g., showing gratitude, listening to other people)

E-Bank Withdrawals

- Yelling
- Hurt Feelings
- Relentless Disrespect
- Negative Body Language
- Unkindness
- Demeaning
- Judging
- Critical with No Solutions
- Trash Talking

IDENTIFY A RELATIONSHIP YOU WOULD LIKE TO IMPROVE.

WHICH CHARACTERISTICS OF EMOTIONAL INTELLIGENCE DO YOU ALREADY BRING INTO THAT RELATIONSHIP? WHAT CHARACTERISTICS DO YOU WANT TO DEVELOP?

USE THE E-BANK TO UNDERSTAND WHEN AND HOW YOU MAKE DEPOSITS AND WITH-DRAWALS. IDENTIFY HOW YOU CAN MAKE IMPROVEMENTS.

Motivation

The following are ways to motivate oneself and others. To harness these approaches, you must first take these three steps: convey an attitude of caring, develop trust, and lower barriers.

As a leader, you are always dealing with Motivation. What came first, the chicken or the egg? You can't separate them. And by motivating people you lead, you help them get what they want and you get what you want too.

The following are ways to motivate:

- Caring
- Helping
- Personal Attention
- Compensation
- Extra Vacation
- Innovation
- Examining and Setting Goals
- Achieving Goals
- Exercising Creativity

- Taking Care of Others
- Positive Self-Projection
- Responsibility
- Comfortable Environment
- Music
- Play
- Compliments
- Dinner Out
- Movies

- Challenges
- Learning
- Excitement
- Love
- Meeting Deadlines
- Day Dreaming
- Visualizing
- Exercise
- Threat of Loss

IDENTIFY THE THREE BIGGEST MOTIVATORS YOU USE DURING YOUR DAY. HOW OFTEN DO YOU USE THEM?

CHOOSE THREE YOU HAVE NEVER USED. YOUR TASK IS TO INCORPORATE THESE THREE NEW MOTIVATORS DURING YOUR DAY.

HOW CAN YOU USE MOTIVATORS TO ACHIEVE YOUR GOALS?

Leadership

There are 200 or more traits that comprise a good leader. While possessing all may be difficult, adding just a few to your leadership repertoire can make a big difference.

I believe the most important quality of a leader is caring about people and having emotional intelligence. Next is being a connector, being able to bring people together. A leader must also be a maven—have knowledge that others need. People will listen only if they trust you. As a leader you must also be a motivator and fire people up.

- Courage to Speak Out
- Emotional Intelligence
- Belief in Your Skills
- A Connector
- A Maven—you've acquired lots of knowledge to share
- A Sender—sending people away with tears in their eyes and fire in their bellies (getting people motivated to pursue goals on their own)
- A Motivator
- Decisive
- Not Intimidated
- Love Challenges
- Display Conviction
- Self-Confidence
- Self-Efficacy (belief in)
- Self-Regulation
- Social Skills

- Empathetic Listening Skills
- Ask Astute Questions
- Non-Interrupting
- Seeking Suggestions
- Control Others in a Nice Way
- Delegating Authority
- Sensitivity
- Awareness
- Recognizing Critical Moment
- Cycling Upward
- Organized
- Flexible
- Adaptable
- Able to Prioritize
- Disciplined
- A Trouble Shooter
- Problem Solver

- Embrace Change
- Establish Relationships
- Positive Attitude
- Works with Others
- Team Player
- Affects Environment
- Loves Controversy
- Accepts New Ideas
- Good Communicator
- Leads with Personal Authority, Not Power of Office
- A Goal Setter
- Helps People Set Goals and Achieve Them
- Pushes beyond Comfort Zone
- Good Interpersonal Skills

- Good Self-Esteem
- Understands Organizations
- Positive Attitude
- Positive Self-Projection
- Capture the Emotions of an Audience
- Connect with Others
- Persuasive
- Commands Respect and Admiration
- Improves Habits
- Has a Personal Mission Statement or Purpose in Life
- Optimistic
- Courageous
- Persuasive

IDENTIFY 3 TO 5 STRONG LEADERSHIP TRAITS YOU ALREADY HAVE.

IDENTIFY THE TRAITS YOU WANT TO DEVELOP.

IDENTIFY SOME AREAS IN YOUR LIFE WHERE YOU CAN EXERCISE AND PRACTICE LEADERSHIP.

ACKNOWLEDGMENTS

The principles used in my motivational speaking were accumulated over a lifetime. They were values and lessons I learned and established on my own, and through messages by other speakers, books, and articles. I used anything I came across to validate my principles and beliefs.

I've been fortunate to have people around me who contributed to my successes and ultimately the writing of this memoir. I am indebted to Ann LoPrinzi, former *Times of Trenton* tennis columnist, and to my editor, Cathy Kreyche. After Ann took my scribbled, handwritten manuscript and brought it to life, Cathy ably and professionally immersed herself into my story, brought out other meaningful life experiences and their relationship to my principles and beliefs, and helped me through the publication process. I also want to thank my good friend, attorney, and author Jack Furlong, who provided much-needed encouragement and feedback, and shared his knowledge on just about everything. I couldn't have done this without my wife Mary Ellen, a master of local and family history and digging up valuable photographs, and my daughter, Tara Devlin, for designing my website and the book cover. And thank you to Rachael Hixon, who designed the book's interior.

I thank all those who influenced and encouraged me on my journey. That includes my coaches and teachers who recognized some talent and leadership in me. Russell Fleishmann helped get me started on the path to motivational speaking. Bill Mountford taught me how to teach tennis. Jim Baugh and Ken Merritt each had an impact on me in conducting tennis clinics. I am grateful for the faith the Dodgers organization, Rider College, Mount Snow, Prince, and the Army put in me, as well as the private clubs that employed me to teach tennis. I thank my wide circle of sports friends who played a major role in my learning processes and served as great sounding boards for developing my principles, including my tag-team buddy, the late Stan Dlugosz, Dave Haggerty, and all the guys who keep coming to "the Swamp" for good tennis and great conversation—Jack, Scott, Carl, Pete, Mike C., Mike E., and Joe. Thanks to Maureen Myers for scheduling my tennis lessons, which gave me more time to write this book, and to Mountain View.

Thank you to all those who contributed to the editing process and provided valuable feedback on an early draft of this book, particularly Mary Reath, Nancy Plum, Julie Durso, Jordan Kreyche, and Tom Bozzone; Gail Palatine made excellent suggestions later in the process.

What I've written describes events and experiences in my life as best as I can remember them. Thanks to Al Sumutka, who dug into important details of my time at Rider as Athletic Director. Whatever I got right here, I owe to you. To Ken Merritt, Steve Davis, and Patti Haggerty, who provided their memories of working at Prince, and to Pete Stratton and Bill Holmes, I thank you for your time, interest, and friendship. I continue to learn from the tennis players I drill with and get to see first-hand just how effective my principles are. And my love and thanks to my family for allowing this "Jackass" to come full circle, and to my grandkids for bringing even more meaning and joy to my golden years.

On the next page is a list of resources I used.

Resources

Antonavosky, Aron. *Unraveling the Mystery of Health: How People Manage Stress and Stay Well.*

Bandura, Albert, Ph.D. *Self-Efficacy in Changing Societies.*

Benson, Herbert, M.D. *Timeless Healing: The Power and Biology of Belief.*

Blakeslee, Thomas R. *The Attitude Factor: Extend Your Life by Changing the Way You Think.*

Chopra, Deepak, M.D. *Ageless Body, Timeless Mind.*

Cousins, Norman. *Anatomy of an Illness as Perceived by the Patient: Reflections on Healing and Regeneration.*

Covey, Stephen R., Ph.D. *The 7 Habits of Highly Effective People.*

Csikszentmihalyi, Mihaly, PhD. *Flow: The Psychology of Optimal Experience.*

Elliot, Robert S., M.D. *From Stress to Strength: How to Lighten Your Load and Save Your Life.*

Flach, Frederic F., M.D. *Resilience: Discovering a New Strength at Times of Stress.*

Gladwell, Malcolm. *The Tipping Point: How Little Things Can Make a Big Difference.*

Goleman, Daniel, Ph.D. *Emotional Intelligence.*

—. *Working with Emotional Intelligence.*

Harvard Study on Adult Development. www.adultdevelopmentstudy.org

Joseph, Rhawn. *The Naked Neuron: Evolution and the Languages of the Body and Brain.*

Loehr, James, E., Ed.D. *Stress for Success: Jim Loehr's Program for Transforming Stress into Energy at Work.*

Nesbitt Shanor, Karen. *The Emerging Mind.*

Pert, Candace B., Ph.D. *Molecules of Emotion: Why You Feel the Way You Feel.*

Prochaska, James, Ph.D. *Changing for Good: A Revolutionary Six-Stage Program for Overcoming Bad Habits and Moving Your Life Positively Forward.*

Sapolasky, Robert M., Ph.D. *Why Zebras Don't Get Ulcers.*

Photo Credits

Thanks to NJ Advance Media for permission to reprint photos published in the *Trenton Times* newspapers. Frank Bauman was the photographer for the photo essay in *Look* magazine, "American Legion Junior Baseball"; special thanks to his granddaughter, Dayna Bauman, for permission to reprint a photo from the photo shoot. Finally, special acknowledgment and thanks to the Mount Snow Ski Patrol and to Darren LoPrinzi.

p. 12

132 Abernethy Drive, Trenton (Devlin Family photo)
Marty Devlin (Devlin Family photo)
Martin P. Devlin, Sr. (Devlin Family photo)

p. 13.

Trish Devlin, Donald Devlin, John Devlin, and Marty Devlin
(Devlin Family photo)
Donald Devlin, John Devlin, Marty Devlin, and Trish Devlin Delahey
(Devlin Family photo)
Viola Mae Attwood Devlin (Devlin Family photo)
Martin P. Devlin, Jr. (Devlin Family photo)

p. 16

Basketball at Junior HS #3 (Collection of Marty Devlin)

p. 20

Parade car (*Indianapolis News,* Collection of Marty Devlin)
The Schroths after the championship game in Indianapolis: In front (from L):
Ronnie Holford, batboy Don Browning, Bernie Groomes, Marty Devlin,
Chuck Lucarella. In back (from L): Lou LiMato, Paul Bodine, Ron Schnorbus,
Leon (Pete) Millington, Andy Greener, Don Minnick, Asst. Coach Al Weiss,
Jim Babashak, Tony Recine, Bill McLaughlin, Coach Carl (Kelly) Palumbo
(*Indianapolis News,* September 11, 1948; Collection of Marty Devlin)

p. 21

Part of the crowd of 5,000 (Collection of Marty Devlin)
"American Legion Junior Baseball" (Frank Bauman Collection)

p. 26

Two-time All-American diver for the swim team (*Trenton Evening Times,* March 2, 1948). Copyright NJ Advance Media. Reprinted with permission.

Leading the blocking (Collection of Marty Devlin)

p. 27

"Trenton Sports Figures, by Joe Masick and Bill Dwyer, (*Trenton Evening Times,* April 12, 1948). Copyright NJ Advance Media. Reprinted with permission.

Baseball at Trenton High School (*Trenton Evening Times,* May 25, 1948). Copyright NJ Advance Media. Reprinted with permission.

p. 29

Marty Devlin at Duke (Gail Palatine)

Marty Devlin with teammates in the minor leagues (Collection of Marty Devlin)

p. 36

Uncle Sam got me! (US Government / Collection of Marty Devlin)

"Devlin, Meningitis Patient, Improved but Still Serious" (*Trenton Evening Times,* March 30, 1953, p. 1). Copyright NJ Advance Media. Reprinted with permission.

39th Infantry Regiment team (US Government / Collection of Marty Devlin)

p. 46

Marty Devlin and Tom Bigham (Collection of Marty Devlin)

p. 47

Letter from Martin P. Devlin, Jr. to the president of the AA Fort Worth Baseball Club (Collection of Marty Devlin)

p. 50

Market in the poor section of Maracaibo (Collection of Marty Devlin)

p. 51

Stadium in Cabimas (Collection of Marty Devlin)

Lake Maracaibo from the Hotel del Lago pool (Collection of Marty Devlin)

p. 52

Little boy on a burro (Collection of Marty Devlin)

Marty Devlin, Cabimas (Collection of Marty Devlin)

Oil rig being built on Lake Maricaibo (Collection of Marty Devlin)
Plane taking the Cabimas Petroleros to an away game (Collection of Marty Devlin)

p. 58

With Martin Patrick Devlin IV ("Butch") (Collection of Marty Devlin)

p. 59

At the orange juice stand in Dodgertown during Spring Training (Collection of Marty Devlin)

pp. 60–61

Marty Devlin managing ("Class D Baseball Manager: A Study," *Orlando Evening Star*, August 22, 1959, pp. 10-A–10-B). Reprinted with permission of the *Orlando Sentinel*.

p. 71

Rider University, *The Shadow* (Lawrenceville, N.J., Trenton, N.J.: 1969), 138, Moore Library Special Collections and University Archives

p. 76

Some of those 500 railroad ties (Devlin Family photo)

p. 86

Mary Ellen and Marty Devlin on wedding day (Devlin Family photo)
Marty Devlin, Kyle Devlin (on Marty's back), and Tara Devlin (Devlin Family photo)
With Mary Ellen Devlin and Tara Devlin (Devlin Family photo)
Mary Ellen Devlin and Marty Devlin, celebration at Prince (Collection of Marty Devlin)

p. 87

Marty Devlin and Mary Ellen Devlin (Devlin Family photo)

p. 96

Marty Devlin instructing during a clinic (Collection of Marty Devlin)
Marty Devlin with the clinic participants (Collection of Marty Devlin)

p. 97

Prince tech reps: (L to R) John Keller, Tommy Judson, Peitre Overbeeke, Marty Devlin, Ken Merritt, Jerome Jones, Dale Hawkins (Collection of Marty Devlin)
Stew Bunn, a tech rep, pulling the ball machine (Collection of Marty Devlin)

p. 98

Tommy Lasorda holding Tara Devlin (Devlin Family photo)

Marty Devlin, Bill Hughes, and Steve Garvey (Collection of Marty Devlin)

p. 99

Jim Baugh, Marty Devlin, and Dave Haggerty (Collection of Marty Devlin)

Ken Wilson and Marty Devlin (Collection of Marty Devlin)

Mary Ellen, Marty Devlin, and Bobby Riggs (Collection of Marty Devlin)

p. 105

Dana skiing on Mt. Snow (Collection of Marty Devlin)

Dana Bezar in an exhibition (Collection of Marty Devlin)

p. 106

Marty Devlin, Ian Bezar, Dana Bezar, and Andrea Bezar
  (Collection of Marty Devlin)

Dana Bezar's prosthesis (Collection of Marty Devlin)

Dana Bezar, Ed Hill, and Steve Davis (Collection of Marty Devlin)

Dana Bezar, Ken Merritt ("Smiley Bones"), and Marty Devlin
  (Collection of Marty Devlin)

Marty Devlin, Ian Bezar, Dana Bezar, and Andrea Bezar
  (Collection of Marty Devlin)

p. 110

My big blue Rube Goldberg van (Devlin Family photo)

Tara Devlin and Kyle Devlin (Devlin Family photo)

Marty Devlin building stone wall at the Swamp (Devlin Family photo)

Marty Devlin digging with Donald Devlin (Devlin Family photo)

p. 111

Autumn at the Swamp (Collection of Marty Devlin)

p. 123

Marty Devlin and Kyla Devlin (Collection of Marty Devlin)

Bill Holmes, Marty Devlin, and Jim McDevitt (Collection of Marty Devlin)

Stan Dlugosz and Marty Devlin (Collection of Marty Devlin)

Mount Snow Ski Patrol (Mount Snow Ski Patrol)

p. 128

A t-shirt from the Ladies of the Court with a some Martyisms
(Collection of Marty Devlin)

p. 129

Some of the Ladies of the Court and Good Buddies (Darren LoPrinzi Photography)
Tennis drill–baby shower (Collection of Marty Devlin)

p. 134

Martin P. (Pat) Devlin V, Marty Devlin, Mary Ellen, Kyla Devlin, Liam Devlin,
Conrad, Scarlett, Liana Devlin (Devlin Family photo)
Martin Patrick Devlin V (Devlin Family photo)
Tara Devlin, with children Conrad and Scarlett (Devlin Family photo)

p. 135

Liana Devlin, Diane Devlin, Kyla Devlin, Liam Devlin, and Kyle Devlin
(Devlin Family photo)

Front Cover

Marty Devlin (Collection of Marty Devlin)

Back Cover

Marty Devlin diving (Collection of Marty Devlin)
Marty Devlin (Collection of Marty Devlin)

ABOUT THE AUTHOR

Marty Devlin grew up in Trenton, New Jersey, served in the U.S. Army, and has led an extraordinary life of diverse experiences and accomplishments. His athletic career spanned several sports and decades. He played and coached professional baseball, was a self-taught tennis player who earned a world ranking in senior tennis, was a ski patrol member, an All-American diver, and an All-City quarterback. Among his many "paid to play" roles were college athletic director, college intramural program innovator and director, and international tennis ball machine clinician. Devlin has impacted many lives through coaching, motivational speaking, and positive thinking and is revered for his contagious enthusiasm. "Hi, I'm Marty Devlin and I'm high on life," is the introduction that thousands of people have heard in his world-famous tennis clinics.

Devlin received his undergraduate and masters degrees in Health and Physical Education from Trenton State College (now The College of New Jersey). He lives with his wife Mary Ellen and has three children and six grandchildren. Devlin continues to teach tennis at "the Swamp," the court he built at his home in Ewing, New Jersey, where he continues to motivate and inspire people.

LIST OF ACCOMPLISHMENTS

Awards and Recognition

Received the James E. Cryan Achievement Award

Charter inductee of Mercer County Tennis Hall of Fame

USTA Middle States Hall of Fame (Tennis)

Rider College Athletic Hall of Fame (Administrator)

Trenton Baseball Hall of Fame as member of the 1948 Schroths Team, 50th Anniversary

Inaugural class of Mercer County Sports Hall of Fame as member of the 1948 Schroths Post 93 American Legion National Championship Team

Member of the American Legion Post 93 National Championship team (Schroths 1948) recognized by the Baseball Hall of Fame

Member of the American Legion Post 93 New Jersey state legion title team (Schroths 1949)

Honored as Middle States Player of the Year

Named Boy Scouts Man of the Year

Acknowledged as the top tennis player of the century in Mercer County and one of the top athletes of all time in Trenton, NJ

Recipient of the Lester J. Fitzgibbon National Grass Court Championship Sportsmanship Award

Received most popular player award with the Greenwood Dodgers, Elmira Pioneers, and Fort Worth Cats

Appeared many times on TV, radio, and in newspapers

Received NJ Sportswriter Achievement Award for tennis achievements

Baseball

Named to all-state team in high school

Played winter baseball (two years) in Venezuela

Played in American Association for St. Paul (AAA)

Played in Canada for Montreal Dodgers in the International League (AAA)

Member of Professional Baseball Association

Was told he was youngest manager in professional baseball

Played all nine baseball positions as a professional

Played two years in the Texas League for the Fort Worth Cats (AA)

First to play baseball for four years with the legendary Post 93 Schroths

Played semi-pro baseball in Clarksburg, VA

Played C baseball in Greenwood, MS, for Greenwood Dodgers, Cotton States League

Took 30-day leave from service and played three games in one day during spring training

Played for Mobile Bears in Southern Association

Hit four home runs in eight years of pro baseball (that's sick!)

Played for Elmira in the Eastern League

Playing manager of Fort Dix Regimental baseball team

Stole 48 bases in one season with the Greenwood Dodgers

Was considered the best second baseman the Texas (AA) League ever had at that time

Voted most popular player several times in Dodgers' organization

College Administration

Instituted Hall of Fame program at Rider College

Instituted a creative program, Arete (Be the Best You Can Be), to market the college through the athletic program and develop the athletes

Developed a very popular Intramural Athletic program at Rider and served as its director for 18 years

Served as Assistant Athletic Director and Athletic Director at Rider College

Family

Married to Mary Ellen and has three children: Martin IV, Tara, and Kyle, and six grandchildren

Motivational Speaking

Gave presentations (without a note) at Columbia, Harvard, Yale, William & Mary, Trenton State, and Rider

Gave presentations at tennis clinics and speaking engagements all over the world

Other Teaching/Coaching/Community

Certified for teaching tennis by the USPTA

Taught health and physical education at Hopewell Valley High School

Coached high school wrestling

Coached high school golf

Tennis coach at Rider College, instituted a no-cut policy, lauded by *NY Times*

Taught a quadruple amputee to play tennis and ski

Chairperson for Mercer County Park Commission (tennis)

Member of advisory staff for two major tennis corporations

Member of State of NJ Governor's Council on Physical Fitness

High school football and swimming official

Skiing

Started skiing at age 26 and was a member of the National Ski Patrol for 35 years at Mount Snow, Vermont

Served as an Ambassador at Mount Snow for 5 years

Rescued some 350 people from every face of Mount Snow in all conditions while on National Ski Patrol

Swimming

Two-time All-American high school diver

Director of swimming program at Greenacres Country Club for 12 summers

Used innovative methods of teaching

Taught brain-damaged person to swim miles

Tennis Clinician

Product Manager for Prince ball machines, including the technological development and marketing for nine years

Developed aerobic and anaerobic tennis programs for Prince Mfg.

Developed endurance, stretching, and power fitness program for Prince Mfg.

Developed testing program to measure tennis skills

International tennis technician for Prince Mfg

Set up dealership network for Prince ball machines throughout USA

Worked with Prince research and development for development of Prince tennis rackets

Performed wheelchair tennis clinics in Dallas

Guest tennis instructor for eight years at Mercer County Community College tennis camp

Represented *Tennis* magazine in monthly clinics in eight major cities, working with Chris Evert, Stan Smith, and others

Ran wheelchair tennis clinics

Tennis Player

Represented USA in Potter Cup in Barcelona, Spain and Stevens Cup in Port Washington, NY (international senior events between countries)

Taught himself to play tennis at age 36 and became the No. 1 player in the U.S. and 10th in the world in the 45-and-over division. This award was presented by *Tennis* magazine for 1981. Legend Rod Laver was ranked No. 9 at the time.

Ranked in the top ten nationally for ten consecutive years

Won three national tournaments on three different surfaces: hard/outdoors in La Jolla, CA, 1981; indoor in Salt Lake City, UT, 1981; and clay in Sarasota, FL, 1981

Finalist in singles two more times in the 45s (clay and outdoors); one more in 45 doubles (clay)

In the 50-and-over division, won singles twice more—indoors and clay

Won national titles three times, was a finalist in six others for a total of 9 championship rounds within a ten-year span

Played tennis in 50 states and 20 countries

U.S. Army

Drafted and spent two years in U.S. Army

Volunteer

James E. Cryan Memorial Tournaments

Nelson Green Memorial Tournaments

National Junior Tennis League of Trenton

Various fundraisers

Local tennis camps

TESTIMONIALS

Marty Devlin is one of the wisest men I know! I was excited to learn he was writing book and sharing his wisdom in his inimitable fashion.

—Eric Scott,
Vice President/Senior Political Director, New Jersey 101.5

Marty Devlin, Mr. Energy, gave a very inspiring presentation at the 2003 USPTA Eastern Division Convention at the National Tennis Center....I think if we all take a step back and look at our lives and our professions, we will see the importance of Marty's subject. Tennis: A curriculum for Life hits home on many fronts. If you get another chance to see him speak, I suggest you jump on the opportunity. It can improve your life both on and off the court.

—Steve Diamond,
former VP of USPTA Eastern and two-time Eastern President

You were the coach who knew his baseball. One day you spent quite a while teaching me how to throw a curveball. You had me stand over a peach basket and another player handed me the ball and had me properly rotate the ball so it would curve downward when pitched. I don't think anyone else came close to my curve. I can remember players swinging at it when it hit the dirt. All thanks to you!

—Bruce Carlson,
Trenton State College Baseball, 1959–61

Everything I learned in life, I learned at the "Swamp." For that, you have my undying gratitude. I feel fortunate to know you.

—*Jack Furlong,*
  Trenton

Fantastic! Greater than expected! Twelve hours of supreme enjoyment! Tactful and effective salesmanship! You must be commended for the greatest promotional vehicle since the "Flying Lady" on the Rolls-Royce. I've been in the club business over 20 years, and I have never had members as excited over a program or a product line.

—*David Saxe,*
  Wisconsin

I was fortunate to be able to work side by side with one of the legendary tennis players in the northeast region. Not only did I have a great mentor in the dynamics of teaching and coaching tennis but a mentor on how to be a positive and productive individual through everyday life. It does not take long to find out that Marty is a great humanitarian.

—*Ric Flagg and Rich Giordano*
  on a Special Recognition, 2003

You are an inspiration to all. You bring talent, humor, kindness, and skill to your coaching. You teach tennis and so much more.

—*Anne & Rich Scheffler,*
  Trenton

From the moment I met you, my life changed. I realized I could do whatever I truly put my mind to with time, effort, and Marty's fabulous coaching skills. Marty, you make the world a better place. Your smile warms my heart and there is no doubt that my tennis game improved.

—*Denise and Jenny,*
  Trenton

That was the most dramatic entrance I've ever seen in my life for a guest speaker It was epic. Just out of nowhere, Marty Devlin walks into the classroom and erupts like a volcano......His story would make an incredible Hollywood film.

–*Daniel Kingsley,*
Rider College

Your "dog and pony show" really gave us a boost this spring. Ball machine interest has never been so high.

–*Betty Kelley Van,*
Washington

Just a note of thanks for the great job you did with the Prince Clinic last Thursday. The women and kids are still talking about what a great time they had.

–*Jimmy Pitkanen,*
Tennessee

Marty continues to amaze me. He had an audience of 90 to 100 Texas teaching professionals on the edge of their seats.

–*Dean Larson,*
Texas

Marty Devlin is not only an inspiration but a tremendous asset to a clinic of this type. When you're around Marty, one cannot help but get enthusiastic about the Prince products and the game of tennis.

–*Nancy Rivenburgh,*
Oregon

Marty's unique personality and his attention to detail resulted in four hours of excellent drilling and, I think, made more than 100 new friends for Prince. It's no wonder that you've become the top racquet company in the world.

–*Don Prial,*
New Jersey

In all my travels, I have yet to encounter or work with a person who can match the raw enthusiasm, the dynamic energy, and the positive impact that Marty Devlin generates during his presentations.

—Bill Tym,
USPTA President, Alabama

The clinic was just sensational!

—Jimmy Pitkanen,
Tennessee

In our market, there is no better effective method of spending money than on Marty and his clinics. The consumer memory of Prince and Marty's clinics will ensure far longer than any other type of promotion we could offer.

—Tim Gehrig,
Hawaii

Marty has to be one of the most dynamic individuals in the tennis industry.

—Ward Phelps,
Colorado

Part of what made the camp so successful were the Prince Clinics put on by Marty Devlin. Marty came to camp once a week each of the three weeks and put on fantastic clinics.

—Nick Bollettieri,
Florida

I just wish we could clone him, and all the reps could buy one.

—Bob Till,
Texas

Not a day goes by that I don't hear your voices and words of wisdom as I move through my day. The Tag Team [Marty and Stan Dlugosz] have set the bar extremely high. We all will continue to work to attain your level of excellence.

   – Pete MacDonald,
     Director of Ambassador Program at Mount Snow, Vermont

Marty joined some pretty talented clinicians for the weekend. His enthusiasm dominated the show, and he was not challenged as the class of this field.

   –Pat Laughlin,
     Hawaii

Dana, Ian, and I wanted to thank the most important person in our ski adventure. You are a very special person to all of our family.

   –Andrea Bezar,
     mother of Dana Bezar

You are a very special person. I can recall thinking to myself when I read the article about you and Dana Bezar that I was so lucky to be able to say that Marty is a friend of mine.

   –Richard Bilotti,
     Publisher of the Times of Trenton

You owe me no thanks. You more than paid me back with your performance when you reached the 39th, both as an athlete and as a soldier. I consider myself lucky to have had an opportunity to work with you.

   –Captain Bob Moorman,
     39th Regiment, C Company

Listening about how he turned nothing into something was amazing and the fact that he did it over and over again was special. Leaving the class that night I had a different perspective on work ethic and attitude.

—Brian Rikkola,
Rider University

An impressive part of his story was the fact that he was always the captain of each team he was on.

—Matthew Gonzalez,
Rider University

Around the age of 40 or 50 is when Devlin started to feel comfortable with himself. This caught my attention because I feel like in your late 20s, early 30s, you're supposed to have everything together.

—Kimberly Ramos,
Rider University

His life stories were really inspiring. He never gave up on anything he did in life, and he always had a positive aspect on life. The one lesson I can take from his speech was to always believe in yourself and to persevere.

—Sarah Kim,
Rider University

We had the pleasure of meeting a Rider University legend who has given back to his community and provided a positive aura which attracted plenty of attention from students and the faculty.... I hope to be as well received by a community as he was because I will feel a much larger purpose for living than my peers.

—John Lansing,
Rider University

Hearing about Marty's life story and his perseverance in sports was remarkable. I hope that one day when I'm 83 I am able to live with just as much excitement and happiness that he does. He preached "marketing yourself" and that is exactly the way he lived his life. He marketed himself through his work ethic and determination. He had a positive attitude that was second to none and he could make any bad situation into a good one.

—Connor Markulec,
Rider University

He was known as an employee and player that will go above and beyond with what he was assigned to do because that's just who he was.

—Salvatore Bivona,
Rider University

This was the best series of clinics that I've ever seen you [Prince] do. Keep up the great work. Both clubs received great comments and want you back again.

—Evie Boone,
Washington